Ctrl + Z

Ctrl +

The Right
to Be Forgotten

Meg Leta Jones

 NEW YORK UNIVERSITY PRESS
New York and London

NEW YORK UNIVERSITY PRESS
New York and London
www.nyupress.org

References to Internet websites (URLs) were accurate at the
time of writing. Neither the author nor New York University
Press is responsible for URLs that may have expired or changed
since the manuscript was prepared.

Library of Congress Cataloging-in-Publication Data
Names: Jones, Meg Leta, author.
Title: Ctrl + Z : the right to be forgotten / Meg Leta Jones.
Other titles: Ctrl plus Z | Right to be forgotten
Description: New York ; London : New York University Press, 2016. | Includes
bibliographical references and index. | Also available as an e-book.
Identifiers: LCCN 2015043578 | ISBN 9781479881703 (cl : alk. paper) |
ISBN 1479881708 (cl : alk. paper)
Subjects: LCSH: Right to be forgotten—United States. | Right to be forgotten—Europe. |
Privacy, Right of—United States. | Privacy, Right of—Europe.
Classification: LCC K3264.C65 J66 2016 | DDC 323.44/8094—dc23
LC record available at http://lccn.loc.gov/2015043578

New York University Press books are printed on acid-free paper,
and their binding materials are chosen for strength and durabil-
ity. We strive to use environmentally responsible suppliers and
materials to the greatest extent possible in publishing our books.

Manufactured in the United States of America

10 9 8 7 6 5 4 3 2 1

Also available as an ebook

with aid from a grant from
Figure Foundation
in the bearing of memory

For David

Contents

Acknowledgments

I have been very lucky to work on this book at Georgetown University, with incredibly caring and supportive departments and colleagues. I'd like to thank my fellow faculty members in the Communication, Culture, & Technology program for their kindness and creating a truly interdisciplinary environment that has stretched and challenged me in ways that inspire and energize. I'd like to thank Carole Sargent, Director of Scholarly Publications, who has guided me through writing my first book, as well as Jen Tobin and Oriana Mastro, who have trudged through it with me week by week. I'd also like to thank Julie Cohen for the many coffees and my editor, Clara, whose enthusiasm for the project proved infectious and got this book to the finish line.

The ideas that form the basis of this book emerged over the course of my graduate work at the University of Colorado. My PhD advisors, Paul Ohm and Jill Dupre, have been nothing short of vital to the completion of this work and my career. Their commitment has included long meetings, hours of editing, and managing numerous frantic communications. For their generous guidance, warm kindness, and immense patience with me, Paul and Jill have my sincerest gratitude. No part of the PhD process was more enjoyable than the time spent with my very large committee. John Bennett fully supported every aspect of my work inside and outside ATLAS. I cannot thank him enough for being my biggest cheerleader and dependable leader. Preston Padden and Dick Green have offered their time, guidance, and experience to this research, as well as guest-lectured classes and brought real-world and international context to the debate. Diane Sieber has been an inspiration and become a close friend. I was honored to have her involved in my PhD. Harry Surden's creativity and thoughtfulness has provided a great deal of depth to this project. Last but not least, Susan Nevelow-Mart played an important role on the committee with endless energy, support, and interest. All of these people have been inspiring teachers and nurturing friends. I will be forever grateful for their reliable support.

A number of fellowships supported my graduate work and my development as an interdisciplinary researcher. I am incredibly grateful to CableLabs and its amazing team, particularly Dick Green, Chris Lammers, Simon Krauss, and Lee Zieroth, for their belief in the work being done at ATLAS and by me. I am also grateful to those at the Harvard Berkman Center for Internet & Society who made my fellowship experience there exciting, enriching, and inspiring. My thanks also goes out to those involved in the Provosts Fellowship in University Libraries, namely, the law librarians in the Wise Law Library and their director, Susan Nevelow-Mart. Finally, I would like to thank the incredible team in computer science that coordinates the NSF eCSite project, including Dirk Gunwald, Debra Goldberg, Clayton Lewis, Jessica Feld, and Sarah Hug.

Portions of the book are adaptions of previously published work, and all of their individual acknowledgments should extend here as well. Those publications include *Speaking of Forgetting: Analysis of Possible Non-EU Responses to the Right to Be Forgotten and Speech Exception*, 38:8 TELECOMMUNICATIONS POLICY 800 (2014); *The Right to Be Forgotten across the Pond*, 3 JOURNAL OF INFORMATION POLICY 1 (2013) (with Jef Ausloos); *Seeking Digital Redemption: The Future of Forgive-*

ness in the Internet Age, 29 Santa Clara Computer and High Technology Law Journal 99 (2012) (with Nicole Friess and Jill Van Matre); and *You Are What Google Says You Are: The Right to Be Forgotten and Information Stewardship*, 17 International Review of Information Ethics (July 2012). A different version of chapter 4 appeared as *It's about Time: Privacy, Information Life Cycles, and the Right to Be Forgotten*, 16 Stanford Technology Law Review 369 (2014). I thank the *Stanford Technology Law Review* for permission to reprint. I benefited from numerous opportunities to present the ideas at workshops and conferences at universities with engaged faculty. I'd like to thank those editors and attendees who refined this work and pointed me in new directions. Specifically, I'd like to thank my European coauthors Paulan Korenhof, Jef Ausloos, Ivan Szekely, Giovanni Sartor, and Ronald Leenes, who taught me much about European law and attitudes toward information rights. Most importantly, I'd like to thank the reviewers of the manuscript and wonderful copyeditor. Your feedback and criticism were monumentally important to getting the book into shape.

Finally, I would like to thank my friends and family. My parents and brothers provide unconditional love and security in life that makes it possible to take the road less traveled. My friends (Madelaine Maior, Nicole Day, Belle Marsh, Carolyn Miller, Joanne White, Leslie Dodson, Kara Behnke, and Heather Underwood) give me constant entertainment, enjoyment, laughter, camaraderie, and motivation. Lastly, I would like to thank my partner in crime and husband, David Jones, for his patience, interest, editing, and love.

Introduction

Two cases addressing the complicated concerns of reputation, identity, privacy, and memory in the Digital Age were decided the same day on opposite sides of the Atlantic with different conclusions. The first began in Spain. In 2010, Mario Costeja González requested that a Spanish newspaper remove information about a sale of his property related to insolvency proceedings. When the paper refused, he requested that Google remove the search results that included the information. Google's refusal led to litigation in the Court of Justice of the European Union. On May 13, 2014, the court ordered Google to edit the results retrieved when González's name was searched because the information about the property sale was "inadequate, irrelevant or no longer relevant, or excessive in relation to the purposes of the processing at issue carried out by the operator of the search engine."[1]

On the same day in the U.S., two *American Idol* contestants brought every conceivable claim against Viacom, MTV, and a number of other defendants over online content that led to their disqualification from the television show.[2] These two contestants made it to the "Top 32" round when information about their earlier arrests was published on websites like Smoking Gun. The hopeful singers had not disclosed their arrests to the show's producers. An unexceptional U.S. case, all of their claims were dismissed by the Tennessee district court for two main reasons. First, some of the claims were too old. Even though the Internet allows for continued public accessibility, under Tennessee state law, defamation claims must be filed within one year from the time the content was published. Second, any lawsuit in the U.S. seeking damages for the publication of true information is not going to get far.

Although the facts of the cases differ in ways that matter to the law as well as to public opinion, both involved parties asking the judicial system to limit the damage of digital content that would otherwise remain available for an indefinite period of time. Policy makers around the globe are being pressed to figure out a systematic response to the threat of digital memory—and it is a complex threat involving uncertain technological advancements, disrupted norms, and divergent values.

On October 12, 2012, fifteen-year-old Amanda Todd took her own life after posting a desperate YouTube video explaining the details of how she was bullied.[3] In the video, the vulnerable girl explained that a scandalous image she was convinced to create led to brutal on- and offline torment.[4] She suffered from depression and anxiety as a result; in the video, she holds a card that reads, "I can never get that photo back."[5] In 2008, Max Mosley, a former head of Formula One racing, was awarded £60,000 in damages by an English High Court in a claim against the British *News of the World* newspaper for publishing a story detailing his involvement in an allegedly Nazi-themed, sadomasochistic, prostitution-filled orgy—complete with video.[6] In an effort to remove the material related to the event, Mosley brought legal action in twenty-two countries and sought deletion from almost two hundred websites in Germany alone by 2011.[7] The most recent of Mosley's claims for removal was filed against Google to hide the remaining links to the story.[8] Just months later, terrorists murdered twelve people in Paris as retribution for satirical depictions of Muhammad published by a French newspaper and circulated online, prompting interior ministers from European Union countries to call for Internet service providers to find and take down online content that "aims to incite hatred and terror" as well as to allow governments to monitor activity to prevent future attacks.[9]

To drive home the importance and difficulty of the issue, imagine the worst thing you have ever done, your most shameful secret. Imagine that cringe-inducing incident somehow has made its way online. When future first dates or employers or grandchildren search your name, that incident may be easily discoverable. In a connected world, a life can be ruined in a matter of minutes, and a person, frozen in time. Keeping that embarrassing secret offline is not as easy as it once was. The wrong button can get pressed, networks can be confusing, people can be misidentified, and sometimes foes—or friends—are vindictive. Your secret may never be disclosed, but it may nonetheless be discovered when the bits of data trails are put together—and you may be the last to know. You may not only suffer dramatically from the discovery and use of your personal information; worry or fear may curb your behavior on- and offline to avoid the risks of unwanted attention, misinterpretation, or abuse. Now imagine the biggest jerk you have ever met, someone you do not want to be able to hide records of his inconsiderate, nasty, spiteful, or twisted behavior. Imagine that no matter what rules you come up with, he will try to abuse them.

The global Internet population is around 2.1 billion people, with over 274 million users in North America and 519 million users in Europe. Every minute in 2012, 204,166,667 emails were sent, over 2,000,000 queries were received by Google, 684,478 pieces of content were shared on Facebook, 100,000 tweets were sent, 3,125 new photos were added to Flickr, 2,083 check-ins occurred on Foursquare, 270,000 words were written on Blogger, and 571 new websites were created.[10] The average webpage has fourteen cookies to track users around this massive information network.[11] Who should be able to hide or delete information? How do we determine when and what is appropriate to keep or discard?

The Right(s) to Be Forgotten

Since Stacy Snyder became the cautionary tale of social media in 2006, it is well known that employment prospects can be negatively impacted by information on the Internet. Snyder was denied her teaching degree days before graduation because an administrator at the high school where she was training in Pennsylvania discovered a photo of her wearing a pirate hat and drinking from a plastic cup, with the caption "Drunken Pirate," on MySpace.[12] Today these stories are a dime a dozen.[13]

Jacqueline Laurent-Auger was disappointed when her contract with the private boys' school where she taught drama for fifteen years was not renewed. The school was concerned about Laurent-Auger's judgment, explaining, "The availability on the Internet of erotic films in which she acted created an entirely new context that was not ideal for our students. After discussion and reflection, we concluded that adult films must remain just that, a product for adults. That's why we decided not to renew Mrs. Laurent-Auger's contract."[14] But it would have been hard for her to predict this consequence of her decision, considering color television was only just becoming available when she filmed the scenes in the late 1960s and early 1970s—nearly fifty years before. On this point, the school stated that the Internet had ushered the "erotic portion of [Laurent-Auger's] career into the present."[15]

In 2010, Mary Bale was caught on video picking up an alley cat and tossing it into a garbage bin. The cat's owners posted the video online, and within hours, Bale's name and address were published online, a "Death to Mary Bale" Facebook page and numerous anti–Mary Bale Twitter accounts were created, and she later received death threats.[16]

When the site Jezebel outed a number of high school students who had posted vulgar, racist tweets after President Obama was reelected, it highlighted many of the controversies and questions at issue with digital memory. The students who were identified deleted the tweets and some their Twitter accounts, but for a number of them, the Jezebel article was already on the first page or the top result when their names were searched on Google. Of course, Jezebel could have covered the story without identifying the teenagers, but as the site explained, "While the First Amendment protects their freedom of speech, it doesn't protect them from the consequences that might result from expressing their opinions."[17]

The web has become a searchable and crunchable database for questions of any kind, a living cultural memory whose implications are complex and wide reaching. The abundance of information online is heavily relied on by prospective professional and social contacts. Around 80 percent of employers, 30 percent of universities, and 40 percent of law schools search applicants online.[18] Before a first date, 48 percent of women and 38 percent of men perform online research on their date.[19] Thanks to the content that users purposefully place online (wisely or not), the growth of surveillance technologies in everyday devices, and free instant sharing platforms, it is increasingly easy to gain and publish harmful information about others online. "Slut-shaming" and "revenge porn" sites dedicated to humiliating women in sexually vulnerable positions are hotly debated and extremely popular. These sites, which encourage users to post sexually explicit photos or videos of a former lover online with accompanying identifying information like name, address, and workplace, receive fifteen to thirty posts and are visited by over 350,000 unique visitors each day.[20] Suicides of cyberbullying victims have been rising and highlight the extreme consequences of online content.[21] With over half of adolescents and teens experiencing some form of online bullying, the ability to remove content is in high demand for some people sympathetic to the poor choices that may occur in youth.[22] Sites like MugshotsOnline.com collect, organize, and publish millions of mug shots acquired from government agency data sources, allow users to "vote for the weekly top 10," and include a disclaimer at the bottom of the homepage explaining that those who are included may or may not have been convicted. Public information such as court filings that has been historically difficult to access is now organized and presented digitally in ways that provide a public service as well as risks to individuals identified through the records. In fact, an industry of online reputation management has emerged to counter negative content and search results.

The Internet law scholar Viktor Mayer-Schönberger has warned that the digitization and disclosure of life's personal details "will forever tether us to all our past actions, making it impossible, in practice, to escape them."[23] The tether is actually a detailed structure of discoverability that relies on a number of technical and social occurrences. All Internet communication—downloading webpages, sending email, transferring files, and so on—is achieved by connecting to another computer, splitting the data into packets (the basic unit of information), and sending them on their way to the intended destination using the TCP/IP standard. When a host wants to make a connection, it first looks up the IP address for a given domain name and then sends packets to that IP address. For example, the uniform resource locator (URL) www.twitter.com/megleta contains the domain name "www.twitter.com." A DNS resolver computer, commonly operated by the Internet service provider, the company providing Internet service, will perform the domain-name-to-IP-address lookup. Content being sent to users making requests within this delivery system is increasingly stored in the cloud, beyond the reach of the creator.

Search engines continually crawl and index the Internet's available content. This content is then ranked, with the results most relevant to the user's search entry appearing first. Search engines have emerged as vital and ubiquitous navigation tools. They compete with one another by refining these ranking systems, but the details of how these systems process and present information are not disclosed. The search giant Google's goal is to "organize the world's information and make it universally accessible and useful."[24] In 2009, the company began offering personalized search results based on the data profiles it had for the individual user.[25] This data collection to serve users' personalized content includes logs of each search request, results the user actually saw, and results he or she eventually clicked on. In 2006, John Battelle discovered that Google could identify the IP addresses (and/or

Google cookie values) of users who have searched for a term as well as a list of terms searched by an IP address (and/or Google cookie value).[26]

Prior to the phenomenon of a "Google account," the company kept the originating IP address, cookie value ID, time, date, search term, and resulting clicks.[27] The infusion of Web 2.0 into the search experience asks the user to sign in to Google as a way to utilize its many social services including email, chat, telephony, photo collection, maps, and a social networking site, as well as its ever-enhanced search engine. The privacy policy now explains that the company collects information you give it and information from the use of its services, including device information (such as your hardware model, operating system version, unique device identifiers, and mobile-network information including phone number), log information (including search queries; telephony log information; IP address; and device event information such as crashes, system activity, hardware settings, browser type, browser language, the date and time of your request and referral URL, and cookies), location information (including GPS, sensor data, and WiFi access point), local storage, and cookies and anonymous identifiers when interacting with partner services.[28] A number of other companies like Facebook and Twitter are similarly adapting business models based on the opportunity to collect, process, and sell user data by partnering with other sites and services to create a web of trackability.

This brings us to what is known as "big data." What makes data big is the amount of data created, the number of partnerships that allow the tracking of data across sites and platforms, and growing data markets and collaborations where this information is shared among interested parties. When a user logs onto the Internet and visits a website, hundreds of electronic tracking files may be triggered to capture data from the user's activity on the site and from other information held in existing stored files, and that data is sent to companies. A study done by the *Wall Street Journal* found that the nation's top-fifty websites installed an average of sixty-four pieces of tracking technology, and a dozen sites installed over one hundred.[29] These are not the cookies of the 1990s, which recorded a user's activity to make revisits more convenient. New tools scan in real time and access location information, income, shopping interests, and health concerns.[30] Some files respawn, known as zombie cookies, even after the user actively deletes them.[31] All of this information is then sold on data exchanges. One of the leading data-trading platforms, BlueKai, which launched in 2008, claimed to have access to over one hundred million unique buyers by 2009.[32]

Due to ubiquitous connectivity, discoverability is not necessarily limited to a personal computer. Sensors creating data about owners and others from phones, cars, credit cards, televisions, household appliances, wearable computing necklaces, watches, and eyewear, and the growing list of "Internet of Things" devices, mean that more personal information is being disclosed, processed, and discovered. All of these nodes of discoverability will be added to the structure of discoverability sooner or later, if they have not been already.

But, as Julian Barnes writes in his 1984 novel *Flaubert's Parrot*, "You can define a net in one of two ways, depending on your point of view. Normally, you would say that it is a meshed instrument designed to catch fish. But you could, with no great injury to logic, reverse the image and define a net as a jocular lexicographer once did: he called it a collection of holes tied together with string."[33] This same structure of discoverability, the net that seems all consuming and everlasting, is full of holes. It is a fragile structure. Digital information is not permanent. Any number of reasons, from lack of interest to site upgrades, can lead to the loss of access to content.

Dependence on digital information puts us at the mercy of bit rot, data rot, and link rot. Bit rot refers to the degradation of software over time. Modern computers do not have floppy disk drives; many of them do not even have compact disk drives. The University of Colorado library has an entire basement space with outdated computer equipment kept just to read old digital formats holding content necessary for research. Data rot or data decay refers to the decay of storage media, such as the loss of magnetic orientation of bits on a floppy disk or loss of electrical charges of bits in solid state drives. Systems that provide growing capabilities to store digital data have been shown also to increase the likelihood of uncorrected and undetected data corruption.[34] Link rot occurs when a hyperlink no longer works, when the target it originally referenced no longer exists. The average life of a webpage is about one hundred days. Users may be presented with the disappointing "404 Error Page Not Found" message, or the original content may have been overwritten. As a recent example, in 2014 a team at Harvard Law School found that approximately half of the URLs in U.S. Supreme Court opinions no longer link to the original information.[35] Moving from paper to digital offers the benefits and drawbacks of increased discoverability, and information has a different life cycle when stored in digital formats that require a computer to interpret the content for a human reader.

The benefits of increased discoverability are rarely overstated. Promises of improved citizen participation and government accountability, use of resources in every area from power to education, scientific discoveries from reproduction to climatology, understanding of humanities research from history to art, and commercial possibilities justifiably drive us to share. The crisis of decreased discoverability, on the other hand, is rarely acknowledged, but it is vital to meeting the promises of data-based progress, as well as to framing the problem of digital memory. This data-driven march is neither good nor bad, but limitations exist and values must be reassessed and reestablished in order to determine what should be preserved and what may be left ephemeral.

One reaction to the outcry over increased discoverability and the permanence of digital information is a demand for what I call digital redemption or digital reinvention, which refers to the willingness and means to transform digital public information into private information upon the subject's request, liberating the individual from discoverable personal information. The legal implementation of digital reinvention, the right to be forgotten, has been described as "the right to silence on past events in life that are no longer occurring."[36] This broad concept is controversial and has been called "rewriting history," "personal history revisionism," and simply "censorship."

In 2009, Viviane Reding, then the European Commissioner for Justice, Fundamental Rights and Citizenship, announced her intention to review the EU Data Protection Directive of 1995 (DP Directive).[37] This review would include special attention to a right to be forgotten. She explained that "a unified approach at the E.U. level will make Europe stronger in promoting high data protection standards globally."[38] On January 25, 2012, the proposal for the new Data Protection Regulation (DP Regulation) to replace the 1995 DP Directive was released. Article 17 addressed "the right to be forgotten and to erasure."[39] For the first time, the world was presented with an explicit legislative right to be forgotten, under which data subjects would have the right to force the deletion of personal data held by data controllers, with certain exceptions for the protection of other rights and interests. Although the Regulation continues to receive updates (e.g., the title of article 17 has since been changed to "The Right to Deletion and Erasure"),[40] the European Union Court of Justice's interpretation of the 1995 DP Directive in May 2014 in favor of González has been considered enforcement of a right to be forgotten, even though the case itself only dealt with deindexing select pages from search results.

Similar legislative efforts have been presented in the U.S. to address threats to children by online content, but the U.S. is generally considered an anomaly in the arena of privacy regulation. While the EU has embraced a uniform approach to legislating data privacy, the U.S. addresses the issue with situation-specific rules, market-based approaches, and voluntary codes of conduct. This is due in no small part to the U.S. concept of the "firstness" of the First Amendment, which places other rights and interests subordinate to First Amendment rights.[41] It is not only the prioritization of expression that divides the U.S. and Europe; variation in treatment of public figures, intimate information, relationships, and context also exists. Differences abound in political structure, administrative procedure, and the role of law itself. These differences between the U.S. and Europe are problematic when one region seeks to protect its citizens with regulations that require the compliance of the other.

Digital Redemption

Mayer-Schönberger describes a shift in how and what we remember in an age of ubiquitous computing. The Digital Age threatens to shift (or already has shifted) the balance between forgetting and remembering: "forgetting has become the exception, and remembering the default."[42] Human memory has many virtues; its fallibility protects us by revising, forgetting, and contextualizing our pasts. Digital memory on the other hand is considered "more comprehensive, as well as more accurate and objective than the fallible memory of the forgetful human mind."[43] Mayer-Schönberger thoroughly traces the rapid advancements in digital memory, explaining that it is now quite possible to digitally capture and remember every aspect of life for very little money. For him, digital memory "negates time."[44] It becomes difficult for people to detach themselves from humiliating or embarrassing past moments, which can make efforts at self-improvement seem futile. The Internet, as an integral piece of external memory, also prevents one from moving to a new community to re-create oneself and start fresh. Digital memory, in short, prevents society from moving beyond the past because it cannot forget the past.

Although Mayer-Schönberger analyzes how memory has changed and why forgetting is cognitively important for psychological health, the social value at play is not just memory. Choosing to allow individuals to move beyond their past is not forgetting. Forgetting is rarely intentional (and in this way the Internet is indeed forgetful, as discussed in chapter 4). Forgetting as it relates to digital privacy and identity is intended to free individuals from the weight of their digital baggage. It is a larger cultural willingness to allow individuals to move beyond their personal pasts, a societal capacity to offer forgiveness, provide second chances, and recognize the value of reinvention. The legal scholar Jeffrey Rosen notes, "Around the world citizens are experiencing the difficulty of living in a world where the Web never forgets, where every blog and tweet and Facebook update and MySpace picture about us is recorded forever in the digital cloud."[45] As we watch search engines and social networks shift their societal roles, we must wonder if forgiveness and reinvention *can* and *should* move into the Digital Age, when information lingers indefinitely and restricts individuals to their pasts. "Forgetting" and "oblivion" are unfortunate, albeit catchy and dramatic, word choices; their negative connotations do no favors to the underlying values they intend to protect. Any manipulation of lingering personal information will threaten numerous interests including technological innovation and economic progress, speech and historical records, and privacy and autonomy, but digital-redemption protects forgiveness.

While definitions of forgiveness vary, most psychologists agree that forgiveness is not forgetting, condoning, excusing offenses, reconciliation, reestablishment of trust, or release from legal accountability.[46] These concepts are related but do not represent synonyms or definitions. Many definitions of forgiveness are laden with normative intent. Instead, I utilize a more descriptive and general definition of forgiveness. Simplified, forgiveness means a decision to forgo negative feelings, retribution, or vengeance.[47] The broader definition embraces popular understandings of forgiveness. When polled, 66 percent of U.S. adults found "very accurate or somewhat accurate" the statement "If you have really forgiven someone, you should be able to forget what they have done to you."[48] The majority also agreed that if a person is to forgive another, he or she must want to release the other from the consequences of his or her actions[49] and that the relationship should be rebuilt.[50] These results suggest that, despite scholarly attempts to precisely define forgiveness as unrelated to forgetting, "many people believe that forgiving implies forgetting, reconciliation, or the removal of negative consequences."[51] Although the decision to relinquish negative feelings toward an individual may satisfy the baseline definition of forgiveness, moving forward is the motivation, focus, and goal of those who engage in the forgiveness process. In order to establish a form of forgiveness in the Digital Age, it is important to recognize popular experiences with, and attitudes toward, forgiveness and to bridge those experiences with the described moral value sought to be preserved.

The range of benefits associated with forgiveness can be seen in the research area of restorative justice, which attempts to establish alternatives to retribution.[52] Advocates of this movement seek to preserve the rights and dignity of victims, as well as of offenders, often providing opportunities for the parties to meet, communicate, apologize, and forgive.[53] Restorative practices result in participants reporting high satisfaction with the process.[54] Victim and offender can benefit from restorative processes, while the social goal of judicial efficiency is also promoted by forgiveness, as shown by research examining how apologies facilitate averting lawsuits.[55] Some perpetrators who acknowledge wrongdoing and are forgiven may experience a gratefulness that motivates them to reciprocate goodwill through improved behavior and reparations, minimizing repeat offenses.[56]

A growing body of research strongly suggests that granting forgiveness to others is beneficial in a variety of ways. Individuals who received treatment to help them forgive through the Stanford Forgiveness Project showed significant reductions in anger, perceived stress, hurt, and physical symptoms of stress.[57] The Mayo Clinic lists six specific benefits to forgiving: healthier relationships; greater spiritual and psychological well-being; less anxiety, stress, and hostility; lower blood pressure; fewer symptoms of depression; and lower risk of alcohol and substance abuse.[58] Being unforgiving can be a core component of stress associated with decreased mental health and increased levels of guilt, shame, and regret.[59]

Particularly relevant are studies on the physical and emotional impact of rehearsing hurt and harboring a grudge. Once hurt, people both intentionally and unintentionally rehearse memories of the painful experience.[60] In this state, individuals remain in the role of the victim and perpetuate negative emotions associated with rehearsing the hurtful offense.[61] Nursing a grudge perpetuates the adverse health effects associated with anger and blame.[62] Generally, releasing a grudge "may free the wounded person from a prison of hurt and vengeful emotion, yielding both emotional and physical benefits, including reduced stress, less negative emotion, fewer cardiovascular problems, and improved immune system performance."[63] One study examined the emotional and physiological effects of rehearsing hurtful memories or nursed grudges compared with cultivating an empathic perspective and imagining granting forgiveness; it revealed dramatic benefits to forgiving.[64] Feelings of valence, control, and empathy all were experienced to a greater degree during forgiving imagery exercises.[65] During unforgiving imagery, participants experienced increased heart rates and blood pressure, significantly greater sympathetic nervous system arousal, elevated brown muscle activity,[66] and skin conductance, many of which persisted into the postimagery recovery period.[67]

On an interpersonal level, those who forgive exhibit greater empathy, understanding, tolerance, agreeableness, and insight, resulting in prosocial transformations.[68] Those who are less forgiving tend to be less compassionate and score higher in depression, neuroticism, negative affectivity, and vengeful motivations.[69] As reported by spouses, one of the most important factors contributing to marital longevity and satisfaction is the capacity to offer and seek forgiveness.[70] Children living in areas characterized by violence and poverty who are introduced to forgiveness in the classroom have shown significantly less anger.[71] Families that report a history of forgiveness have better individual member mental health and higher levels of family functionality.[72] These findings add to a growing body of knowledge and have led some psychologists to explore lack of forgiveness as a public health problem.[73]

The United Nations has been heavily involved in the promotion of forgiveness and related research, hoping to refine its amnesty practices and establish peaceful civil and international relationships.[74] Research demonstrates that "forgiveness programs can restore healthy emotions, thus potentially aiding social reconstruction and dialogue."[75] This is true of mothers who lost sons due to conflicts in Northern Ireland and underwent the Stanford Forgiveness Project's six-day forgiveness training.

The mothers showed a 50 percent reduction in perceived stress, a 40 percent reduction in depression, a 23 percent reduction in anger, a significant reduction in hurt, and a significant increase in physical vitality.[76] For groups, reminders of historical victimization, such as the horrific events of the Holocaust, have been shown to result in legitimization of actions taken toward a new enemy, such as violence against Palestinians in the present.[77] Forgiveness intervention in Rwanda—where violence between groups had decreased dramatically but attitudes between members of the groups had not changed and future violence was likely to occur—has promoted structural and institutional stability in the country's justice system and educational system, leading toward sustained mutual acceptance.[78]

In addition, wrongdoers benefit from being forgiven by others. Individuals value the goodwill of their fellow human beings, and many of those who have transgressed "feel the bite of conscience for their misdeeds."[79] "Forgiveness may lighten the burden of guilt from their shoulders, making it easier for them to move on with their lives."[80] Those who avoid denying their mistakes and "ask for and receive forgiveness are more likely to learn their lessons."[81] The desire to earn forgiveness can be a catalyst for healthy, positive change.[82] Like the process of forgiving another, being forgiven aids psychological healing, improves physical and mental health, promotes reconciliation between the offended and offender, and promotes hope for the resolution of real-world intergroup conflict.[83] Forgiving oneself is also beneficial. Lower self-esteem, greater depression, and increased anxiety and anger are associated with difficulty forgiving oneself.[84] Self-forgivers report better relationships with their victims, as well as less regret, self-blame, and guilt.[85]

Although forgiveness may be good for us individually and socially, it is difficult to obtain any level of forgiveness when we cannot escape reminders of the violation. "The capacity to forget aspects of the past (or remember them in a different way) is deeply connected to the power to forgive others."[86] As one scholar notes, the "inability to modulate the emotional content of the memory of an affront severely diminishes the capacity to forgive it."[87] In fact, those who have been wronged are "less likely to forgive to the extent that they exhibit greater rumination and recall a greater number of prior transgressions, and are more likely to forgive to the extent that they develop more benign attributions regarding the causes of the perpetrator's actions."[88] The ability to forgive oneself and to accept the forgiveness of others depends, in part, on escaping memories of wrongs or indiscretions: "the capacity to let go of the painful emotions associated with our memory of wronging others is integral to accepting their forgiveness for our faults."[89] Assuming that information remains indefinitely accessible to a search engine, "forgiving" anyone, including oneself, may be incredibly challenging.

The Internet can be a harsh place, and the "perpetual memory" of the Internet hinders forgetting, thereby stifling forgiveness. Kashmir Hill, a journalist specializing in privacy matters, explains:

> Online, the past remains fresh. The pixels do not fade with time as our memories do. . . . Since we live in a world where we tend to choose "archive" instead of "delete," everything is saved, and memories have a way of forcing themselves to the surface in the most unexpected ways. If memories are painful, that can be paralyzing, like a digital PTSD, with flashbacks to events that you can't control. Depending on how much you turn to Facebook for the chronicling and journaling of your life, this might unearth some powerful moments you hadn't expected, or wouldn't have necessarily wanted, its algorithms to serve up to you.[90]

Increasing aggregation and availability of information online means that the past can be stirred with greater frequency, triggering memories that would otherwise have been forgotten. As individuals will acutely reexperience the humiliation or pain of their indiscretions, offenses, or tragedies when memories of them come to mind, the Digital Age has decreased the chances of successful forgiveness.

The benefits of forgiveness have been shown to "spill over" into situations and relationships outside the original conflict; those who are forgiven engage in more volunteerism, charity donations, and other altruistic behavior.[91] But forgiveness can also be dangerous. Philosophical writings on the subject promote forgiveness as a virtue[92] but are found alongside writing addressing the moral value of retribution and revenge.[93] Forgiveness has the ability to cause its own injustices, particularly when offered by a third party, as opposed to the wronged.[94] A victim or offended observer may feel that the offender has not had to feel the proportional repercussions of his or her actions or that the act was simply unforgiveable.[95] The most severe threat of disrupting the benefits to forgiveness is from offering or receiving it too quickly or too late.[96] "Self-respect, respect for the moral order, respect for the wrongdoer, and even respect for forgiveness itself" may be undermined by hasty forgiveness.[97] Forgiveness may be individually and socially beneficial but must be crafted and implemented carefully.

Cultural Specificity

Current debates surrounding international privacy issues often make two improper assumptions. The first assumption is that the same technology presents societies with the same problems. In research on the growth of European significance in international privacy regulation over three decades, the political scientist Abraham Newman states, "The proliferation of computer technology poses the same challenges in civil liberties for all policymakers across the advanced industrial democracies, but the type of privacy regimes adopted in response differed dramatically."[98] The renowned legal historian Lawrence Friedman similarly explains, "An automobile is an automobile is an automobile, whether it is in Tokyo or Moscow or Buenos Aires or New York. A cell phone is a cell phone; a computer is a computer. There is no such thing as a Chinese cultural cell phone, or a Brazilian style of computer."[99]

In Friedman's view, regulations must account for cultural context, but technology is the same everywhere. This view is strange to those who study technology. As the science and technology studies (STS) scholar Sheila Jasanoff articulates,

The world is not a single place, and even "the West" accommodates tech-nological innovations such as computers and genetically modified foods with divided expectations and multiple rationalities. Cultural specificity survives with astonishing resilience in the face of the leveling forces of modernity. Not only the sameness but also the diversity of contemporary cultures derive, it seems, from specific contingent accommodations that societies make with their scientific and technological capabilities.[100]

Although the power of social construction and technological deter-minism remain popular topics in science and technology studies, both forces are recognized as impactful and important.[101] Technologies are "co-produced" by what behaviors they make newly possible (here, increased discoverability) and socially constructed within cultures that make sense of and respond to them within specific contexts.[102] In short, a computer in Moscow is not a computer in New York. A computer may be materially the same and constrain or afford certain behaviors, but placed in different cultures, technologies hold different meaning, pro-vide different use, and carry different norms and expectations shaped by numerous factors including the legal culture in which the computer sits. These in turn may result in the design of country-specific versions of different websites and services.

Related is the second assumption that harmonization is necessary or desirable for regulatory efficiency. If everyone were dealing with the same problems presented by a new technology, conceptualized and used in the same way, harmonization could make sense. But the conceptual-ization, use, problems, and pressures put on citizens are not the same. Hurried harmonization risks placing efficiency over problem solving and giving the false impression of consistency where significant variety remains. The past two decades have put in place a structure of diverse socio-technical compliance that relies heavily on design adjustments, institutions, and public and private actors; there are avenues forward that do not require harmonization.

Continued access to personal information will be understood and responded to differently depending on the particular culture and legal regime. "At least as far as law goes, we do not seem to possess general 'human' intuitions about the 'horror' of privacy violations."[103] This introduction began by shamelessly appealing to readers' anxieties by asking you to imagine your own exposure. Yet it does not presume what information or circumstances the incident would entail or where or how exposure would occur. Irwin Altman has theorized the ways in which privacy is culturally universal and the ways in which it is culturally specific.[104] Privacy, according to Altman, is dynamic boundary management in which people use a mix of behaviors to achieve a desired level of privacy depending on the situation. Altman concludes that privacy is a universal process but involves culturally unique regulatory mechanisms. Although forgiveness, reinvention, and redemption are also universal processes to some extent, we do not possess a general intuition about who, what, where, when, and why an individual should be relieved from his or her past.

While the United States and European countries have conversed extensively on the subject of information policy, their differences have become more apparent as the Internet has made them more relevant. Exotic legal terms like "personality" and "private life" are laced throughout European law, but as James Whitman explains in "Two Western Cultures of Privacy," "one's sense of personhood can be grounded just as much in an attachment to liberty as in an attachment to dignity."[105] U.S. personhood is the protection of individual development that occurs in an outward fashion, by expressing oneself and socially engaging in the marketplace of all things, including ideas. In contrast, the EU Charter states flatly, "Human dignity is inviolable." According to Whitman, who focuses on the relative differences in German, French, and U.S. law, this dignity is rooted in the very old body of Continental law of "insult" that protects personal honor.[106] For a long time, only high-status individuals in Europe were treated with a certain level of respect, explains Whitman.[107] In France, one's honor was defended by the duel throughout this period, but by the mid-nineteenth century, the exposure of private life became a legal issue.[108] The protection of the press in the 1791 French constitution was quickly followed by the protection against "calumnies and insults relative to private life."[109] A free press was conceived as vital to self-governance, but the "private person" could not be left vulnerable.[110] Developed as an alternative to English notions of liberty, German privacy was established and protected within the "personality" right. Personality can be described as the "Inner Space" in which people "develop freely and self-responsibly their personalities."[111] The German emphasis was placed on crafting a system that protects an unfettered creation of the self, as opposed to an emphasis on consumer sovereignty.[112] Both France and Germany distinguish between privacy violations and insults but package them as dignity rights intended to protect against the untrustworthy (France) or simply unworthy (Germany) press and free market. "Privacy is an aspect of personal dignity within the continental tradition, and personal dignity is never satisfactorily safeguarded by market mechanisms."[113] Whitman continues, Europeans have slowly granted *all* individuals the right of dignity. Americans, in contrast, grant privacy to those who make choices to retain their privacy, protect against government invasions into recognized private spaces (most notably their homes) and subjects (like health or financial information), and preserve reputations against only the most severe falsehoods and financial damage. The distinction between the two regions is a stark one and says a great deal about their respective historical roots: one cannot alienate one's dignity, but one can alienate one's liberty.

Digital redemption and digital reinvention can be understood similarly. They are extensions of culturally entrenched and dynamic concepts. Although privacy, reinvention, and redemption are firmly rooted in each country's cultural norms, expectations, and values, it is unclear which information rights will remain regulated in culturally specific ways and which will become universal fundamental human rights. Countries currently protect and balance reputation, identity, cultural history, corporate power, expression, access, and exceptions differently, but these balances and governance structures are constantly in flux. All countries reflecting on what types of restraints and freedoms should be placed on the Internet are considering which values must be preserved, how those values should be preserved, and what can be left behind.

Arguments and Caveats

The central thesis of *Crtl+Z* is that a digital right to be forgotten is an innovative idea with a lot of possibilities and potential. The idea simply needs to be opened up, reframed, and restructured. The extreme options currently on the table limit the many ways to think about digital redemption and polarize regions. By utilizing new theories of privacy, breaking down the concept to organize its many meanings, and reframing the problem as one of information stewardship instead of information permanence, a host of choices become available for consideration. In order to make these difficult choices once they are on the table, the issues must be configured to fit within a digital discourse, existing legal cultures, and the international community.

My approach to analyzing digital redemption is inherently comparative. The right to be forgotten is indisputably a European creation, but there is a great deal to be gained from studying digital redemption beyond European borders. The right to be forgotten sits at the intersection of change: change in national and transnational policy and change in everyday information technology practices, demands, and expectations. Situated in this unique position, the right to be forgotten encompasses many of the big questions surrounding information technologies and offers a particularly valuable site and moment for comparison of democratic information societies. Comparison among regional treatments of information technology should help us make sense of legal particularities and assumptions that otherwise go unnoticed.

Cross-regional policy comparison may even inform a course forward for political communities. With that hope, I undertake the type of comparative work that describes a foreign jurisdiction (Europe) in relation to one's own legal system (the United States). The comparative research that follows exposes distinct legal cultures[114] across the pond that create very different landscapes from which a right to be forgotten can emerge. However, a digital right to be forgotten is a governance proposal for a socially and technologically connected world and, therefore, must also be assessed globally. And so the analytical framework is not the perfect right to be forgotten nor ways to achieve certain forms of social progress. The goal is to provide insight and an approach for considering the right to be forgotten and to encourage pluralistic development based on the situated use and users within diverse legal cultures that remain interoperable.

Finding extreme existing responses to digital redemption in the EU and U.S., four remaining steps take a pragmatic, prospective turn, seeking to provide new perspectives and possibilities. The first is theoretical, the second technical, the third socio-legal, and the fourth international. The steps reflect the broad range of disciplines and sources used, as well as the intended audience. Communication and media studies, computer and information studies, science and technology studies, comparative law, law and technology, and comparative and international technology policy research have all contributed to this project, and I hope these disciplines will find a valuable contribution in the following pages. For this reason, I have tried to boil down points, show parallels where helpful, and limit legal and technical jargon.

Chapters 1 and 2 describe existing and proposed options for those who seek legal and nonlegal recourse when personal information haunts them, tracing the socio-technical-legal roots in the U.S. and European countries. Chapter 1 concludes that digital redemption is offered quite freely under the EU system, and instead of recognizing the pluralistic nature of new technology and societal disruption, the EU has sought to assert the right to be forgotten as a universal solution to a universal problem. The window of opportunity for digital redemption in the U.S., on the other hand, is far too small, as I assert in chapter 2. The silver-bullet alternatives to a legal digital right to be forgotten—namely, alternatives in the form of norm evolutions, market solutions, and technological responses—are similarly and significantly limited.

Chapter 3 works through the theoretical and conceptual muddles surrounding the right to be forgotten. Utilizing new concepts of privacy and breaking down the right to be forgotten, a new set of possibilities emerge. Chapter 4 criticizes the way in which the technical issue has been framed. Although both European and American commentary have similarly framed the problem as "digital permanence," such framing is understood and responded to differently by each and ignores the materiality of digital information. The chapter reframes the problem that the right to be forgotten seeks to solve. It argues that digital information is actually quite impermanent and should be considered through a lens of information stewardship. Web decay and link rot plague our networks and require conversations about digital redemption to account for the fact that digital information is not permanent—it is just different. The chapter assesses the new digital information landscape and outlines an information life cycle to support debates about discoverability of lingering information and the implementation of information stewardship.

Chapter 5 discusses how to construct digital redemption within existing legal systems by applying these tools to the U.S. system. It pulls out elements of the United States' legal culture of forgiveness in order to determine how information stewardship may be embraced within the U.S. using an information life cycle approach. It concludes that while the First Amendment places significant hurdles in the way of establishing a digital redemption, narrow exceptions may provide room for such a right under certain circumstances. Finally, chapter 6 argues that technical, social, and legal interoperability are necessary for the development and viability of the right to be forgotten. The chapter recognizes that the information regulations of one country can no longer be ignored by others in a networked world and proposes ways in which diverse structures and procedures can protect digital redemption in one region while respecting its development in another.

This text carries with it a certain level of tentativeness based on the difficulty in comparing technology policy. Each region's data-protection laws are built on more than formal, written legal instruments and function within various administrative, procedural, and corporate cultures. The variation in available explanatory documentation or case law works against presenting sound conclusions about all legal cultures. In light of these limitations, the comparisons are best considered explorations as opposed to accurate measures of different legal cultures. My own limited language skills and experience with particular jurisdictions and legal cultures also contribute to an appropriate tentativeness. These limitations leave some aspects of the debate less examined than others and many specific areas of law and society largely unexplored.

Given the nature of my subject, which grows and changes every second, this book has the common problem of making any claims about a moving target. This text is only a snapshot in a moment of international popular and regulatory debate during a significant shift in sociotechnical practice and expectations. The dynamic nature of technology policy results in frequent revisions and adjustments and is difficult to assess. The European Union may have passed its Data Protection Regulation by the time this text is in print, but if not, criticism of its intent to harmonize the right across member states and its choice of procedural execution may remain relevant as the Regulation is assessed. However, its implementation and interpretation may negate such criticism. The text may contribute to such implementation and interpretation and may provide guidance to jurisdictions at the early stages of developing a right to be forgotten. The technology policy landscape is not static, and so the text may only represent details available as of winter 2015.

For Americans and much of the rest of the world, the Internet has always been a wild and weird place—we love it for that. Yochai Benkler explains in his book *The Wealth of Networks* that networked participation has unleashed an unparalleled level of creativity and innovation into the world.[115] The Internet used to be described as virtual place where anyone could go try on a new identity or test a new idea.[116] It has become increasingly identifying, which has its pros and cons (victims are more easily identified, but transgressors are as well).[117] And the online is spreading into the offline—or offline spaces and moments are simply disappearing. Technology-saturated societies are full of mediated and connected spaces and people generating more and more data by the second to add to the various record books. Google CEO Eric Schmidt described the setting as "living with a historical record" and warned that people will need to be "much more careful how they talk, how they interact, what they offer of themselves."[118]

Responding to this new and changing setting requires a closer look at what living with a historical record really means and what role the law plays in shaping it. We must ask under what conditions we will flourish within cultural definitions of human freedom.[119] It is not an easy question to answer, and it deserves reflective, thoughtful treatment and more than a simplistic choice between preserving speech or privacy—saving or deleting.

Forgetting Made Easy

In the landmark case *Google v. AEPD*, handed down in May 2014, citizens of the European Union were granted one version of a right to be forgotten based on portions of the 1995 European Union Data Protection Directive. Within the first thirty-one days, Google received a reported 70,000 requests to remove 250,000 search results linking individuals in the EU to information they would rather be dissociated from. That is a lot of lost information. Responding quickly to technological threats is admirable, but extreme responses that do not account for social variation and legal uncertainty can lead to internal injustices and cross-cultural struggles.

Europe has a long history of privacy regulation,[1] much of which is relevant to the right to be forgotten. A number of unifying documents have been passed in the twentieth century and continue to be refined and interpreted through two main braches: the Council of Europe and the European Union.[2] The Council of Europe's European Convention on Human Rights (ECHR) is over sixty years old and conveys the "right to respect for private and family life" in article 8. The Council's Convention for the Protection of Individuals with regard to Automatic Processing of Personal Data (Convention 108) proactively addressed computational data processing in 1981. Since 2000, article 7 of the Charter of Fundamental Rights of the European Union has protected "respect for private and family life." Additionally, the Charter explicitly denotes the protection of personal data in the next article (8). Arguably the most influential privacy regulation ever conceived, the EU Data Protection Directive (DP Directive) was passed in 1995 and is the core of the European data-protection framework. It directed all EU member countries to create data-protection agencies and establish means of protecting specified data rights granted to citizens. It has significantly influenced most, but not all, data-protection laws around the world. The two organizations exist as cooperative partners, engaging in joint programs and initiatives, but have complementary roles. All twenty-eight members of the EU are members of the forty-seven nations of the Council of Europe, and so privacy regulations and rights must account for article 10 of the ECHR, the right to "receive and impart information and ideas," and its corresponding right found in article 11 of the Charter. Most importantly, in comparing European and U.S. legal cultures, each right must be accorded "equal respect" as courts seek to strike a "fair balance" when presented with controversies involving multiple rights, interests, and circumstances as directed by the European Court of Human Rights (ECtHR).[3] These and other agreements have had important impacts on the protection of privacy in European countries. Each European country briefly surveyed in the following pages has a different relationship to, role within, and adapted legal structure for these regional intergovernmental organizations, laws, and rights. I have chosen to limit discussion of these interplays for the sake of brevity and to focus on the way in which the national systems have developed and deployed protection of information privacy and redemptive concepts.

Before looking at individual European countries, an important difference between European and American information policy to keep in mind is the default for sharing. The default in the U.S. generally permits the collection and transfer of personal information and prevents abuse through self-regulation and market forces. National systems within Europe operate under comprehensive regimes that protect personal information across both the public and private sectors and are enforced by specialized data-protection agencies. The structure, resources, regulatory tools, and enforcement tactics of data-protection authorities, as well as their place within the national regulatory system, vary across nations, but the default is generally not open sharing. For instance, cross-marketing efforts in the 1990s between financial services and insurance companies in Germany required each customer to consent to the transfer.[4] Many countries restrict the transfer of publicly available data and protect information in public registries, such as voting records, real estate transactions, and judicial decisions. Because this approach applies to both the public and private sectors, sharing between the two types of institutions also is restricted. Another example is the injunctive relief based on a violation of intimacy of private life in France, ranging from the destruction of art to the suppression of books, which is extended to information prior to disclosure.[5] This difference in default matters greatly to the right to be forgotten and is entangled with the way in which countries have navigated their relationships to intergovernmental organizations and laws.

Many national legal systems in Europe embrace a notion of redemption by which an individual may preclude another from identifying him or her in relation to his or her past. While the initial release of personal information may be warranted, over time the justifications for continuing to make available or to disclose old data wane as privacy rights gain legitimacy. This dynamic is essentially a right to be forgotten and finds different roots, interpretations, and enforcement across European countries. It is no surprise that countries with rich personality rights like Germany, France, and Italy—those that encompass and firmly protect dignity, honor, and the right to private life—have had established and evolved forms of the right to be forgotten for decades. What is somewhat surprising is that privacy rights in all three of these influential civil law countries (wherein codes and statutes intended to reach every eventual-ity are the main source of law) derived from common law (wherein the main source of law is judicial opinions that ensure consistency through adherence to precedents) judicial developments at various time periods, a characteristic not shared by the UK.

The United Kingdom, while part of the European Union, is unique within Europe because it is a common law legal system, as opposed to the rest of the countries of Europe (with the exception of Ireland), which have civil law systems. This difference is emphasized by the United Kingdom's lack of a single constitutional document. The country has of course protected privacy, reputation, and speech through other claims and rights but has done so utilizing its "uncodified constitution." Like many of the other countries in Europe, the UK has relied heavily on defamation law to protect reputation, as a right recognized within the right to respect for private and family life. The United Kingdom's bal-ance between the preservation of reputation and freedom of expression has shifted, particularly because the Defamation Act of 2013 made a number of changes that brought the tort closer to a U.S. version.

While defamation now provides less control of individual reputation than in the past, the Human Rights Act of 1998 and the Data Protection Act of 1998 have increased the UK's recognition and enforcement of pri-vacy rights through tort actions. Prior to the Human Rights Act, which was passed in the UK to give full effect to the ECHR and stated that it is unlawful "for a public authority to act in a way which is incompatible with a Convention right," the UK protected privacy through an expan-sion of its law of confidentiality.[6] Confidentiality claims center around the inappropriate sharing of personal information, which historically required the claimant to have an expectation of trust based on the na-ture of the relationship and information exchanged but has since been expanded to reach incidents where no prior relationship exists.[7]

A series of relatively recent opinions from English courts, most in-volving claims filed by celebrities like Michael Douglas and Naomi Campbell trying to prevent or be compensated for the publication of their personal information, reveal the doctrinal shift prompted by the need to fit national legal protections within the ECHR.[8] By the time Max Mosley sued over the publication of video and pictures taken of him engaging in sexual acts under uncommon circumstances, the groundwork had been laid for his victory.[9] Mosley's claim that he had an expectation of privacy in information regarding his sexual activity was easily accepted.[10] Additionally, the court rejected the publisher's argument that the criminal element (prostitution) necessarily meant the information was of public interest.[11] Finally, the aspect of the Nazi theme, which according to the court might have been of public interest, was dropped due to lack of evidence.[12] The court balanced article 8 (right to respect of one's privacy and family life) and article 10 (freedom of expression and information), diminishing somewhat the unique distinction that England possessed in regard to protecting privacy interest.[13]

The UK's data-protection regime, in place since 1984, has been similarly altered to fit within broader European goals. Senior High Court Justice Tugendhat explained in 1999, "It is vital to note that the 1984 Act created, and the 1998 Act continues, concepts entirely new to English law. These rights do not depend on whether the data subject . . . would have rights under the existing law of confidentiality or defamation or any other tort or statute."[14] The implementation of the DP Directive required certain updates to the Data Protection Act of 1984, which were put in place by the Data Protection Act of 1998. Enforced by the UK's data-protection agency, the Information Commissioner's Office (ICO), the privacy regime is overseen by the Information Tribunal. While British jurisprudence experienced a bit of a jolt and data protection was restructured slightly, the UK has not embraced the right to be forgotten. The UK's House of Lords EU Home Affairs, Health and Education Sub-Committee has fought against the incorporation of a right to be forgotten into EU law, calling it "misguided in principle and unworkable in practice."[15]

Postwar Germans have embraced the protection of personal information more directly.[16] Although reluctant to recognize expansive personality rights in the nineteenth and early twentieth centuries, German courts actively and consistently emphasized individual human dignity as the guiding principle of the Basic Law, which was drafted and instituted in response World War II and serves as constitutional law in Germany.[17] Additional judicial steps were taken in *Schacht* (1954) when a newspaper published portions of a letter to the editor that created misleading impressions about the attorney who had written it on behalf of his client. The Federal Supreme Court found that the version of the publication was a gross misrepresentation and had not been consented; it ordered that the paper print the full statement.[18] In 1973, when Princess Soraya, ex-wife of the shah of Iran and a German resident, sued a weekly paper for publishing a wholly fabricated interview with her, the Federal Constitutional Court upheld prior court decisions awarding damages for defamation and privacy invasions. Previously, in the prewar era, such cases were heard only by criminal courts and punished with a fine.[19] The court found that the Basic Law protected "above all . . . a person's private sphere, i.e. the sphere in which he desires to . . . remain free from any outside interference,"[20] and in a controversial exercise of power, awarded substantial damages beyond the civil code for the violation of human dignity.

The German right to be forgotten is a personality right situated in the principle of informational self-determination; it incorporates the right to decide for oneself how one will be portrayed to third parties or the public, as well as what and to what extent personal information is made available and to whom. This principle is an extension of other rights, namely, articles 1 ("right to human dignity") and 2 ("right to free development of one's personality") of the German constitution. A new, extensive national census in 1983 provoked public indignation and resistance that led to one of the most important early European data-protection cases. Suspending the census, the German Constitutional Court (BVerfG) interpreted the rights in light of technological innovation: "The worth and dignity of individuals, who through free self-determination function as members of a free society, lie at the core of the constitutional order. In addition to specific guarantees of freedom, the general right of personality guaranteed in Article 2.1 in conjunction with Article 1.1 of the Basic Law, which can also become important precisely in view of modern developments and the concomitant new threats to the personality, serves to protect that worth and dignity."[21] This 1983 ruling also mentions the obligations to provide details and clarification on data collected and stores, as well as to delete data.[22] Most importantly, the ruling is foundational to the principle that "every use of personal data intrudes upon personal freedom and therefore requires legal justification."[23]

Although Germans have a very different twentieth-century history than other European countries do, Germany, like all countries, must draft or interpret its own laws and jurisprudence in light of unifying European documents like the European Convention on Human Rights—a feat of legal reasoning handled by ECtHR judges who hear allegations of violations of the ECHR by Council of European state actors. One of Germany's, and Europe's, most important privacy cases involved a 1999 German BVerfG ruling against Caroline von Hannover (princess of Monaco), who had sought relief for the magazine publication of pictures depicting her going about her daily life (leaving restaurants or walking on the sidewalk).[24] The BVerfG reasoned that she was a public figure and had to tolerate publication of images taken in public so as not to infringe on the freedom of the press and the public's legitimate interest in her.[25] However, the ECtHR overturned the decision, arguing that the German court had deprived von Hannover of her right to privacy and to respect for her family life.[26] After dismissing another of von Hannover's claims for injunctive relief in 2008 for another set of photos, the BVerfG's decision was upheld by the ECtHR because the accompanying story discussed Prince Rainier's illness, which was of legitimate public interest as opposed to a publication for entertainment purposes alone.[27]

Specifically, the German right to informational self-determination entered the conversation about the right to be forgotten when Wolfgang Werlé and Manfred Lauber started filing lawsuits against websites to have their names disconnected from the murder of the actor Walter

Sedlmayr, of which they were convicted in 1993. The conviction is a matter of public record, and because of the actor's fame, numerous news stories were drafted and disseminated about the crime. The two successfully convinced some sites to remove their names and sued a number of other media outlets, including the German-language Wikipedia.[28] Lower courts were split on whether online archives were a current dissemination of a story, which would have violated Germany's interpretation of its right to the development of one's personality as it had been extended to other individuals who had served their time.[29] But when the cases reached the Federal Court of Justice of Germany (BGH) in 2009, it found against Werlé and Lauber by focusing on whether the information was clearly marked as old and outdated, in which case it could be retained.[30] This case, discussed later in chapter 4, takes into account not only the public interest but also the user experience with the information and the expressive interests of the data controller; it represents a refreshingly nuanced approach to privacy.

Franz Werro has investigated the "transatlantic clash" of the Swiss right to be forgotten and the right to inform in the U.S.[31] Switzerland, a member of the Council of Europe but not part of the European Union, holds a strong right to be forgotten based on the country's recognition of a general right to personality, which is similar to the right in Germany and has been interpreted repeatedly to protect criminally prosecuted individuals from being associated with the proceedings once the individual is considered rehabilitated (usually after the judicial proceedings or time served).[32] Although the Swiss civil code and federal law recognize the primacy of the ECHR, national decisions on the right remain the dominant source on the subject because the right to be forgotten has yet to be heard explicitly by the ECtHR.[33] Under Swiss law, publishing the name of an individual in relation to his or her criminal past is only acceptable if the conviction remains newsworthy, and even then it will not be permissible if significant rehabilitation efforts have been made. For instance, the Swiss Federal Court has prevented the publication of white-collar crimes[34] and armed bank robbery,[35] as well as preventing the broadcasting of a 1980 documentary on a man sentenced to death in 1939, an action brought by his son.[36]

French privacy rights are, like others, one in a bundle of personality rights that also include moral rights of creators for the purposes of copyright, the right to control the use of one's image, and the right to protect one's honor and reputation. Although France, too, is a civil law system, its privacy rights developed in a "remarkably uncivil" way.[37] Without legislation on the books, French judges essentially created a right to oppose the publication of private facts through common law based on tort principles and expanded into recognition of a substantive right to privacy in the 1950s and 1960s. A right to be forgotten of sorts developed through extensive case law on various aspects of French personality rights and modern data-protection reform. In what is known as the *Rachel* affair of 1858, a famous actress was photographed on her deathbed at the request of the her sister with the express agreement that the photographs would not be shared with third parties, but a sketch of the deathbed scene appeared shortly after for sale in local stores.[38] Rachel's sister successfully sued to have the sketches seized and destroyed. A number of French privacy attributes are revealed through analysis of the case. The attorney and lecturer in law Jeanne M. Hauch has explained that, prior to legislation and convergence through France's participation in the United Nations, Council of Europe, and European Union, French courts found "liability without much discussion of the reasonableness of the defendant's conduct,"[39] focused on the suffering of the plaintiff, preferred specific rather than monetary relief, and found that the right of privacy trumps the personality rights of expression and informational interest. The *Rachel* decision uses words like "absolute right" and "[no matter] the celebrity of the person involved," reflecting "a feeling that protection tempered by a requirement of negligence or recklessness is simply not stringent enough where the human personality is at issue."[40]

One of the most prominent privacy cases in the country's history illustrates the development of a unique protection of private life. In 1867, the famous *Three Musketeers* author Alexandre Dumas père filed a claim revolving around a set of untoward photos disseminated by the photographer. Dumas admitted that he had sold his rights in the photographs to the man he was suing for publishing them.[41] The *Dumas* court adopted ideas regarding private life that were expressed when the first law lifting post-Napoleonic censorship of the press was passed in 1819.[42] The court explained that even if a person had consented to exposure, that person must retain the right to withdraw in order to protect his or her dignity.[43] Only upon dissemination of the information may the person realize its ramifications, particularly when it violates the expectations that the subject had in mind upon its release. Although Dumas "had forgotten to take care of his dignity, [exposure may] remind him that private life must be walled off in the interest of individuals, *and* often in the interest of good morals as well."[44]

Preliminary injunctive relief that would prevent the disclosure of information to avoid privacy violations was questioned and established nearly one hundred years later in the *Philipe* affair, after several reporters bombarded the hospital room of the nine-year-old son of the famous actor Gérard Philipe. Philipe's widow brought an action to have the publications, set to come out in the next weekly issue, seized prior to hitting newsstands. Even though the article was supportive of the boy and most of the pictures in the article had already been published, the lower and appellate courts found the intrusion of the press intolerable, and the injunction was upheld by the highest court in 1966, further solidifying a strong privacy right that would restrict expression where necessary.[45] A host of privacy claims that were decided through the 1950s and 1960s further refined levels of violations on the basis of the circumstances and associated relief. While the French maintained a newsworthiness component, they did not extend it to a number of things happening in the public view, because the public's legitimate interest does not extend to knowing about personal interests or activities like hobbies or relationships.

Judicial interpretations of personality rights were codified in article 9 of the French Civil Code in 1970, which explicitly guarantees individuals the right to demand respect for his or her private life and grants judges the power to prescribe "all measures" to avoid or remedy a violation of intimacy of private life.[46] In the late 1970s, France also enacted its first data-protection laws. Chapter 5 of Law 78–17/1978 included a right of individuals to demand erasure of personal data that is no longer relevant.[47] Additionally, "numerical oblivion" is a notion adopted specifically for the banking sector and provides individuals with a right to erase personal information from databases after a reasonable period of time.[48]

Fast-forward to 2012: a Parisian civil court ordered Google.com and Google.fr to remove from search results all links to Diana Z and her past as a porn star.[49] French President Nicolas Sarkozy declared, "Regulating the Internet to correct the excesses and abuses that come from the total absence of rules is a moral imperative!"[50] France was among the first countries to enact data-protection laws, and the 1978 legislation was amended in 2004 to meet EU standards. In the amended legislation, article 38 provides a right to object to personal data processing for legitimate reasons, and article 40 provides a procedural right to rectify, complete, or erase "incomplete" data.[51] The French data-protection agency (CNIL) pioneered recognition of a right to be forgotten for a digital world. In 2010, France gave the concept of *le droit a l'oubli* (right of oblivion) momentum. The campaign, led by the French secretary of state, Nathalie Kosciusko-Morizet, who was heading developments in the digital economy, drafted codes of conduct, one for behavioral advertising and one for social networks and search engines, to be signed by industry members.[52] The charter was signed by a number of actors but did not include Google or Facebook. France has remained relatively isolated from industry pressure not only because of its fierce cultural and legal protection of individuals but also because many of the information sectors were nationalized in France during the mid-twentieth century.

The Italian legal culture has embraced as part of its personality rights what is called the right to personal identity, an individual's right "to appear and to be represented in social life (especially by the mass media) in a way that fits with, or at least does not falsify or distort, his or her personal history."[53] The Italian legal scholar Giorgio Pino explains that the Italian Civil Code of 1942 explicitly recognizes only the right to one's name and pseudonym, likeness, and moral copyright and that the Italian constitution is less explicit in its recognition of a right to the development of the person than are other national constitutions such as those of Germany and Spain. Nonetheless, Italian judges, not unlike French and German judges before them, interpreted these rights to craft a right to personal identity using common law techniques in a civil law system.[54] For instance, in *Pangrazi and Silvetti v. Comitato Referendum* (1975), a photograph of an unmarried farming couple was used without their consent on posters supporting a traditionalist, antidivorce movement to which they were opposed.[55] The judge expanded on the plaintiff's claim that the poster violated their likeness rights by adding that the image violated the individuals' right to have their personal identity protected from misrepresentation by widespread publication. Pino further explains that judicial developments have given the Italian right to personality distinct features: misrepresentation of the person must be made public to be actionable; it does not protect privately held ideas or thoughts; and the right is flexible, covering various contexts such as political, sexual, and professional identities. As an example of the right-to-oblivion context, a convicted murderer who was later pardoned and then the subject of a newspaper trivia game thirty years later successfully challenged the publication. The Tribunale Roma ruled that the paper "shed 'false light in the public eye' about the actual personality of the subject" and had not proved justifiable public interest.[56]

The Italian courts and data-protection agencies have focused on time and data quality to extend protection to citizens in a related way. In 1984, the Italian Court of Cassation established a balancing test for old information when 1972–1973 newspaper reports concerning the fund of two real estate companies were claimed to be continually damaging a decade later.[57] The court used three criteria to weigh article 2043 of the Italian Civil Code, providing for recourse when loss is suffered, in light of article 21 of the Italian constitution, providing for freedom of the press (codified in the Italian Press Act): (1) the information must be of social or public interest, (2) the coverage must be correct or at least lead to serious investigation toward discovering truth, and (3) the information must be presented objectively and civilly.[58] The court considered the social utility of the information, its incompleteness, and the harm and potential harm, with a special focus on time.[59]

In 2004, the Italian data-protection agency (Garante) interpreted the data-quality principle in article 11 of its data-protection legislation to mean that data quality is not preserved when personal data that no longer meets the initial objective associated with its collection is not deleted, particularly upon notification from the data subject.[60] In 2005, the Garante dealt with the online retrieval of an Italian Antitrust Authority decision against a company for misleading advertisements.[61] The agency determined that external search engines should be restricted from crawling the information by applying "Robot Meta Tags" to certain pages and asked the Antitrust Authority to create a time-based policy for hiding the sanctions.[62] After five years, the Antitrust Authority would apply metatags to the pages to signal to external crawlers that the pages should not be indexed.[63] In a decision out of the Third Civil Division in April 2012, the Italian Supreme Court of Cassation in Rome ordered online news archives to be kept up-to-date so that the right to be forgotten could be enforced in terms of keeping personal data accurate and timely.[64] The ruling was directed at Italian newspapers like the *Corriere della Sera*, one of Italy's most dominant news sources.[65] The case arose when search engines were connecting a politician from Lombardy to news coverage of his 1993 arrest and charges of corruption for which he was later acquitted.[66] Finding no recourse with the Garante or the Court of Milan, the claimant filed suit with the Court of Cassation to at least resolve the incompleteness of the information in the digital news archives.[67] The court agreed that the information was incomplete in light of later events and that archived articles must be accompanied by relevant updates.[68]

The Spanish data-protection agency (AEPD) has ardently recognized and extended the right to be forgotten. With a firm constitutional foundation in article 10, which provides a right to the free development of personality, the AEPD established the Spanish right to be forgotten in the principles of collection limitation, purpose specificity, and data quality. However, Spain expanded the concept on the basis of its particular privacy position. The AEPD had no problem providing data subjects who were not public figures or part of a news story the right to correct or respond to personal data online.[69] More so than any other country, Spain relies on the right to withdraw consent, found in article 6.3 of its data-protection law.

Gaining substantial U.S. attention, the AEPD brought the initial suit against Google to remove URLs from its index that point to personal information that the AEPD had determined should appropriately be forgotten.[70] More than ninety citizens filed formal complaints with the AEPD about online information, including a domestic-violence victim's address and an old college arrest.[71] After assessing the privacy concerns of each complaint and failing to persuade the source of the content to take action, the AEPD ordered Google to stop indexing the information. Google challenged the order, saying that editing the index "would have a profound chilling effect on free expression without protecting people's privacy"[72] and would violate the "objectivity" of the Internet.[73]

The dispute involved information like a notice of home repossession for nonpayment of social security and a reference to a plastic surgeon's alleged botched operation that was settled out of court; both are information produced and maintained by traditional news sources and retrieved by Google's search engine when the individuals' names are entered.[74] Google appealed five of the determinations to the Audiencia Nacional, which in turn referred the matter to the European Court of Justice (CJEU) for clarification.[75]

In the midst of these distinct national efforts, the European Commission announced in 2009 that it would be reviewing and updating the 1995 Data Protection Directive.[76] After more than three years of reflection, consultation, and debates, the European Commission published its proposal for a new European Data Protection Regulation (DP Regulation) in January 2012.[77] As promised, the draft included a right to be forgotten. All of the aforementioned laws are relevant to the right to be forgotten in one way or another, but the DP Regulation contains an explicit, formalized, and mechanical right to erase personal data held by another party. The proposed DP Regulation, discussed more fully shortly, was met with great resistance and skepticism in the U.S.

But then, in the spring of 2014, something unexpected happened. It turned out that every European Union citizen had a right to be forgotten of sorts all along—well, since 1995 at least. The decision in the *Google Spain and Google Inc. v. AEPD and González* (*Google v. AEPD*) case that had been appealed through the Spanish court system and referred to the CJEU was handed down March 13, 2014; it interpreted the 1995 DP Directive to grant a right to be forgotten across the European Union.[78] The named plaintiff in the case was Mario Costeja González, who had complained about a 1998 *La Vanguardia* notice regarding a real estate auction related to his social security debt. Although long since resolved, the notice came up when people searched him on Google. González first contacted Google Spain with a request to remove the notice from search results but was told that all search results are handled at Google headquarters in California. Unsuccessful, he took his issue to the AEPD. The AEPD pursued his claim against both Google Spain and Google but rejected González's claim against the newspaper on grounds it had "lawfully published" the content.

When the Spanish court referred the question to the EU's high court, the CJEU decided that Google's search activity met the definition of a "data controller" under article 2(d) of the DP Directive because its collection, storage, analysis, and rank of content were acts that "determined the purpose and means" of the personal data in its system. The court also found that, as a data controller, Google was "processing" personal data under article 2(b), which defines the term as "any operation or set of operations which is performed upon personal data, whether or not by automatic means, such as collection, recording, organisation, storage, adaptation or alteration, retrieval, consultation, use, disclosure by transmission, dissemination or otherwise making available, alignment or combination, blocking, erasure, or destruction."[79]

The CJEU next determined that the right to access in article 12 and the right to object in article 14 enable a data subject to address the search engine directly in order to prevent indexing. Article 12(b) grants each data subject the right to rectify, erase, or block data processing that does not comply with the Directive in articles 6 and 7. Under article 6, data processing is incompatible with the Directive if the data is inadequate, irrelevant, or no longer relevant; excessive in relation to the purposes of the processing; or kept after it has been used for the purpose for which it was collected. Article 7 provides the acceptable justifications for processing.

Additionally, article 14 provides a right to object to data processing. Article 14 requires member countries to provide a right to object for at least those data-processing practices that are legitimized as tasks of public interest (article 7(e)) or necessary for the legitimate interest of the data controller (article 7(f)) *and* when the data subject has "compelling and legitimate grounds." This means that member states may not be required to provide a right to object when data processing is legitimized under the other justifications in article 7: the data subject has given his or her unambiguous consent, the processing is necessary to perform a contract, a legal obligation exists, or a vital interest of the data subject is being protected (article 7 (a)–(d)). Although it may read as a fairly limited right, the CJEU pointed out that "in each case the processing of personal data must be authorized . . . for the entire period during which it is carried out."[80]

Substantively, the court offered very little guidance on implementing the rights it uncovered in the Directive. It did, however, find that data subjects cannot just delete something they dislike—they do not even need to dislike it. While González and the Spanish and Italian governments argued that data subjects should be able to enforce their right when search results are prejudicial against them (overriding the interest of the operator and general interest of freedom of information),[81] the CJEU agreed with Google and the Greek, Austrian, and Polish governments and the European Commission, which all argued for a seemingly more limited interpretation: in order to force removal, an individual's personal data must only have lost its adequacy, relevance, or original purpose or its processing lost its authorization.[82] The court was frank but not clear:

> As the data subject may, in the light of his fundamental rights under Articles 7 and 8 of the Charter, request that the information in question no longer be made available to the general public by its inclusion in such a list of results, it should be held . . . that those rights override, as a rule, not only the economic interest of the operator of the search engine but also the interest of the general public in finding that information upon a search relating to the data subject's name. However, that would not be the case if it appeared, for particular reasons, such as the role played by the data subject in public life, that the interference with his fundamental rights is justified by the preponderant interest of the general public in having, on account of inclusion in the list of results, access to the information in question.[83]

Google argued—supported by Austria and Greece—that the publisher of the website is in the best position to assess the lawfulness of the content, to address its importance to the public, and to easily make the content inaccessible by making small technical adjustments that would prevent Google's crawlers from indexing the content at issue.[84] According to the opinion, Poland agreed that if the content is lawfully and truthfully published on the original page, a search engine is released from obligations to remove links to it.[85] The CJEU did not see it this way, insisting that reaching search engines was vital to ensuring a high level of protection for fundamental rights in the Digital Age.[86]

Procedurally, having categorized Google's search activities as those of a data controller under the Directive, the court established a direct line between EU users and Google. It created a subject-to-controller takedown system for personal information. It is similar to the U.S. Digital

Millennium Copyright Act (DMCA), discussed further in chapter 2. A takedown-notice system is more efficient than having to go through an administrative or judicial proceeding of some kind. The takedown system also has the benefit of avoiding the unwanted publicity that filing a privacy claim can bring. We can conclude that a takedown regime for the right to erasure would be (and is proving to be, as Google receives more takedown requests every day from the EU) relatively cheap, efficient, and privacy preserving. All a data subject must do is contact a data controller that would exercise removal of the information, and the data controller must comply unless retention would fall under one of the exceptions. Efficiency comes at a cost, and the DMCA has offered a lesson when it comes to the threat of litigation that hinges on data controllers' and site operators' interpretation of and reaction to uncertain legal exceptions. One study from 2006 found that a third of the DMCA takedown notices in the Chilling Effects database presented obvious questions for a court, such as fair-use determination or the legitimacy of the copyright.[87] Additionally, 57 percent of notices were sent to target content of a competitor.[88] While not substantially effective, safeguards are included in the DMCA to prevent abuse, such as penalties for misrepresenting content or activity as infringing (17 U.S.C. § 512(f)). The right to erasure has no such safeguards.

The potential for abuse in user-initiated takedown systems is already incredibly high, but the added element of international uncertainty regarding the interpretation of numerous digital rights to be forgotten across the EU and their exceptions make widespread abuse inevitable. Arguably, every right-to-be-forgotten takedown request would involve a substantive legal question related to the underlying claim. As a data controller, Google is obligated to consider each and every removal request from data subjects. It must do so with only the aforementioned minimal guidance offered and across twenty-eight different legal cultures. Each country will find different answers as to when and why the interference with a data subject's fundamental rights under the Directive is justified in light of the general public interest to access the information.

Most importantly, no country has a richly developed digital right to be forgotten. No data controller could receive a right-to-be-forgotten request from any EU country and find clear guidance in legislation, regulation, or jurisprudence and know how to respond legally. In the *Future of Reputation*, Daniel Solove argues, "The goal of the law should be to encourage the development of norms and to spur people to work out their disputes informally."[89] However, informality must take into account a lack of legal certainty and chilling effects. Attempting to knock Google down a few pegs, the CJEU instead further empowered the search giant by essentially putting the right to be forgotten in the company's hands to be shaped. Google's policies, instead of a data-protection agency or court, now serve as the jurisprudence for the right to be forgotten in Europe.

The decision was surprising because both the Directive and Google have been around for some time without this determination having been made. The opinion of the advocate general, a preliminary opinion generally relied on by the CJEU, came to an almost completely opposite conclusion less than a year earlier. Advocate General Jääskinen highlighted the many changes that had occurred since the 1995 Directive and stated that search engines were still "at their nascent stage. . . . The provisions of the Directive simply do not take into account the fact that enormous masses of decentrally hosted electronic documents and files are accessible from anywhere on the globe and that their contents can be copied and analysed and disseminated by parties having no relation whatsoever to their authors or those who have uploaded them onto a host server connected to the internet."[90] Jääskinen found that the objectives of the Directive required an interpretation that had balanced and reasonable outcomes[91] and that to find Google a data controller would be a "blind literal interpretation" of the controller concept.[92] Additionally, he found no right to be forgotten in the Directive. He stated that "a subjective preference alone does not amount to a compelling legitimate ground within the meaning of Art. 14 (a)," and he was not inclined to agree that a data subject is entitled to restrict or delete disclosed personal data "that he considers to be harmful or contrary to his interests."[93] This was the general understanding of data subjects' right to object in article 14 and right to erasure in article 12. In fact, at the time, the European Commissioner stated that the DP Regulation would *introduce* the right to be forgotten when she discussed the Commission's intentions to revamp the Directive with a Regulation in 2010.[94]

Although doubts about the advisability of a right to be forgotten exist after the CJEU opinion, there can be no doubt about the demand for digital redemption after the flood of requests that followed. Once Google created an online form for EU citizens to fill out describing their claim to be forgotten and verifying their identity, the company received 12,000 requests in the first day, 40,000 requests over the first four days, and 70,000 requests to remove 250,000 links by the end of the first month. The surge of requests settled into about 1,000 requests per day, with France submitting the most requests of the total figures at 14,086, followed by Germany with 12,678, and the United Kingdom at 8,497 requests (half of which reportedly came from those related to criminal convictions).[95] Faced with mounting compliance costs, Google's team granted the removal of 70,000 links within the first month and created a committee to help the company "be more European."[96]

The decision does not mean that the inclusion of the right to be forgotten in the DP Regulation is now irrelevant—far from it. The Directive required each member country to provide protection for certain rights within its own national legal framework. There is a great deal of variation, as the input from various countries in the *Google v. AEPD* case illustrates. As the foregoing cursory look at only a few EU countries reveals, each European country has a different history when it comes to data, speech, access, public interest, public figures, privacy, identity, reputation, self-determination, and self-presentation. Some of these countries may be similar and their treatment appropriately converged into one, but others will not merge seamlessly. The point of the DP Regulation is to update the DP Directive from 1995 to meet the technological realities of today and the future, as well as to harmonize data-protection regimes throughout the EU in order to streamline compliance. The DP Regulation intends to set forth a single set of rules, with national data-protection agencies coordinated by a European Data Protection Board to resolve fragmentation and incoherence.

As mentioned, the European Commission has proposed its long-expected draft revision of the European data-protection legal framework.[97] Although a final version is not expected to be adopted until the end of 2015 or early 2016, it is useful to evaluate the current DP Regulation proposal, which already represents four years of reflection and three stages of EU legislative decision making, in order to assess how it may resolve the issues that have already presented themselves since the *Google v. AEPD* case.

The DP Regulation's objectives can largely be divided into two main categories: (1) the proposal tries to strengthen individuals' control over their personal data, and (2) it tries to provide legal certainty and minimize administrative burdens for businesses. One of the elements included to achieve the first objective is the introduction of an explicit "right to be forgotten and to erasure," building on the existing right of erasure in the DP Directive. In the Commission's words, this provision is intended "to ensure that when an individual no longer wants their personal data to be processed, and if there is no legitimate reason for an organisation to keep it, it should be removed."[98]

When the Commission's proposal was sent to the next phase in the EU legislative process, the title of article 17 was changed to just "the right to erasure" by the Civil Liberties, Justice, and Home Affairs (LIBE) committee.[99] The language I quote shortly is the language in the LIBE draft accepted by the EU Parliament. It will proceed to the EU Council, which may make additional alterations, but an agreed-on text must be established between Parliament and the Council in order to be enacted.

It is important to consider the overall scope of application of the DP Regulation itself. The right does not create obligations for activities that fall within the "household" exception, which is defined as "a natural person without any gainful interest in the course of its own exclusively personal or household activity" (art. 2(d)). Besides this personal use or household exemption, the Regulation is also *not* applicable to data processing in the context of national security issues or criminal investigations. Otherwise, article 17 is far reaching.

The first paragraph describes four situations in which the data subject has "the right to obtain from the controller the erasure of personal data relating to them and the abstention from further dissemination of such data":

> (a) the data are no longer necessary in relation to the purposes for which they were collected or otherwise processed; (b) the data subject withdraws consent on which the processing is based . . . , or when the storage period consented to has expired, and where there is no other legal ground for the processing of the data; (c) the data subject objects to the processing of personal data pursuant to Article 19 [right to object]; (c)(a) a court or regulatory authority based in the Union has ruled as final and absolute that the data concerned must be erased; (d) the data has been unlawfully processed.

Thus, dependent on verification of the data subject's identity, the right can be invoked whenever (a) the purpose-limitation principle is breached, (b) consent is withdrawn or the legitimate storage period has been exceeded, (c) the right to object to data processing has been legally exercised or ordered by a court or agency, (d) the processing of data is illegal (i.e., does not comply with the Regulation).

The purpose-limitation principle is not a new concept and can be found in the current DP Directive (art. 6), although it is rare to find in practice. The third and fourth grounds, too, can be found in the current framework. When data is processed illegally, the controller must remove it, and when an individual exercises his or her right to object, this renders further processing illegal (and thus removable) as well. However, the second ground is more novel: consent withdrawal and expiration. The new Regulation tries to deemphasize reliance on a one-time consent framework, for example, by explicitly allowing for its withdrawal (art. 7(3)). The proposed right to erasure also follows this trend, seeking to establish a balanced environment where individuals can continually and effectively reevaluate their consent.[100]

The second paragraph,[101] however, is the source of significant dispute, bringing to the forefront drastic differences between European and U.S. legal and cultural treatment of information privacy. This paragraph grants a right to the data subject that extends to circumstances in which the data controller has disclosed the personally identifiable information to the public (e.g., by publishing it on a website) or when publication is delegated to a third party. It reads, "Where the controller referred to in paragraph 1 has made the personal data public without a justification based on Article 6(1), it shall take all reasonable steps to have the data erased, including by third parties, without prejudice to Article 77. The controller shall inform the data subject, where possible, of the action taken by the relevant third parties" (art. 17(2)). The vagueness of the obligation to take "all reasonable steps to have data erased" is challenging. But the LIBE committee did edit the language that previously stated, "Where the controller has authorised a third party publication of personal data, the controller shall be considered responsible for that publication." It was unclear when a publication would be considered "authorised" and what "responsible" duties and liabilities entailed—the nature of data sharing today made that obligation unworkable. The second paragraph is also puzzling when read in conjunction with article 13 of the proposed Regulation. This article already provides for a more general rule on data subjects' rights to trace their data. This provision states that the controller has to communicate erasure requests to all recipients to whom personal data was disclosed, unless this proves to be impossible or disproportionate. The relationship between article 13 and article 17(2) is unclear. The current draft leaves much open to interpretation.

Most wanting for clarity is article 17(3), which outlines the exceptions to the right to be forgotten. In cases where the erasure request is based on a withdrawal of consent, personal data should not be erased when other legal grounds for processing the data exist. Furthermore, paragraph 3 determines that the data controller may retain the personal data at issue if it is necessary (a) to protect the right of freedom of expression, (b) for reasons of public interest in the area of public health, (c) for historical, statistical, and scientific research purposes, or (d) for compliance with a legal obligation to retain the personal data by Union or Member State law.[102] The exceptions will define the right to be forgotten. It is not hard to establish a historical, statistical, or scientific justification for keeping any data. However, no further guidance on how to balance these vital, numerous, and circumstance-specific interests is provided. Personal data can also be retained—although the controller does have to restrict its processing[103]—(a) when its accuracy is contested by the data subject (for a period enabling the controller to verify the accuracy of the data), (b) for purposes of proof, (c) when the data subject is opposed to erasure (even though the processing is unlawful) and requests that the use of the data be restricted instead, and (d) for data-portability purposes. Although the applications of all these exceptions are not clear, their interpretations will make or break the right to be forgotten.

All of this vagueness is particularly troublesome in light of the chilling effects associated with user takedown systems and because of the Regulation's stern penalties, which the Commission had set as a fine up to €1 million or up to 2 percent of its annual worldwide turnover and the LIBE Committee raised to a fine up to €100 million or up to 5 percent of the annual worldwide turnover, whichever is greater (art. 79(2a)(c)). At this point, article 17(9) may be the most important part of the entire section; in it, the Commission reserves the right to adopt "delegated acts" in order to specify criteria and requirements for the application of the right in specific sectors and situations but also to specify conditions with regard to the enigmatic second paragraph.

There are also international measures designed to *guide* all countries that participate in the councils and groups that craft the measures. The Fair Information Practice Principles (FIPPs) lay some foundation on which a right to be forgotten may find footing. The FIPPs have gone through many iterations and vary by sector. The Organization for Economic Cooperation and Development (OECD) proposed privacy guidelines[104] similar to those developed by the Council of Europe,[105] both in 1980. The principles in the OECD *Guidelines on the Protection of Privacy and Transborder Flows of Personal Data* are as follows:

▷ Collection Limitation Principle. There should be limits to the collection of personal data and any such data should be obtained by lawful and fair means and, where appropriate, with the knowledge or consent of the data subject.

▷ Data Quality Principle: Personal data should be relevant to the purposes for which they are to be used and, to the extent necessary for those purposes, should be accurate, complete, and kept up-to-date.

▷ Purpose Specifications Principle: The purposes for which personal data are collected should be specified not later than at the time of data collection and the subsequent use limited to the fulfillment of those purposes or such others as are not incompatible with those purposes and as are specified on each occasion of change of purpose.

▷ Use Limitation Principle: Personal data should not be disclosed, made available or otherwise used for purposes other than those specified in accordance with [the Purpose Specification Principle] except: a) with the consent of the data subject; or b) by the authority of law.

▷ Security Safeguards Principle: Personal data should be protected by reasonable security safeguards against such risks as loss or unauthorized access, destruction, use, modification or disclosure of data.

▷ Openness Principle: There should be a general policy of openness about developments, practices and policies with respect to personal data. Means should be readily available of establishing the existence and nature of personal data, and the main purposes of their use, as well as the identity and usual residence of the data controller.

▷ Individual Participation Principle: An individual should have the right: a) to obtain from a data controller, or otherwise, confirmation of whether or not the data controller has data relating to him; b) to have communicated to him, data relating to him within a reasonable time; at a charge, if any, that is not excessive; in a reasonable manner; and in a form that is readily intelligible to him; c) to be given reasons if a request made under subparagraphs (a) and (b) is denied, and to be able to challenge such denial; and d) to challenge data relating to him and, if the challenge is successful to have the data erased, rectified, completed or amended.

▷ Accountability Principle: A data controller should be accountable for complying with measures, which give effect to the principles stated above.[106]

This version of the FIPPs explicitly gives the individual user a right to delete personal data, but only when denial of a request is successfully challenged. The OECD's principles have been widely embraced, including by the Asia-Pacific Economic Cooperation (APEC) Privacy Framework. The FIPPs were most recently utilized by the Obama White House in a report by the National Strategy for Trusted Identities in Cyberspace (NSTIC).[107] However, the NSTIC set of FIPPs does not include user-initiated deletion in the individual-participation or data-minimization principles, but as we have seen, the combination can offer users a claim to delete data that has fulfilled its original purpose depending on how these principles are to be enforced. Again, though, these are principles to be incorporated and enforced (or not) by various legal cultures around the world. All of the mentioned FIPPs have been offered to members as guidelines.

There is no international law currently used to implement digital redemption, but there may be one on the books. The 1966 International Covenant on Civil and Political Rights (ICCPR) has since its adoption included a right to privacy in article 17. It reads,

1.) No one shall be subject to arbitrary or unlawful interference with his privacy, family, home, or correspondence, nor to unlawful attacks upon his honour and reputation.
2.) Everyone has the right to the protection of the law against such interference or attacks.[108]

Although this reads similarly to the ECHR's article 8 and the Charter's article 7, General Comment 16 of 1988 distinguishes the UN's focus from these two European documents, which are much more encompassing. The ICCPR's article 17 refers to the need for limits on collection, security measures, and access to collected data but little else relative to the principles that had already been stated prominently elsewhere. The UN is not perceived as a strong source of data privacy; even still, the General Comment on article 17 explicitly states, "Every individual should also be able to ascertain which public authorities or private individuals or bodies control or may control their files. If such files contain incorrect personal data or have been collected or processed contrary to the provisions of the law, every individual should have *the right to request rectification or elimination*."[109] There may be a right to be forgotten written into the ICCPR, making it an international human right, but the right to be forgotten is not likely the UN's highest priority in terms of protecting information privacy, family privacy, or individual honor; nor has the UN taken the lead on data privacy issues. Furthermore, the ICCPR also mandates the freedom of expression in article 19, and the U.S. has made an official reservation that none of the articles should restrict the freedom of expression.

Forgetting Made Impossible

Since the conversation about the right to be forgotten began in Europe and particularly after *Google v. AEPD*, many observers in the U.S. have perceived digital redemption as entirely unworkable and ridiculous, while others have begun to consider the idea more seriously. Although many Americans may want some kind of structure for digital redemption, the commentary surrounding digital redemption stops the conversation before it starts, in large part due to the weight placed on the freedom of expression in the U.S. When Wolfgang Werlé and his lawyers were contacting media outlets to have his name dissociated with his crime, they attempted to do the same for the English-language Wikipedia entry by sending a cease-and-desist letter to the Wikimedia Foundation, explaining, "[Werlé's] rehabilitation and his future life outside the prison system is severely impacted by your unwillingness to anonymize any articles dealing with the murder."[1] The Electronic Frontier Foundation rebutted the argument: "At stake is the integrity of history itself."[2] In the U.S., solutions in the form of nonlegal governance are popular approaches to the harms caused by increased discoverability, but these silver bullets are no more successful than are other simplistic responses.

Though a number of state constitutions expressly provide for a right to information privacy, the U.S. Constitution does not; as we have seen, this is not actually unusual. The right to privacy crafted by the Supreme Court in 1965 in *Griswold v. Connecticut*, which stated that "specific guarantees in the Bill of Rights have penumbras, formed by emanations from those guarantees that help give them life and substance. . . . Various guarantees create zones of privacy," serves only to protect against an overbearing and too powerful government, offering no protection against private intrusion.[3] Any protection against private entities, therefore, is derived from common or statutory law. "Dignity" has not made its way into either. Although the Supreme Court used the term "human dignity" or its equivalent in 187 opinions between 1925 and 1982 and 91 times between 1980 and 2000, the references have been "inconsistent and haphazard," and the cases involve bodily searches, treatment of prisoners, marriage, and abortion.[4] In the context of information privacy, Samuel Warren and Louis Brandeis in their monumental 1890 law review article "The Right to Privacy," which launched the expansion of common law privacy actions in the U.S., envisioned a right to privacy that was "a part of a more general right to the immunity of the person, the right to one's personality."[5] In 1960, William Prosser's classic article "Privacy" analyzed and organized hundreds of privacy cases and found four distinct torts,[6] which were eagerly and obdurately put into practice, but in doing so, Prosser "stripped out any high level concepts of *why* privacy should be protected."[7] This operationalistic approach was reiterated by Chief Justice of the Seventh Circuit Frank Easterbrook, who stated frankly, "When we observe that the Constitution . . . stands for 'human dignity' but not rules, we have destroyed the basis for judicial review."[8]

The conflict between expression and privacy is inevitably lopsided, as it is one of constitutional versus common or statutory law. The values of privacy and the First Amendment have been "balanced," and lines have been drawn between negligence and actual malice,[9] public figures and private citizens,[10] and public concerns and private interests[11] to guide lower courts. The attempts by judges, legislators, and advocates to etch out some space for privacy concerns in light of the reverence for expression, explicitly granted in the Constitution, have been woefully unsuccessful.

There are four key legal mechanisms utilized by those who want to control or limit the flow of information about them once it is released: intellectual property restrictions; contractual obligations; defamation; and the privacy torts: (1) intrusion upon seclusion, (2) public disclosure of private facts, (3) misappropriation, and (4) false light. Copyright restrictions are very useful for preventing the replication of content created by the information subject, but they only reach the creative aspects of that work and do not reach information created by another person related to the subject. European countries offer similar protections but under the umbrella of certain rights, as opposed to four separate civil claims. While avenues for protecting privacy are available in both regions, we will see that in the U.S. these options have been significantly weakened, offering little recourse once information is considered public.

To say that Americans do not remove information from the Internet would be disingenuous. Copyrighted material is regularly removed at the request of the copyright holder. Section 512 of the DMCA grants safe harbor from secondary copyright liability (i.e., responsibility for copyright infringement of an end user) to online service providers (OSPs) that remove content in response to a takedown (cease-and-desist) notice from the copyright holder (17 U.S. Code § 512). This can be the removal of an image, song, or video or a link that simply directs one to the complained-of content. There is no judicial oversight involved in this initial takedown-for-immunity arrangement. Use of copyrighted material may be permitted in situations that are considered fair use, found in section 107 (17 U.S. Code § 107). These exceptions include criticism, comment, news reporting, teaching, scholarship, or research and are subject to a balancing test applied on a fact-specific, case-by-case basis. If a user believes his or her use of content falls within a fair-use exception, he or she can file a counternotice, but the OSP is required to keep the content offline for a week (17 U.S.C. § 512(g)). Wendy Seltzer, policy counsel to the World Wide Web Consortium (W3C), explains the way a takedown system can significantly chill speech: "The frequency of error and its bias against speech represents a structural problem with secondary liability and the DMCA: the DMCA makes it too easy for inappropriate claims of copyright to produce takedown of speech."[12] It is too easy for two main reasons: (1) even good-faith claims involve legal uncertainty; (2) speedy removal creates an incentive to file dubious claims.[13] The chilling effects of the DMCA system have not resulted in further alterations to copyright law. A data subject who owns a copyright in the information he or she is trying to remove will be able to address the copyrighted material itself but not commentary surrounding the material or use that falls into one of the exceptions.

Often the disclosure of information online is covered by the terms of service of the site; but these contractual obligations only restrain those who are privy to the contract, and much of the information disclosed about an individual is outside this relationship. So, while information flow can be controlled through legal mechanisms like intellectual property laws and terms-of-service agreements, these options leave holes for personal information from the past to easily slip through, in which case filing a tort claim may be the only option. Even then, looking more closely at available tort claims reveals that suing someone where truthful information is involved will not likely be successful in the United States.

The privacy torts are not entirely relevant to the goal of digital reinvention as they address false impressions or the improper disclosure of information, whereas digital reinvention relates to the invasion that results from continued access to personal information. But the privacy torts are the options that Americans have when they seek to protect against the unwanted dissemination of information by others, and they have been significantly restricted to protect free speech. Intrusion upon seclusion protects one from the intentional invasion of solitude or seclusion through physical or nonphysical means like eavesdropping, peeping through windows, or opening another person's mail. The public disclosure of private facts is a cause of action against one who disseminates generally unknown private information, even if it is true. One may also be sued for using another person's name, likeness, or other personal attributes without permission for exploitative purposes, or misappropriation. In states that recognize a claim for false light, it can be brought if a defendant publishes information that places the subject in a highly offensive light, but this claim addresses false impressions as opposed to false statements. In order for one of these claims to be successful and prevent, hinder, or punish the dissemination or access to information in the U.S., it is the interest of the public, not the interest of the individual, that matters.

Public interest is built into information disputes through the protection of "newsworthy" content or content that "the public has a proper interest in learning about."[14] Many victories over privacy have been won with a blow from First Amendment newsworthiness. But newsworthiness is not impenetrable and has not *always* trumped privacy claims. If we look back far enough, we can find cases wherein the public's interest would not necessarily override an individual's privacy interests. For example, in *Melvin v. Reid* (1931), the court found that the movie depiction of a former prostitute's real-life involvement in a murder trial impinged on the positive reinvention of the woman and overpowered the public's interest in her past. "One of the major objectives of society as it is now constituted . . . is the rehabilitation of the fallen and reformation of the criminal. . . . We believe that the publication by respondents of the unsavory incidents of the past life of appellant after she had reformed, coupled with her true name, was not justified by any standard of morals or ethics known to us and was a direct invasion of her inalienable right."[15] After *Melvin*, the rehabilitative function of privacy began to dwindle, and the definition of newsworthiness began to grow. In 1971, in *Briscoe v. Reader's Digest Assoc.*, California's highest court recognized a common law cause of action for invasion of privacy for a magazine's publication of circumstances that occurred a decade earlier, ordering that the magazine could be liable if it published the material with reckless disregard for facts that a reasonable person would find highly offensive. The plaintiff had been convicted of hijacking trucks in the 1950s. Upon serving his sentence, he reformed his life, but his past was revealed to the world when *Reader's Digest* published a story on hijacking and identified the plaintiff in relation to the crime. The court found this identification potentially actionable: "One of the premises of the rehabilitative process is that the rehabilitated offender can rejoin the great bulk of the community from which he has been ostracized for his anti-social acts. . . . In return for becoming a 'new man' he is allowed to melt into the shadows of obscurity. . . . Human forgetfulness over time puts today's 'hot' news in tomorrow's dusty archives. In a nation of 200 million people there is ample opportunity for all but the most infamous to begin a new life."[16] Even still, the plaintiff ultimately lost. When the case went back to the trial court, it was removed to the federal Central District of California, where the story was found newsworthy and the magazine's motion for summary judgment was granted in an unpublished opinion.[17]

Time does not have the same impact on the public interest in the U.S. as it does in some European countries. More specifically, time does not generally transform a once-famous person, a former public official, or those who are thrust into a public issue into not being of interest to the public later. This becomes clear when we look at defamation standards. Defamation claims create a cause of action to protect one's reputation from false statements of verifiable fact, as long as the individual is not a public figure or considered one for the limited purpose of an event that is of public interest. Truth is an absolute defense in a defamation claim, and so it is not an available avenue for pursuing digital redemption of properly disclosed information; but because public-figure plaintiffs suing for defamation must meet a higher standard ("actual malice"— that the defendant published with either knowledge of falsity or in reckless disregard for the truth),[18] case law on plaintiffs who are no longer in the spotlight is relevant. Anita Wood Brewer, a television performer and recording artist and Elvis Presley's "no. 1 girl" in the late 1950s, had retired to private, married life when an article in 1972 mistakenly reported a romantic reunion with Presley. A unanimous Fifth Circuit panel held that Brewer remained a public figure, at least in regard to a report revolving around the source of her fame.[19] In *Street v. National Broadcasting Co.*, the Sixth Circuit held that Victoria Price Street was a public figure over forty years later on the basis of her involvement as a victim in the famous Scottsboro Boys case, a controversial trial of nine black young men who were convicted and sentenced to death for raping two white women on a freight train in 1931. Street was portrayed as a prostitute, a perjurer, and dead in the NBC "docudrama" aired in 1976. Though the trial court found that Street was no longer a public figure,[20] the Sixth Circuit held that her public-figure status was not changed by the passage of four decades.[21]

Courts have maintained this stance in the privacy context. Newsworthiness and public interest are not necessarily, or likely, diminished with the passage of time. *Sidis v. F-R Pub. Corporation* (1940) illustrated the beginning of a trend away from *Melvin*. In it, a child prodigy who was profiled in 1910 brought a claim for intrusion upon seclusion when the *New Yorker* published an intimate "where are they now?" story, with the subtitle "April Fool!," profiling him as an odd, recluse adult in 1937. The Second Circuit established that Sidis remained a public figure and explained that it could not confine "the unembroidered dissemination of facts" unless the facts are "so intimate and so unwarranted in view of the victim's position as to outrage the community's notion of decency."[22] In *Estill v. Hearst*, the Seventh Circuit decided a case regarding the publication of an image taken fifteen years prior depicting then Indiana prosecutor Robert Estill in a friendly pose with John Dillinger in jail. The picture was described as "literally a fatal mistake. Following Dillinger's epic crashout with a wood-carved gun, Estill lived long enough to be laughed out of office. Then, a broken man, he died."[23] Estill was neither laughed out of office (he had maintained active political life, held public office, and practiced law for twenty-five years after Dillinger escaped) nor dead, but because the court found that the plaintiff had been a public figure at the time the photo was taken, no invasion occurred a decade and a half later. In *Perry v. Columbia Broadcasting Sys.*, the actor Lincoln Theodore Perry, who went by the stage name Stepin Fetchit, argued that the 1968 CBS series *Of Black America* "intentionally violated [his] right of privacy and maliciously depicted [him] as a tool of the white man who betrayed the members of his race and earned two million dollars portraying Negroes as inferior human beings."[24] The Seventh Circuit held in 1974 that forty years after Perry filmed his last movie, he remained a public figure.

In the end, most privacy tort claims result in losing plaintiffs and unscathed defendants who were allowed to expose the private idiosyncrasies of the subjects; the facts are rarely offensive enough, and the public interest is easily satisfied. As the Indiana Supreme Court held in 1997 that an HIV-positive postal worker could not sue a coworker for invasion of privacy after she shared his health information, it explained, "Perhaps Victorian sensibilities once provided a sound basis of distinction, but our more open and tolerant society has largely outgrown such a justification. In our 'been there, done that' age of talk shows, tabloids, and twelve-step programs, public disclosure of private facts are far less likely to cause shock, offense, or emotional distress than at the time Warren and Brandeis wrote their famous article."[25] If society finds disclosure unobjectionable, the dissemination of private facts will not be hindered based on real implications for the individual.

It is difficult to imagine what facts could be more private, morbid, or sensational than those intertwined in rape cases, but these disclosures are nonetheless protected as long as they are obtained legally. In *Cox Broadcasting Corp. v. Cohn*, the U.S. Supreme Court decided that truthful publication of a rape victim's name obtained from public records was constitutionally protected.[26] A similar set of facts led to the same result in *Florida Star v. B.J.F.*, in which the Court addressed the issue of whether information obtained from the public domain—subsequently published by the press—created liability under the public disclosure tort, narrowly deciding favorably for the press.[27] The "zone of privacy surrounding every individual, a zone within which the State may protect him,"[28] recognized by the Court in *Cox* has not developed clearly defined boundaries, but generally, the right to know has trumped privacy interests.

Deference to journalists to determine what is newsworthy and assurance that the long tail of the Internet creates an audience for everything make for a very convoluted notion of newsworthiness as a standard for the proper and continued dissemination of private information. Of course, today the disclosure of private details that reach the masses can originate from any number of sources including the individuals themselves. Cringe-worthy personal information may reach the press last (after having been passed from email or smartphones to social media posts to blogs), reporting on how a file has gone viral. U.S. law reinforces the notion that we are at the mercy of the people around us. After all, "exposure of the self to others in varying degrees is a concomitant of life in a civilized community. The risk of this exposure is an essential incident of life in a society which places a primary value on freedom of speech and of press. 'Freedom of discussion, if it would fulfill its historic function in this nation, must embrace all issues about which information is needed or appropriate to enable the members of society to cope with the exigencies of their period.'" While courts have gone back and forth on elements of privacy tort law, this quote—the second half originally handed down by the Supreme Court in *Thornhill v. Alabama* in 1940,[29] the first half added in *Time v. Hill* in 1967,[30] and used again in 2001 in *Bartnicki v. Vopper*[31]—represents a consistent aspect of American legal culture.

The difference between the foregoing information disputes and those related to digital redemption is that in the former cases, there is nothing necessarily illegal or undesirable about the information when it is initially collected or published online. The right to be forgotten addresses information that has become outdated, irrelevant, harmful, or inaccurate. This information haunts individuals, causing undesirable repercussions for them. An interesting attempt at digital forgetting occurred in the lower state courts in California. In 2006, the *Daily Californian* published, against the pleas of a student's parents, a story about his suspension from the Berkeley football team because of his actions at an adult club; a downward spiral ensued, and in 2010 he died. The parents sued after the newspaper refused to remove the article from the website. Its perpetual existence had caused a great deal of emotional pain, but the court found that the two-year statute of limitations in the Uniform Single Publication Act begins upon the first publication. Moreover, the court took issue with the assertion of intentional infliction of emotional distress derived from libel of the memory of a deceased family member, preventing the case from moving forward.[32] More of these creative claims should be anticipated.

One such claim was rejected by the Second Circuit on January 28, 2015. The court was asked to interpret Connecticut's Criminal Records Erasure Statute in relation to a newspaper's right to distribute content about the original arrest. In August 2010, Lorraine Martin was arrested with her two sons on drug-related charges. After the state of Connecticut decided not to pursue charges against her in January 2012, her criminal case was nolled, meaning it would no longer be prosecuted, and thus she was "deemed to have never been arrested within the meaning of the general statutes with respect to proceedings so erased and may so swear under oath," in accordance with the statute.[33] Martin sued multiple news sources that had published stories about the arrest, arguing that the publications were defamatory after the incident was nolled. The Erasure Statute requires destruction of "all police and court records of any state's attorney pertaining to such charge" but does not impart erasure obligations on anyone else. Martin contended that the continued discoverability of the news story, made possible by the news sites' hosting of the content, constituted the publication of false information, but the court explained that the statute "does not and cannot undo historical facts or convert a once-true fact into falsehoods."[34] Essentially, the court interpreted the Erasure Statute in relation to the First Amendment as allowing for multiple legal truths. Martin may say she was never arrested as a legal truth, and the newspapers may legally publish the fact that Martin was arrested. Because the content accurately portrayed Martin's arrest, all of her claims failed. Beyond her libel and false-light claims, which failed because the stories contained no falsehoods, the claim of negligent infliction of emotional distress failed because there was no negligence in the publication of truthful newsworthy information, and the appropriation claim failed because the paper did not improperly appropriate her name by reporting criminal proceedings to the public. Similar conclusions have been reached by state courts, including the New Jersey Supreme Court, which explained, "The expungement statute does not transmute a once-true fact into a falsehood. It does not require the excision of records from the historical archives of newspapers or bound volumes of reported decisions or a personal diary. It cannot banish memories. It is not intended to create an Orwellian scheme whereby previously public information—long maintained in official records—now becomes beyond the reach of public discourse on penalty of a defamation action."[35]

U.S. cases, with few exceptions, are markedly distinct from *Google v. AEPD* for two reasons. The first is that most of the U.S. claims have been unsuccessful. The second is that all the U.S. cases involve removal from the original source of publication. The lack of success is explained by the First Amendment's interpreted priority in relation to the press, privacy, and reputation. The second distinction is a result of Google's immunity from liability as a search platform. Section 230 of the Communication Decency Act (CDA) prevents interactive computer service providers (platforms and service providers) from being held liable as a publisher for content posted by users of the service. It reads, "No provider or user of an interactive computer service shall be treated as the publisher or speaker of any information provided by another information content provider" (47 U.S. Code § 230). U.S. courts have not been inclined to hold intermediaries accountable for information created by a user and have extended § 230 immunity to a wide range of scenarios, including claims for invasion of privacy, misappropriation, and even negligent age-verification procedures.³⁶ In the U.S., platforms and service providers are considered simply conduits for content provided by someone else, with the exception of copyrighted material, of course.

Data trails that are not publicly disseminated fall outside these legal tools. Priscilla Regan succinctly describes the way data protection works in the U.S.:

> Generally it takes an incident to focus attention on the issue of information privacy—and such incidents tend to focus on one type of record system at a time. . . . There is always vocal and well-financed opposition to privacy protections, generally from business and government bureaucrats who do not want to restrict access to personal information. Their opposition is usually quite successful in weakening the proposed privacy protections and in further narrowing the scope of such protections. And after passage opponents are likely to challenge legislation in courts, often on the basis of First Amendment grounds that any information, including that about individuals, should flow freely and without government restriction.³⁷

Detailing the murder of an actress that led to restrictions on the release of vehicle-registration information, the disclosure of a Supreme Court candidate's movie rentals that led to the Video Privacy Protection Act, and concern about the ease with which health and financial information could be shared that led to legislation, Regan concludes that in the rare instances when self-regulation is not available and legislation actually passes, the individual is handed the burden.³⁸ "In most instances, the costs associated with protecting privacy are shifted to the individual in terms of time to monitor privacy notices and practices and time and often money to pursue redress of grievances, which rarely benefit the consumer in a meaningful way."³⁹

The dissemination of data collected through sites and services is governed by the terms of service set by the sites and services themselves, which are enforced by the Federal Trade Commission (FTC) and by internal policies enforced by what Jeffrey Rosen calls "delete squads."[40] These are the teams of people hired by large platforms that interpret and enforce sites' internal policies on the removal of certain content. The FTC acts under its authority to combat unfair trade activities, to bring actions against deceptive digital information operations, and to guide corporate policy through workshops and best practices. In the end, there is currently very little legal support for individuals who seek to curate their digital profiles and to delete old information.

Children, however, are a little different. With regard to data-protection regimes, the U.S., unlike other countries, carves out special privacy protections and detailed procedures for children online. The Children's Online Privacy Protection Act (COPPA) regulates information collected from children, as opposed to what they are exposed to. The FTC is responsible for the enforcement of COPPA, which requires parental authorization before commercial operators may collect personal data from children under thirteen if the site or service targets children or has actual knowledge of preteen users. Most sites that do not intend to be "kid" sites either do not collect birthdates (which would put them on notice of users under thirteen) and inform users in their terms of service that those under thirteen are not allowed, or collect birthdates at registration and do not allow accounts to be created for children under thirteen who put in their real birthdate. Needless to say, there are a lot of workarounds at registration.[41] The disclosure of children's data collected by rare governed operators requires additional consent to be obtained.

While COPPA gives children and parents the right to actively participate in the collection, use, and retention of children's personal data, it does not protect children from themselves. COPPA is intended to protect children from unscrupulous data-hungry adults working in an asymmetric information landscape, as described earlier. In fact, COPPA stops providing protection to children just when they need it most, as teenagers.

The gap left by COPPA, in both age and protection, was filled by a California state law, Privacy Rights for California Minors in the Digital

World.[42] Signed in September 2013, the law grants minors under eighteen the right to remove information that they themselves post online. There are some important caveats to the law. First, the California law applies only to

▷ sites and services directed at minors or those with actual knowledge that a minor is using the site or service;

▷ minors that have registered with a site (unless the operator prefers to extend the right to nonregistered users); and

▷ nonanonymized posts that do not individually identify the minor.

The right does not extend to content posted by another user, posts that have been copied or reposted by a third party, anonymous posts, or content removed from visibility but still stored with the site or service.

The state law does not require an "eraser button," meaning that this is not a technology-forcing law. Rather, it grants the substantive right to remove content that has been disclosed (arguably) to the public and asserts the associated procedural requirements to effectuate that right. Procedurally it is similar to laws that ensure information controllers provide means to correct information in certain settings (included in most policies based on the Fair Information Practices Principles). The law requires that sites and services must provide notice of the right and clear instructions for exercising the right and must explain that exercising the right does not ensure complete or comprehensive removal of the information.

The right granted to California minors is novel in the U.S. Under only a few circumstances does U.S. law allow truthful information to be retracted from the public domain once it is released (e.g., copyright). The law grants this right only to minors in California but intends to hold any site that is accessible to people in California responsible for any violations. The law took effect January 2015 and has not yet been challenged in court, so it is still unclear whether the forced removal of content that has been made publicly available violates a First Amendment right to

access such information. The juvenile cases that supported the dissemination of B.J.F.'s identity by the *Florida Star* newspaper involved striking
down a pretrial order that enjoined the publication of the name and
photograph of a boy in connection with proceedings attended by journalists[43] and overturning an indictment of two newspapers for violating
a state statute that forbade the publication of names of youths charged
with crimes prior to being granted permission by the juvenile court.[44]
In 1962, facts from juvenile court records that detailed a boy's sexual
assault of his younger sister were printed in a "daily record" column of
a newspaper and were determined to be newsworthy.[45] Thus, it is not
entirely clear that a California minor has a right to remove a newsworthy comment he or she posts online, particularly one on a traditional
newspaper story page.

While the disclosure of the identities of juveniles and rape victims is
much more easily prevented and punished elsewhere, COPPA remains
a unique and pioneering approach to protecting children. The European
Union is often considered to have no special protections for minors,
but that is not entirely true. The DP Directive may not provide specific
treatment for children, but a child's right to development is protected as
a fundamental right—so much so that it is stated in the Universal Declaration of Human Rights (art. 25), the International Covenant on Civil
and Political Rights (art. 24), the International Covenant on Economic,
Social and Cultural Rights (art. 10), and the EU Charter of Fundamental
Rights (art. 24).

Children's data-privacy rules for the age of consent and additional
parental consent differ in somewhat informal ways across Europe. In
the UK, the Data Protection Authority's Guidance states that parental consent is generally required to collect data from children under
twelve years old. Germany requires parental consent for children under
fourteen, and Belgium for those under twelve. In Spain, a royal decree
requires verifiable parental consent in order to process data for children under fourteen. France requires compliance closer to COPPA.
The French data-protection agency requires parental consent to collect

data from minors under eighteen. Only email addresses and age can be collected for email subscriptions. It is illegal to use a minor's image or transfer a minor's data to third parties when obtained through games. In Denmark and Sweden, data cannot be collected from children under the age of fifteen as a general rule. None of these countries provide extensive procedures like those outlined in COPPA or an explicit digital right to be forgotten specifically for children.

A few other efforts should be mentioned that pointedly address information with significant psychological effects or social stigma. The first is an anti-cyberbullying movement. Cyberbullying is harassment using information technologies to send or post hurtful, hateful, or embarrassing content. The issue has given rise to numerous nonprofit foundations, initiatives, and workshops, as well as laws and policies.[46] These proposed and codified laws have limitations and variations because cyberbullying is difficult to define, affects speech, and involves removal of content.[47] Still, this is one type of content, depending on the age and educational affiliation of the subject, that may (possibly) be forgotten.

Although there is no U.S. federal law for cyberbullying specifically, states have taken up the challenging task of drafting laws that address real and lasting harms without inviting government censorship. Currently, forty-one states have online-stalking laws, and thirty-seven have online-harassment laws. The trick is differentiating between harassment and protected speech. For instance, the New York State Court of Appeals struck down a county cyberbullying statute that criminalized electric or mechanical communication intended to "harass, annoy, threaten, . . . or otherwise inflict significant emotional harm on another person."[48] The statute was challenged by a fifteen-year-old boy, who pled guilty after creating a Facebook page that included graphic sexual comment next to photos of classmates at his school. Judge Victoria Graffeo explained, "It appears that the provision would criminalize a broad spectrum of speech outside the popular understanding of cyberbullying, including, for example: an email disclosing private information about a corporation or a telephone conversation meant to annoy an adult."[49] In dissent,

Judge Robert Smith stated that he believed the law could stand if applied only to children.[50]

A second movement is the anti-revenge-porn movement. Revenge porn is the disclosure of sexually explicit images, without consent of the subject, that causes significant emotional distress. Also called "nonconsensual pornography," revenge porn is often the product of a vengeful ex-partner or opportunistic hacker, and most victims suffer the additional humiliation of being identified with the images, leading to on- and offline threats and harassment.[51] As of 2015, sixteen states have criminalized revenge porn. A number of scorned lovers have been prosecuted under New Jersey's revenge-porn statute, which prohibits the distribution of "sexually explicit" images or videos by anyone "knowing that he is not licensed or privileged to do so" and not having the subject's consent.[52] Dharun Ravi, a Rutgers University student who distributed webcam footage of his roommate engaging in sexual activity, was also convicted under the law after his roommate killed himself.[53] These laws have been criticized as unnecessary because legal remedies like the privacy torts and copyright, criminal extortion, harassment, and stalking statutes cover the aspects of revenge porn that do not infringe on free speech rights. For instance, the ACLU is challenging the Arizona revenge-porn statute, which makes it a crime to "intentionally disclose, display, distribute, publish, advertise, or offer a photograph" or other image of "another person in a state of nudity or engaged in specific sexual activities" if the person "knows or should have known" that the person depicted has not consented to the disclosure, arguing that it is unconstitutionally broad and captures First Amendment–protected images.[54]

The third is a smaller movement, directed at sites that post mug shots and arrest information about individuals. These mug-shot websites may simply be conveying public information, but when they started charging upward of four hundred dollars to remove pages, state legislators responded.[55] A few states have passed laws limiting the commercial use of mug shots. The Oregon law, for instance, gives a site thirty days to take down a mug shot once individuals prove that they were exonerated or that the record was otherwise expunged.[56] In light of the Second Circuit's *Martin v. Hearst* case, discussed earlier in this chapter, the constitutionality of these statutes is questionable and may hinge on a distinction between the press and other types of sites.

Recognition by some U.S. courts that these narrowly tailored legislative efforts do not violate the First Amendment suggests that when communication is gossipy, vindictive, or coercive (as opposed to published by the press), the public may not have a right to know it. These laws are designed, however, to punish the disclosure of only specific and extreme content: (1) nonconsensual, highly intimate images, (2) psychologically detrimental communication directed at children, and (3) communication that reaches the level of harassment, stalking, or extortion. They do not cover your run-of-the-mill bankruptcy notice in an old newspaper or protected expression that was rightfully disclosed but may no longer be of legitimate interest to the public. The ability of these movements to decrease discoverability of the information hinges on whether disclosure of the content can be punished within the limitations of a given interpretation of the freedom of expression, whether they are properly enforced, and whether removal can be effectuated.

European laws that protect against cyberbullying and revenge porn are similarly situated in national and local harassment, privacy, and defamation laws, but no Europe-wide law exists. Instead, the EU, equally concerned and involved in these movements, has supported research to understand the extent of the cyberbullying problem, has developed guidelines for ISPs to keep children safe online, and has started a #Deletecyberbullying campaign.[57] A number of European countries are considering whether they need new laws to deal with cyberbullying given the existing protections provided by other legal mechanisms. In November 2014, Ireland's Law Reform Commission asked for public comments on an issue paper addressing the subject of cyberbullying.[58] Revenge-porn laws were passed in the UK in October 2014, defining the content as "photographs or films which show people engaged in sexual activity or depicted in a sexual way or with their genitals exposed, where what is shown would not usually be seen in public."[59] Each European country has laws for handling criminal records, and unlike the multiple truths allowed by the U.S. Second Circuit, many of these countries prevent references to criminal pasts. In January 2014, a French art dealer demanded that his criminal record be deindexed from his Google search results and received a favorable ruling from a Parisian lower court, which explained that he had a right to protect his reputation under French data-protection laws.[60] For the most part, special laws to address the aforementioned movements have been deemed unnecessary by European countries.

For good reason, then, nonlegal options are often put forth in the U.S. as the key to solving the problems of digital memory; after all, law can be a heavy-handed response to a socio-technical problem when compared to technical solutions or the quick action of the market. Values, including forgiveness, may need to be governed and preserved differently in the Digital Age. Lawrence Lessig, whose work on the governance of technology is considered foundational, explains that online, much like in the offline world, computer code, norms, markets, and law operate together to govern values and behaviors.[61] Computer code, the pressure of adhering to social norms, and the invisible hand of market-based solutions may address the problems that the right to be forgotten seeks to address, but none are the silver bullet their advocates purport them to be.

Lessig succinctly argues in his book *Code* that the future of cyberspace will be shaped by the actions we take to define and construct it and that action will need to be taken to safeguard cherished values. Lessig describes the four methods of regulation as the market forces that invisibly meet the demands of society; norms and other social regulators that pressure individuals to behave appropriately; technical design that affects behavior; and government regulation. Although law is the most effective form of regulating behavior, according to Lessig, all of the first three methods are regularly suggested as more suitable responses to persistent personal information. But none will save the day on its own.

Markets are looked to more readily to solve problems in the U.S. than in the EU.[62] And in fact, the market has answered the call regarding the tarnishing of reputation. Companies like Reputation.com, TrueRep.com, and IntegrityDefender.com offer services to repair your reputation and hide your personal information. On the "Suppress Negative Content Online" page of Reputation.com, the site explains, "You're being judged on the Internet," "The Internet never forgets," "The truth doesn't matter," and you are "guilty by association."[63] These statements may seem dramatic, but for those who live with a nasty link on the first page of a Google search for their name, they probably feel very accurate. The fact that these businesses are successful suggests that there is a market of users with injured online reputations who are seeking redress and that search results are already gamed. Only Americans with means can remove themselves from the record of the Internet, and those who are less powerful can only hope for an opportunity to explain their digital dirty laundry. While it may be appealing to demonize the "privacy for a price" approach in favor of one based on privacy for all, these services provide privacy from past negative information, a very complicated task, starting at the low price of fifteen dollars per month.

Markets have other limitations for addressing a society that is incapable of forgetting. Certainly, reputation systems[64] like those for sellers on eBay and Amazon allow for reputational cure by performing a large number of trust-affirming transactions, making the poor review less representative of the seller's commercial conduct. The equivalent solution for personal reputation is to try to get negative information pushed off the first few pages of search results by bombarding the Internet with positive content. Those who suffer from negative online content can and do hire reputation management companies, presenting positive information about the client as opposed to presenting the confidences and character testimony of others.[65] Relying on the market, however, runs the risk of endangering users because it allows for those subjects whose information is socially vital (i.e., politicians and professional service providers) to be hidden.[66] By allowing the market to effectively suppress

content to the last few pages of a search result, censorship is administered without any oversight or safeguards. This type of manipulation
also may further victimize those who have been harmed by a subject,
making them feel as though the subject suffered no social ramifications
because he or she could pay to avoid them. Finally, the market ignores
privacy as a right, providing forgetting services only to those who can
afford it and those who are comfortable with a large online presence.

This form of intervention may promote the goals of reputation rehabilitation but does not serve the Internet as a socially valuable information source or provide privacy. The easiest way to make negative
information less accessible is to bury it under highly ranked positive
information—and lots of it. Though a reputation service can add content that adds context, it is not necessarily more accurate, relevant, or
valuable. Additionally, this solution does not offer real seclusion or the
feeling of being left alone or any other privacy definition related to autonomy. If users are interested in being left alone, paying for a service
that will plaster information about them all over the Internet does not
support their goals of regaining a private existence. If users seek to control information communicated about them, the pressure to fill the web
with positive information in order to place a piece of information back
in a sphere of privacy is more like strong-arming users than empower-
ing them with privacy.

Norms have been suggested as an answer to addressing digital memory and preserving moral dignity in cyberspace.[67] Actually, this is the
most common response I hear from college students. The argument is
that society will adjust as they—the understanding, empathetic, tech-
savvy population—take on positions of power. It is a nice idea. Julian
Togelius, a professor and artificial-intelligence researcher in Copenha-
gen, argues that "we have to adapt our culture to the inevitable presence
of modern technology. . . . We will simply have to assume that people
can change and restrict ourselves to looking at their most recent behavior and opinions."[68] According to danah boyd, "People, particularly
younger people, are going to come up with coping mechanisms. That's

going to be the shift, not any intervention by a governmental or technological body."[69] Jeffrey Rosen argues, "The most practical solution to the problem of digital forgetting . . . is to create new norms of atonement and forgiveness."[70] Essentially these scholars argue that we will all begin to accept seeing previously closeted skeletons revealed digitally and become capable of ignoring them or judge them less harshly.

Other authors and commentators question the success of relying on social adaptation to preserve forgiveness in the age when it is impossible to forget. Viktor Mayer-Schönberger appreciates these ideas but argues that reliance on norms will take too long to avoid significant social damage or is simply an attempt at unattainable social changes.[71] The philosophy professor Jeffrey Reiman challenges reliance on social adaptation as it relates to privacy by explaining that "even if people should ideally be able to withstand social pressure in the form of stigmatization or ostracism, it remains unjust that they should suffer these painful fates simply for acting in unpopular or unconventional ways."[72] Ruth Gavison also refutes these arguments, noting that "the absence of privacy may mean total destruction of the lives of individuals condemned by norms with only questionable benefit to society."[73]

Human memory and the ability to forget may not be susceptible to alteration. The brain's management of information is a result of evolution over a long period of time as it adapts to the context and environments in which it is processing.[74] This view is shared by many leading psychologists, including the Harvard University professor David Schacter, who agrees that memory and forgetting mechanisms are deeply embedded in brain functionality.[75]

Bad events experienced by individuals have stronger impacts on memory, emotion, and behavior than good events do.[76] Negative impressions and stereotypes form quicker and are more resistant to being disconfirmed than positive ones are. The brain reacts more strongly to stimuli that it deems negative, a reaction termed "negativity bias."[77] This is bolstered by behavioral research. For example, the PhD candidate

Laura Brandimarte at Carnegie Mellon University measured how people discount information with negative and positive valence.[78] These experiments supported the conclusion that bad information is discounted less and has longer-lasting effects than good information does.

The idea that we will all be used to seeing indiscretions online and will not judge people too harshly for those exposed indiscretions challenges our capabilities as humans. The opposite of large-scale acceptance is also possible. Norms of nondisclosure may present themselves.[79] Users may self-censor not only because it is difficult to predict who will see their expression but also because norms may change and their expression may become unpopular in the future. Time, then, may add an additional layer of inhibition to what is known as the "spiral of silence," wherein individuals who believe that their opinions are not widely shared are less willing to speak up and engage on the topic.[80] Relying on norms of acceptance to develop is a risky proposition.

In *Forgetting as a Feature, Not a Bug: The Duality of Memory and Implications for Ubiquitous Computing,* the professor of computer science and information systems Liam Bannon warns that "the tendency to use the power of the computer to store and archive everything can lead to stultification in thinking, where one is afraid to act due to the weight of the past."[81] Bannon insists, "What is necessary is to radically re-think the relation between artefacts and our social world. The aim is to shift attention to a portion of the design space in human-computer interaction and ubiquitous computing research that has not been much explored—a space that is supportive of human well-being."[82] One of the more interesting solutions to privacy problems that are not easily or appropriately addressed by the law alone is the concept of privacy by design.[83] Building the value of privacy into the design of a system offers a preventive measure, establishes standards, and potentially lightens the load on government oversight and enforcement. Forgiveness by design or automated forgiveness would be a code-based solution but, at this point, an inappropriate one.

The popularity of ephemeral data technologies became obvious, at least in one area of information sharing, when Snapchat took off. Snapchat is an app that allows users to send photos and videos that are visible to the recipient only for a specified amount of time (up to ten seconds). After the specified time, the recipient cannot access the file through the Snapchat interface, but the file is not deleted from the device. Ephemerality is the fun of Snapchat. The app is so fun that over twenty-seven million users (half of whom are between thirteen and seventeen years old) send more than seven hundred million snaps every day.[84] However, research on users' attitudes toward and behavior on Snapchat suggests that screenshots of messages are common and expected.[85] Senders are notified by Snapchat when this happens, but few are upset about it.[86] So while the ephemeral nature of Snapchat is what makes it popular, norms of lasting content have also become part of the application's use. Other forgetting technologies include Wickr (whose slogan is "leave no trace" and which offers Snapchat-like service in a more secure form) and Silent Circle (which offers a "surveillance proof" smartphone app that allows senders to automatically delete a file from both the sender's and the receiver's devices after a set amount of time). However, with regard to data trails collected by sites and services, technologies that block data from being collected and those that automatically clear history data are currently the only available tools for users.

Computer scientists have also begun to play with coding forms of forgiveness, each outlining variables of forgiveness and reestablishing trust. DigitalBlush is a project designed to support technology-mediated facilitation of forgiveness, focusing on the importance of the human emotions of shame and embarrassment.[87] The researchers developed a formal computational model of forgiveness and designed a tool to support rule-violation reports and link victim with offender to facilitate forgiveness.[88] This required the researchers to categorize elements of human forgiveness. The first, violation appraisal, accounts for the severity, intent, and frequency of the exhibited behavior.[89] The second, reversal, addresses the role of apologies and acts of restitution.[90] Last, preexisting factors like the familiarity with and level of commitment to the offender are considered.[91] Then the project collected user-generated information on rule violations in specific communities.[92]

Other researchers have focused on the role that forgiveness plays among artificial-intelligence agents by portraying the reestablishment of trust as an assessment of regret that can be cured or diminished over time depending on the conduct of the offending agent.[93] The model is particularly valuable because it accounts for the limits of forgiveness (conduct that is unforgivable) and the importance of time.[94] Mayer-Schönberger argues that these code or technical manipulations are the solution to the permanent memory of the web. Users should be able to attach an expiration date to information, after which it would no longer be accessible.[95] Applying an expiration date would be available only for information created by the subject and would require predicting a useful life span at the time of creation.

The process of coding forgiveness of harmful online information carries the same issue as coding to remove unauthorized use of copyrighted material in such a way that also protects fair use: there are too many human elements. That being said, when the right to be forgotten has developed some definition and certainty, it may be much easier to automate significant portions of the determination. Elements of time, fame, and public interest can all be supported by automated systems. The delicate nature of human forgiveness and its implications for censorship require a nonautomated response until a system can be designed to know when an individual feels extreme shame or harm from information online and whether that information can be appropriately removed or deindexed. If not done thoughtfully, manipulation of this content or the system that preserves it in the name of forgiveness may threaten the openness and robustness of the Internet. This conclusion is not to suggest that technology cannot be used to support norms of forgiveness or that code is not an integral part of any effort at digital redemption but only that a singularly technological effort will not solve the problem of personal stagnation.

The foregoing mechanisms are simply ill equipped to handle forgetting, forgiving, or reinvention on their own in the Digital Age. They will all play an important role, but no single response, from law or otherwise, has really taken a close look at the opportunities available to address the issues. Finding innovative, nuanced responses requires going back to the drawing board and looking at new theories, breaking down concepts, and reframing the problem.

Innovating Privacy

The polarizing nature of digital redemption is due in part to its odd relationship to privacy, a polarizing subject in and of itself. The particular issues raised by the right to be forgotten are difficult to understand as *privacy* issues because they are about information that has been properly disclosed but has become or remained problematic. Conceptualizing privacy is perhaps as endless a task as keeping track of the ways in which technology challenges it, but new theories focused on the new information landscape have opened up possibilities for reconceptualizing what privacy can mean in the digital world. The right to be forgotten may be one of those possibilities, but the particular issues raised by the right are also difficult to understand as *manageable* issues. Like privacy, the right to be forgotten can mean too many things that need to be sorted and organized in order to move forward.

To some people, access to old personal information may be a privacy violation or form of injustice—but not to others. Privacy today is most often discussed in terms of a liberal political philosophy that understands society as a collection of somewhat autonomous individuals with stark differences in interests and priorities regarding what boundaries they maintain. Under a liberal notion of privacy, the protection of these differences in boundary management serves to support the goals of civil society. Privacy has been summarized by Alan Westin as "the claim of individuals, groups, or institutions to determine for themselves when, how, and to what extent information about them is communicated to others."[1] His focus on control is different from Samuel Warren and Louis Brandeis's "right to be let alone,"[2] developed only decades before, but neither seems easy to achieve in the twenty-first century. Fortunately, a number of theories have been developed since to meet the demands of a changing socio-technical landscape.

Information privacy is an evolving concept.[3] In 1928, Justice Brandeis called privacy "the most comprehensive of rights and the right most valued by civilized men."[4] Seventy-one years later, Scott McNealy, the CEO of Sun Microsystems, declared, "You have zero privacy anyway. Get over it."[5] The juxtaposition of these quotes represents the current state of privacy. Technological change has seemingly shaken up society and privacy along with it, but not for the first time.

In 1966, Westin wrote, "The very novelty of [the development and use of new surveillance devices and processes by public and private authorities] has allowed them, thus far, to escape many of the traditional legal and social controls which protected privacy in the pre–World War II era."[6] He was referring to a slew of "new" technologies: the radio transmitter microphones that allow conversations to be overheard without the consent of both parties to a conversation (phone tapping), a "radio pill" that emits a signal from within the body, secret "miniature still and movie cameras with automatic light meters" that can be triggered by movement (motion-detection cameras), long-range photography equipment and closed-circuit television units the size of a cigarette pack, beepers smaller than a quarter that transmit a signal for several city blocks, audial surveillance that can be built into one's attire, photochromic microimages, computer storage and processing, credit and debit card systems, polygraphs, and personality tests.[7] New ways to capture and communicate information about more aspects of life from novel places and sources test our notions of and protections for privacy.

Three categories of technological advancement have bent these notions out of shape once again. The Internet allows for instant, cheap, and widespread publication of and access to information. The collection of information through computer code captures our attributes and movements through the network, sensors capture our attributes and movements outside the network, and numerous recording devices (from the personally wearable to the static, publicly situated) capture glimpses of us as we move throughout both realms. The storage, aggregation, and processing of all this information is organized and analyzed to provide utility and efficiency. Together these technological advancements have contributed to incredible social shifts in the way information is created, shared, and understood, leaving overwhelming informational vulnerabilities.

Recent informational threats seem to come from everywhere at all times but can be organized into four categories: threat of limited foresight, threat of rational ignorance, threat of others, and threat of others like us. The right to be forgotten is an attempt to address these threats. It assumes that information will be leaked, collected, shared, and analyzed by individuals and about individuals and seeks to limit the impact by protecting individuals through digital redemption, which incorporates values associated with and the vulnerability of identity, reputation, autonomy, and privacy.

As the Jezebel example in the introduction exemplifies, two important questions for the many countries considering a right to be forgotten are how long consequences should last and why. How should information we actively create and intend to share be assessed and addressed? Thus, the first threat to our digital records comes from our own actions. The social media scholar and youth researcher danah boyd explains, "In unmediated spaces, structural boundaries are assessed to determine who is in the audience and who is not. . . . In mediated spaces, there are no structures to limit the audience; search collapses all virtual walls."[8]

The intended or expected audience is not always the actual audience. The teens in the Jezebel case were probably not expecting the site to read their tweets. They also probably did not expect the tweets to be used by Jezebel in a way that could jeopardize their futures.

Adults and experts are also susceptible to limited foresight in the Digital Age. No matter how much one knows, it can be incredibly difficult to foresee the impact of shared data. The pseudonymous author "George Doe" recounted his family's experience with 23andMe, a service that has offered genetic testing since 2007, in an article titled "With Genetic Testing, I Gave My Parents the Gift of Divorce."[9] 23andMe does more than provide genetic reports and raw genetic data; it connects users who have opted to participate in the "close relatives finder program," which suggests similar genetic history and possible common ancestry.[10] Through the service, George Doe learned that he had a half brother, a discovery that threw his family into upheaval. George Doe is not a child fumbling around a complex social networking site or an adult oblivious to the field of bioinformatics; he is a stem cell and reproductive biologist with a doctorate in cell and molecular biology.

We also passively create potentially regrettable information passively as we spend time as networked individuals. Little lines of code are created to note, measure, and categorize our computationally perceived movements, interests, and characteristics. These digital footprints are meant to be read, aggregated, and analyzed by machines, which makes them hard for users to understand and manage. Processing and use are detailed in long and difficult-to-decipher terms of service. Digital footprints are rarely disclosed to the public, but even when they are disclosed anonymously, a surprisingly small amount of combined information can lead to reidentification of the persons belonging to those footprints.[11] Moreover, the results of processed digital footprints are often presented to the user in the form of predicted content, like an advertisement or news story that is likely of interest. In 2007, the Facebook user Sean Lane bought an engagement ring for his girlfriend online without knowing about or understanding the agreement between the site and Facebook.

He was horrified to find the headline "Sean Lane bought 14k White Gold 1/5 ct Diamond Eternity Flower Ring from overstock.com" presented in his Facebook newsfeed to all of his friends, coworkers, and acquaintances and, of course, his girlfriend.[12] "Thus, the decision not to protect oneself paradoxically may be considered as a rational way to react to these uncertainties: the 'discrepancies' between privacy attitudes and privacy behavior may reflect what could at most be called a 'rational ignorance,'" explains the privacy economist Alessandro Acquisti and the information scientist Jens Grossklags.[13] The difficulties in calculating risk, exercising choice, and initiating control over so much personal data (in combination with the novel uses of old information, creating an incentive to keep all information)[14] have led some observers to argue for a right to be forgotten as an effective way to enforce user participation in data-protection regimes.

The other threats come from what other people do. People have posted some pretty bad stuff about other people on the Internet. Daniel Solove's *Future of Reputation* is chock full of examples of people taking to the Internet to express their disdain for others. An ethically interesting (and PG) example occurred when an everyday breakup between two noncelebrities in Burger King was live tweeted by a stranger, complete with photos and video. The eavesdropping prompted an article in *Cosmopolitan* to warn, "Let this be a lesson to all of you airing your (very) dirty laundry in a public place. You never know who's nearby and ready to broadcast your life to the interwebs."[15] The threat of others is hard to ignore. Content may seem harmless or mundane, or it may be clearly malicious or spiteful; but all can cause real problems down the line. Being at the mercy of strangers, friends, and enemies will cause most of us to be hyperaware and fall in line—or so the chilling-effects argument goes.

Predictive analytics often fill in the blanks we leave in our data trails. These are not characteristics that are expressed or collected through our actions but holes in our digital dossiers that get filled on the basis of the characteristics of others like us. At age eight, a kid named Mikey Hicks found himself on the Transportation Security Administration selectee list that subjects him to higher security scrutiny when he travels. His father, who has the same name, was also on the list. No one was clear as to why they were on the list, and the family was told it would take years to get off the list; but it was likely the actions of a third Mike Hicks were to blame. Netflix will recommend a musical because people who watched some combination of other films and television shows like musicals. Target might label me, as it has others,[16] as pregnant (to the precise trimester, in fact) if I buy a certain set of products because so often women who buy that set of products are pregnant. We are not only at the mercy of our own pasts; we are at the mercy of pasts of others who are like us. How can we charge anyone with guarding against machine inferences made about us on the basis of the data of others? This is, therefore, a more technical question than any of the others, and this threat will be intertwined with broader debates about big data. How can you find and understand, let alone delete, data created about you on the basis of the history of others?

There are a number of ways that the concept of privacy has broken down in light of these shifts and vulnerabilities and reasons why it is being reconceptualized. Central to this breakdown is the "privacy paradox," which describes the apparent inconsistency between Internet users' actions and feelings about privacy.[17] Most claim to care about protecting information and to value personal data but do not take steps that reflect these values and give away their data freely. In a paper and analog world, consent could more easily be granted for a more manageable amount of data after notice has been given regarding the terms of data collection and use. Individuals were more in control and aware of the personal data they disclosed—a sentiment that each generation seems to longingly hold about those prior.

Today, the information landscape places an extraordinary and unrealistic burden on the user. Lorrie Faith Cranor and Aleecia McDonald determined that it would take seventy-six work days to read the privacy policies users encounter in a year.[18] Relying on privacy policies as a form of notice is ineffective because of what Helen Nissenbaum calls the "transparency paradox": if data controllers accurately and comprehensibly describe data practices, the policy will be too long and complicated to expect a user to read it.[19] Users exercise rational ignorance when they do not diligently protect their data.[20] Trading small pieces of data for a service may lead to harms, but these harms are abstract and stretched over time, making them difficult to calculate. The promised convenience, however, is concrete, immediate, and very easy to calculate. Weighing trade-offs within a structure of so many entities collecting, using, and trading data at new, technically sophisticated levels is simply too much to ask.

Additionally, relying on individual choice may not promote the social values that make privacy a core concept of liberal society. Robert Post argued in 1989 that privacy "safeguards rules of civility that in some significant measure constitute both individuals and community."[21] A few years later, Priscilla Regan argued that the lesson of the 1980s and early 1990s was that privacy loses under a cost-benefit analysis when weighed against government-agency needs and private-institution utilization; she argued that privacy is not about weighing trade-offs but about focusing on the social structures and values supported by privacy. "Privacy is important not only because of its protection of the individual as an individual but also because individuals share common perceptions about the importance and meaning of privacy, because it serves as a restraint on how organizations use their power, and because privacy—or the lack of privacy—is built into our systems and organizational practices and procedures."[22] Privacy protects social values that may not be preserved in the hands of individuals making decisions about the benefits and harms of sharing information.

It has been a challenge to theorize information privacy and conceptual tools that accommodate these changes in information flows. Some theories of privacy lend themselves to digital redemption more than others do. For instance, the right to be left alone provided by Warren and Brandeis is about preventing invasions[23] and does not easily reach information that is properly disclosed but becomes invasive as time goes on. Similarly, theories of secrecy and intimacy are about concealing certain information from others. Ruth Gavison's theory of privacy revolves around access to the self. "Our interest in privacy . . . is related to our concern over our accessibility to others, . . . the extent to which we are the subject of others' attention."[24] Digital redemption in many ways is about preventing access to part of one's past that receives more attention than the individual feels is appropriate. Those theories that relate to personhood and control can supplement this notion to further support digital redemption. Westin describes the personal autonomy state of privacy (one of four), in the following way:

> Each person is aware of the gap between what he wants to be and what he actually is, between what the world sees of him and what he knows to be his much more complex reality. In addition, there are aspects of himself that the individual does not fully understand but is slowly exploring and shaping as he develops. Every individual lives behind a mask in this manner. . . . If this mask is torn off and the individual's real self bared to a world in which everyone else still wears his mask and believes in masked performances, the individual can be seared by the hot light of selective, forced exposure.[25]

Westin follows this passage by describing the importance of personal development and time for incubation, warning against ideas and positions being launched into the world prematurely. Neil Richards has developed the concept of "intellectual privacy," which recognizes the need for ideas to incubate away from the intense scrutiny of public disclosure in order to promote intellectual freedom.[26] Once one presents oneself to the world, however, it is unclear whether privacy would allow for the mask to be put back on and another round of incubation to ensue. Charles Fried explains, "Privacy is not simply an absence of information about what is in the minds of others; rather it is the *control* we have over information about ourselves."[27] Digital redemption could be understood as exercising control over one's past information to foster the development and projection of a current self. But even personhood and control do not necessarily provide for retroactive adjustments to information.

Finding that each theory of privacy comes up short in embracing the numerous privacy problems experienced regularly, Solove takes a different, bottom-up approach to understanding privacy.[28] He creates a taxonomy with four main categories to guide us through privacy issues: information collection, information processing, information dissemination, and invasion. Information collection refers exclusively to problems that arise from information gathering, such as surveillance by watching or listening and interrogation used to elicit information. Information processing denotes problems that arise from the storage, organization, combination, modification, and manipulation of data, which incorporates security issues, secondary uses, and ignorance of the user. Information dissemination describes the privacy harms that follow the disclosure of information and includes breaches of confidentiality and trust, the release of truthful information to a wider audience, exposure to an individual's intimate or bodily details, and the distortion and appropriation of an individual's identity. Finally, invasions include harms resulting from disturbances to peace and solitude as well as interference with an individual's decisions about private affairs.

Solove's bottom-up approach to privacy is not normative but is a guide to determining where a violation falls within a more exhaustive, categorized concept of privacy and how to form solutions. It is not clear, however, whether or where the right to be forgotten fits in Solove's taxonomy. It is difficult to fit into one of Solove's categories information that is legitimately disseminated but eventually prevents a person from moving on from the past.

One novel model that does leave room for a right to be forgotten assesses privacy violations on the basis of what Nissenbaum calls "contextual integrity."[29] Nissenbaum outlines a privacy framework based on expected information flows. When the flow of information adheres to established norms, the unsettling emotions of a privacy violation rarely occur. Therefore, a jolting realization that your personal information has reached an unintended audience or has been used in an unforeseen way is probably a visceral signal indicating that contextual integrity was not maintained.[30]

Nissenbaum's framework assesses a socio-technical system within the existing norms pertaining to the flow of personal information; for a particular context, we maintain values, goals, and principles by focusing on the appropriate and expected transmission of information even when technological advancement and new uses change how the transmission is executed. Like Solove, Nissenbaum does not need a fundamental principle of privacy to be put into practice. The lack of this central underpinning can make contextual integrity problematic when contexts are dynamic or even volatile, unsettled, or questioned.

Still, a right to be forgotten is not necessarily excluded and is potentially even supported by contextual integrity. Noëmi Manders-Huits and Jeroen van den Hoven explain, "What is often seen as a violation of privacy is oftentimes more adequately construed as the morally inappropriate transfer of personal data across the boundaries of what we intuitively think of as separate 'spheres of justice' or 'spheres of access.'"[31] Information may be placed in a particular sphere of access that prevents informational injustice—it could also be moved to a different sphere of access over time.

Previously, access to old information about an individual was restricted to information that was recently distributed and for a limited time thereafter. A newspaper article was easily accessible for a few days before it went into a single or a small number of basement archives. Gossip ran its course, and details were quickly lost. Letters and diaries were packed away in drawers and shelves. In contrast, old information today lingers much longer than expected. Facebook's Timeline is an example of easier access to old information that disrupts the expected information flow and causes the unsettling effect of a privacy violation. MyTweet16 does nothing but present any user's first sixteen tweets. Google pulls up old personal commentary, photos, posts, profiles—any file that can be crawled by the search engine with your name in it. Specialized search sites like Pipl.com retrieve a one-page report on the searched individual that digs into the deep web, pages that no other page links to.

If access to aged information continues in a way that disrupts contextual integrity, restrictions to the information can be developed to limit access or use to those who need the information. Drawing these lines is important, because expectations change if integrity is not reinforced. Although it may be possible to identify access to old data that violates contextual integrity, it is still a difficult question whether we are willing to move information into another sphere of access when a privacy violation has been identified—necessarily complicating public access. Growing interest in the right to be forgotten from policy makers, industry, and users suggests that many governments may be willing to move information into different spheres of access. The trouble with contextual integrity is that it is based on norms—as the folk musician Bruce Cockburn sings, "The trouble with normal is it always gets worse."[32] When contexts are dynamic, unsettled, or disrupted, it is difficult to ascertain the integrity of a transmission, providing an opportunity for norms to develop in a less intentional fashion. Supporting digital redemption with other theories that are not based solely on norms helps to reinforce the novel idea.

One of the biggest critics of the right to be forgotten, Jeffrey Rosen, offers another useful conceptualization of privacy as "the capacity for creativity and eccentricity, for the development of self and soul, for understanding, friendship, and even love."[33] Shaping and maintaining one's identity is "a fundamental interest in being recognized as a self-presenting creature," according to the philosopher David Velleman.[34] These theories of privacy focus on threats to the self. The traditional liberal self is one that focuses on protecting "personhood," which Paul Freund has described as emerging in 1975 and defined as "those attributes of an individual which are irreducible in his selfhood."[35] Expanding on this conception of privacy as protector of individuality, the legal theorist Stanley Benn argues that this must be effectuated as "respect for someone as a person, as a chooser, impl[ying] respect for him as one engaged on a kind of self-creative enterprise, which could be disrupted, distorted, or frustrated even by so limited an intrusion as watching."[36] Irwin Altman describes the privacy function of developing and maintaining self-identity:

> Privacy mechanisms define the limits and boundaries of the self. When the permeability of these boundaries is under the control of a person, a sense of individuality develops. But it is not the inclusion or exclusion of others that is vital to self definition; it is the ability to regulate contact when desired. If I can control what is me and what is not me, if I can define what is me and not me, and if I can observe the limits and scope of my control, then I have taken major steps toward understanding and defining what I am. Thus, privacy mechanisms serve to help me define me.[37]

"Personhood" as a theory of privacy involves the protection of one's personality, individuality, and dignity—the protection of the autonomy necessary to choose one's identity. These are relatively new ideas. Julie Cohen takes issue with the "traditional" liberal political theory relied on by modern privacy theorists as a theory that seeks to protect the *true*, autonomous self. Cohen focuses on the importance of understanding humans in a networked system as socially constructed, dynamic, and situated. She argues, "The self who benefits from privacy is not the autonomous, pre-cultural island that the liberal individualist model presumes. Nor does privacy reduce to a fixed condition or attribute (such as seclusion or control) whose boundaries can be crisply delineated by the application of deductive logic. Privacy is shorthand for breathing room to engage in the processes of boundary management that enable and constitute self-development."[38] This breathing room for the self evolves through what Cohen calls "semantic discontinuity," defined as "the opposite of seamlessness: it is a function of interstitial complexity within the institutional and technical frameworks that define information rights and obligations and establish protocols for information collection, storage, processing, and exchange."[39] Semantic discontinuity promotes emergent subjectivity—a subjectivity that is socially constructed, culturally situated, and dynamic. Emergent subjectivity promotes the self that is socio-technically constructed but not socio-technically deterministic—the actual self around which to build technological and legal systems. Under Cohen's theory of privacy, an ongoing record of personal information may create seamlessness. For the dynamic self, creating gaps over time may be as important as creating gaps in any type of informational seamlessness. The right to be forgotten can be understood as the right to retroactively create gaps or boundaries to promote emergent subjectivity and the dynamic self.

"Obfuscation" is the way many users maintain contextual integrity and create gaps and variability for their dynamic selves. While most users do not vigilantly protect against the disclosure of personal information in many settings (discussed previously as a rational decision, considering the amount of work it would entail and the limited ability to see or assess potential harms), users do actively exercise obfuscation by posting pseudonymously, monitoring privacy and group settings in social networks, deleting cookies, lying to websites, utilizing password and encryptions protections, and maintaining multiple accounts and profiles. Woodrow Hartzog and Frederic Stutzman recognize these tactics as natural and important forms of selective identity management. They argue that online information may be considered obscure if it lacks search visibility, unprotected access, identification, or clarity.[40]

This is a rather broad definition of obfuscation, however. More precisely, it is understood as creating noise in datasets by producing false, misleading, or ambiguous data in order to devalue its collection or use. Being shackled to one's past can be prevented by actively obfuscating personal data when it is created, but the right to be forgotten is intended to address information created without such foresight. If that were easy to do, the socio-technical problem at issue would be easier to solve. Instead of retroactively turning personal information into false or misleading information, the right to be forgotten seeks to diminish the ease of discoverability of old personal information. I refer to this closely related concept as *obstruction*. Obscurity by obstruction is simply any means of creating challenges to the discoverability of personal information. Users' reliance on obscurity makes it a natural place to look for answers as well as highlights the importance of context. Obscurity offers an opportunity to have privacy in public, but only if it is respected or protected.

Obstruction allows for information to be gray (somewhat private and somewhat public) and adheres to the idea of "good enough" privacy. The law professor Paul Ohm argues that instead of perfection, privacy- and transparency-enhancing technology should require seekers to struggle to achieve their goal.[41] A common response to digital-redemption initiatives is that there is no way to find and delete all the copies of the relevant personal information, but for most users, only easily discoverable information matters. If the right to be forgotten sought perfect erasure from all systems everywhere, it would not have a leg to stand on. Instead, obstruction clearly signals something more measured than complete forgetting. And so new theories of privacy and information protection allow the right to be forgotten to be considered retroactively, creating gaps using obstructions to support the dynamic self and maintain contextual integrity.

Using these theories of privacy, we can start to break down the right to be forgotten into workable concepts, an exercise it desperately needs. Generally, the right to be forgotten "is based on the autonomy of an individual becoming a rightholder in respect of personal information on a time scale; the longer the origin of the information goes back, the more likely personal interests prevail over public interests."[42] It has been conceived as a legal right and as a value or interest worthy of legal protection. The right to be forgotten represents "informational self-determination" as well as the control-based[43] definition of privacy and attempts to migrate personal information from a public sphere to a private sphere. It represents too much.

Bert-Jaap Koops draws three conceptual possibilities: (1) data should be deleted in due time, (2) outdated negative information should not be used against an individual, (3) individuals should feel unrestrained in expressing themselves in the present without fear of future consequences.[44] Paul Bernal[45] and Jef Ausloos[46] emphasize that the right is only meant to offer more user control in big-data practices. Bernal argues that the right to be forgotten needs to be recast as a right to delete to combat negative reactions and focus on the most material concerns. This should be done as a part of a paradigm shift: "the default should be that data can be deleted and that those holding the data should need to justify why they hold it."[47] Ausloos similarly argues that the right to be forgotten has merit but needs a refined, limited definition. He argues, "The right is nothing more than a way to give (back) individuals control over their personal data and make the consent regime more effective"[48] and should be limited to data-processing situations where the individual has given his or her consent.

On the other end of the spectrum, Napoleon Xanthoulis argues that the right should be conceptualized as a human right, not a "control" right,[49] and Norberto Andrade argues that the right should be one of identity, not privacy, stating that the right to be forgotten is the "right to convey the public image and identity that one wishes."[50] Xanthoulis explains that rights require an important interest and that a human right requires something more; human rights are only human interests of special importance.[51] Xanthoulis succinctly explains that privacy has been proclaimed a human right, so reinvention has to be firmly situated within privacy to qualify as a human right. Andrade conceptualizes the right to be forgotten as one established under an umbrella right to identity, that data protection is procedural and a method to fulfill other rights, but that the right to identity is the "right to have the *indicia*, attributes or the facets of personality which are characteristic of, or unique to a particular person (such as appearance, name, character, voice, life history, etc.) recognized and respected by others."[52] It is therefore not a privacy right exactly, because it does not deal with private information, but as an identity right, the right to be forgotten could assist the "correct projection and representation to the public."[53] None of these conceptualizations is necessarily right or wrong; they are simply talking about different things.

The right to be forgotten is a concept that needs to be broken apart to be manageable. Efforts to address the potential harms derived from numerous collections of digital pasts in both the U.S. and the EU have been discussed, specifically the proposed language in the EU's Data Protection Regulation and the U.S.-proposed Do Not Track Kids legislation. The proposed regulations focus on the individual's rights that remain with a piece of information after it leaves the individual's control. These developments have resulted in inappropriate conceptual convergence. Breaking down the concepts and applications within the right to be forgotten helps to more effectively consider these inevitable issues.

Two versions of the right to be forgotten provide for muddled conceptions and rhetoric when they are not distinguished. The much older one—*droit a l'oubli* (right to oblivion)—has historically been applied in cases involving an individual who wishes to no longer be associated with actions as well as rare other circumstances, as discussed in chapter 1. The oblivion version of the right to be forgotten finds its rationale in privacy as a human/fundamental right (related to human dignity, reputation, and personality). A second version of the right is one offering deletion or erasure of information that has been passively disclosed by the data subject and collected and stored without providing public access. In the second context, a description of the right to be forgotten could instead be called a right to deletion. A handful of scholars have commented on each version separately and both together.

Compare two UK cases that struggle to delineate between interests related to content and data. *Quinton v. Peirce & Anor* involved a local election in 2007 when one politician, Quinton, claimed that his opponent, Peirce, had published misleading (not defamatory) information about Quinton in campaign materials. Quinton claimed both malicious falsehood and violations of the accuracy and fairness provisions of the DPA (recall that this is Britain's national data-protection law, adopted to comply with the 1995 DP Directive). Malicious falsehood of course requires the plaintiff to prove malice, which is quite difficult and therefore rarely successful; Quinton did not sufficiently establish this element of his claim. Justice David Eady then applied the DPA, finding that Peirce was a data controller and that the journalism exemption was not applicable, but Eady would extend this argument no further. To the accuracy claim, he saw "no reason to apply different criteria or standards in this respect from those . . . applied when addressing the tort of injurious falsehood."[54] On the fair-processing claim, which was argued to require that the data subject be notified in advance of the leaflet's distribution, Eady declined "to interpret the statute in a way which results in absurdity."[55]

In *Law Society, Hine Solicitors & Kevin McGrath v. Rick Kordowski*, plaintiffs sought to prevent the defendant from publishing the website Solicitors from Hell, which intended to expose "corrupt, negligent, dishonest, crooked, fraudulent lawyers," and similar websites in the future. Plaintiffs sued for libel, harassment, and violations of the DPA's accuracy and fairness requirements. The claim was initially rejected by the information commissioner, who explained,

The inclusion of the "domestic purposes" exemption in the Data Protection Act (s. 36) [which excludes data processed by an individual only for the purposes of that individual's person, family, or household affairs] is intended to balance the individual's rights to respect his/her private life with the freedom of expression. These rights are equally important and I am strongly of the view that it is not the purpose of the DPA to regulate an individual right to freedom of expression—even where the individual uses a third party website, rather than his own facilities, to exercise this. . . . The situation would clearly be impossible were the Information Commissioner to be expected to rule on what it is acceptable for one individual to say about another be that a solicitor or another individual. This is not what my office is established to do.[56]

Justice Michael Tugendhat disdainfully disagreed: "I do not find it possible to reconcile the views on the law expressed in the Commissioner's letter with authoritative statements of the law. The DPA does envisage that the Information Commissioner should consider what it is acceptable for one individual to say about another, because the First Data Protection Principle requires that data should be processed lawfully."[57] Tugendhat did not grant the website domestic purpose or journalistic exemption, leaving a lot of the web fair game for data-protection claims. It is unclear how privacy and defamation civil claims are to be integrated with data protection when these types of information are not separated.

The right to be forgotten could be applied in an absurd number of circumstances and cannot apply to all information related to all individuals in all situations, no matter in what jurisdiction the right is established. Possible applications of the right illustrate the very different circumstances that the right to be forgotten attempts to take on and supports an argument for conceptual separation. The chart in figure 1 represents all of the possible situations in which a right to be forgotten *could* apply. The chart headings should be read as follows:

▷ *Data* is passively created as a user (automated "clickstream" data).

▷ *Content* is actively created information (nonautomated "expressive" content).

▷ *Internal* designates information that is derived from the data subject whose personal information is at issue.

▷ *External* information is that which is produced about the user by someone else.

▷ *Initial* location is where the content was originally created or collected (e.g., Twitter).

▷ *Downstream* is where it may end up (e.g., retweets, data broker).

Data about a user may also be generated by the data collected and analyzed by another user if the two share similarities such as gender, age, geography, shopping or searching habits, personal or profes-

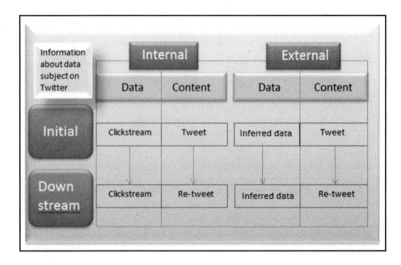

Information about data subject on Twitter	Internal		External	
	Data	Content	Data	Content
Initial	Clickstream	Tweet	Inferred data	Tweet
Down stream	Clickstream	Re-tweet	Inferred data	Re-tweet

FIGURE 1. Organization of potential application of the right to be forgotten

sional connections, or any number of data points; this is called inferred data. The data is generated *passively* by another user and may remain with the *initial* collector to provide more personalized service or be traded *downstream* to assign data to the data subject.

The right to be forgotten may apply to any or all of these cells, columns, or rows, depending on the legal culture seeking to establish it. However, distinctions between legal cultures have been ignored. The conflation of the right to oblivion and the right to deletion has led to much confusion and controversy. Under this conceptual divide, a right to deletion could only be exercised to address data. A right to oblivion would apply to content, such as social media posts, blog entries, and articles. Oblivion is founded on protections of harm to dignity, personality, reputation, and identity but has the potential to collide with other fundamental rights. However, oblivion may be relatively easy to exercise in practice, because a user can locate information he or she would like the public to forget by utilizing common search practices. A right to deletion, on the other hand, would apply to data passively created and collected. It is meant to shift the power between data users and controllers. Deletion is a data-participation right, allowing a data subject to remove the personal data he or she has released to companies that collect and trade data for automated processing, and it may be easier to implement legally because few users have access to this personal information.

The problem with conflating the concepts of deletion and oblivion within the right to be forgotten is that both treat all data in the matrix shown in figure 1 the same way, but the concepts are very different. This is particularly problematic when applying the same analysis and procedures to content (actively created, available online) and data (passively created, privately held). Circumstances surrounding passively created data, which is collected, processed, and stored with consent (to use the term loosely) and privately held, have different interests associated with them than does actively expressed content created online—and therefore, they deserve different treatment.

On the basis of the distinctions just drawn, the right to deletion could be applied to data that is passively created internally by the data subject and that is held by the initial controller or passed downstream, without initiating the more troubling act of deleting publicly available information from the Internet. And more precise procedures for removal or limiting access could be constructed for the right to oblivion that would take into account the more numerous users and uses associated with disclosed personal content.

Versions of Fair Information Practice Principles that include a right to deletion as one of the user-participation principles fall within the concept of the right to deletion applying to data held by the initial data controller and likely applying to downstream data controllers. California's child privacy law falls squarely within the oblivion conception of the right to be forgotten, focusing on reputation and development by offering a right to delete damaging content. The CJEU's interpretation of the EU DP Directive and DP Regulation combines oblivion and deletion—a problematic combination.

The proposed Regulation still refers in paragraph 1 to data collected for specific purposes that have expired (conjuring up notions of data traders and behavioral advertising) and then in paragraph 2 includes information that has been made public (suggesting that a blog entry that identifies the data subject must also be erased or at least obstructed upon request). The right to be forgotten would be well served by language delineating clear conceptual bases in order to anticipate the way in which the right and exceptions will be applied in relation to the various interests they represent.

Even with these options, there is a lot of uncertainty surrounding digital information. We do not really know what types of digital information are intended to be temporary. Certain print information eventually became categorized as temporary; it is called ephemera. A man named John de Monins Johnson (1882–1956) made a hobby of collecting printed ephemera, things like advertisements, menus, greeting cards, posters, handbills, and postcards. These are pieces of paper information intended to be short-lived and discarded. The collection is held in an esteemed library because it provides valuable insight into the past on a variety of fronts. It is mentioned here because it represents a category of momentary human communication and the reasons to hold onto it. By choosing categories in the chart, we utilize the law to label pieces of information as digital ephemera and will need to also find ways to preserve its future value.

Digital Information Stewardship

Achieving a rich discussion of digital redemption and finding a way forward will require not only theoretical innovation and conceptual refinement but also framing work. The main narrative that drives digital-redemption policy choices is permanence. Even when two groups frame a technological problem the same way, it does not mean the technology carries the same meaning or presents the same problem to the two groups. Here, both the U.S. and EU have framed the digital information as permanent but diverge on the type of problem that permanence presents and how to solve it. There is a missing piece to the puzzle. Digital information is not permanent—it sticks around and is accessible in different ways, but it is not permanent. By acknowledging the materiality of digital information and reframing the problem, new approaches to digital redemption open up. Adjusting the framing to be more technically accurate, the problem is less "new," and principles that have been developed in other areas of preservation, stewardship, and privacy can be informative to shaping the right to be forgotten.

In the late 1990s, Brewster Kahle, the famed computer scientist, network engineer, and digital librarian, warned that the web's future could be similar to the lost Library of Alexandria if measures like the Internet Archive were not taken. About ten years later, the polar opposite of Brewster's concern was voiced. In July 2010, Jeffrey Rosen's "The Web Means the End of Forgetting" was published in the *New York Times Magazine*. In it, Rosen asks how we can "best . . . live our lives in a world where the Internet records everything and forgets nothing—where every online photo, status update, Twitter post and blog entry by and about us can be stored forever."[1] If content generated through the web is to be regulated, we must understand and articulate the technical landscape accurately, as well as the extent of the harms caused. Any limitations on access to content may then be appropriately and tightly tailored to that content that truly lasts beyond its utility.

"The Internet is a moving target. Every minute, thousands of Web pages are updated or abandoned," read the headline of an article in *Slate* magazine from 1997.[2] There may be nothing less natural than permanence. The web, of course, is not really permanent. On the one hand, fourteen years later, I still find these articles readily accessible online. On the other hand, who knows how many more sources there once were?

As early as 1985, those who were concerned with preservation were readying the troops, creating reports, conferences, and strategies to handle this new electronic "crisis." That year, the Committee on the Records of Government proclaimed, "The United States is in danger of losing its memory."[3] And over a decade later, the term "digital dark ages" was coined at a 1997 conference of the International Federation of Library Associations and Institutions. In 1998, a collection of librarians, archivists, and computer scientists joined for a project, "Time and Bits: Managing Digital Continuity," the proceedings of which were collected, were posted online, and disappeared within a year. "Digital documents last forever—or five years, whichever comes first," joked the computer scientist Jeff Rothenberg in 1998.[4]

Digital librarians seek to maximize access to their society's cultural treasures, which were once reserved for only a few, as well as to collect our born-digital cultural representations. Culture depends on the quality of its records. Today, records depend not on brittle papyrus or the acid decay of paper but the decay of the digit. Generally, the problem is twofold. First, technology advances so rapidly that the time before a technology becomes obsolete is decreasing. Second, digital resources are less stable than their analog counterparts were, resulting in the corruption of the integrity and authenticity of the resource. As Roy Rosenzweig explained, "The most vexing problems of digital media are the flipside of their greatest virtues. Because digital data are in the simple lingua franca of bits, of ones and zeroes, they can be embodied in magnetic impulses that require almost no physical space, be transmitted over long distances, and represent very different objects. . . . But the ones and zeros lack intrinsic meaning without software and hardware, which constantly change because of technological innovation and competitive market forces."[5]

A laundry list of errors prevent long-term access to digital content: media and hardware errors, software failures, communication channel errors, network service failures, component obsolescence, operator errors, natural disasters, internal and external attacks, and economic and organizational failures. An endeavor to preserve the 1960 U.S. Census data provides a good example of the basic issue. It was widely reported that computers could no longer read the data, but by 1979 the Census Bureau had successfully transferred almost all of the records to newer compatible tapes (1,575 records were lost to deterioration). While persistence is not impossible, it is a major engineering effort. Kevin Kelly, cofounder of *Wired*, explained, "The Internet is basically the largest Xerox machine in the world. If something can be copied it will be copied. On the Internet, it goes everywhere. But what it doesn't do is it doesn't go forward in time very well."[6]

This crisis certainly seems counterintuitive in light of the warnings consistently doled out regarding recording any personal information.

The decay rates, however, are dramatic. In 1997, Kahle estimated that based on the Internet Archive data, the average URL had a lifespan of forty-four days, and in 2004, the average lifespan of a page was about one hundred days. The Frequently Asked Questions section of the Internet Archive today states that the average life of a webpage is seventy-seven days.[7] This ephemerality has continued to motivate digital preservationists and archivists to create management and tools to locate and preserve content before it is gone. It also has motivated computer scientists to measure and understand web persistence.

"The World Wide Web still is not a library," stated Wallace Koehler in the last of a three-sequence study published in 2004 that had tracked URLs since 1996. "It is well established that Web documents are ephemeral in nature." Koehler measures persistence in terms of half lives, "that period of time required for half of a defined Web literature to disappear."[8] A number of studies were being conducted over shorter time periods than Koehler's project. These studies questioned printed Internet guides and web resources,[9] one finding attrition rates of 28 percent and 50 percent over two- and three-year periods.[10] Others concerned themselves with URL citations in scholarship, measuring their increased use and declining viability. URLs cited in legal scholarship were tested in mid-2001 and produced the following results: 39 percent dated 2001 failed, 37 percent dated 2000 failed, 58 percent dated 1999 failed, 66 percent dated 1998 failed, and 70 percent dated 1997 failed.[11] When URLs fail as access points to content, they have suffered "link rot." Much of the persistent web that does not suffer from link rot comprises navigation pages (those that serve to guide the user though a site), as opposed to content pages (pages providing information).[12] In 2003, two-thirds of Koehler's original sample, which was about half navigation and half content pages, were gone, and three-quarters of pages that remained were navigation pages.[13] Koehler notes that there is a steady state after an initial rapid decline in URL link rot and that more research needs to be done on resource life time.[14]

A 2000 study by Junghoo Cho and Hector Garcia-Molina down-loaded 720,000 pages from "popular" web servers daily for four months to study whether the documents changed.[15] More than 20 percent of all pages changed between each crawl (daily); more than 40 percent of .com pages changed daily, but less than 10 percent of .edu and .gov pages changed daily.[16] It took fifty days for 50 percent of the web to change or be replaced by new pages.[17] Brian Brewington and George Cybenko built a web clipping service that collected about 100,000 pages per day from March through November 1999; 56 percent of pages did not change over the duration of the study, while 4 percent changed every single crawl.[18] Another study that crawled 151 million pages once a week for eleven weeks attempted to measure frequency and degree of change and found that most changes were minor modifications.[19]

"Despite the ephemeral nature of the web, there is persistent informa-tion."[20] Daniel Gomes and Mario Silva collected data between 2003 and 2006, measuring the lifetime of URLs and content, as well as synthesiz-ing and comparing their findings to previous research.[21] They found that of the fifty-one million pages harvested from the Portuguese na-tional community, web URLs had a half life of two months and a site half life of 556 days.[22] The most common reasons for URL death are replace-ment or recycling of URLs and site death.[23] The half life for content was two days.[24] These findings suggest a decreased lifetime of content when compared with previous studies.[25] At the rate of disappearance found by Gomes and Silva, none of the originally collected information would remain after approximately 8.42 years. According to the body of research just outlined, around 10 to 15 percent of content persists after a year.[26] Additionally, research on the stability of search results over time found that approximately 90 percent of the 12,600 queries collected had their top-ten results altered within a ten-day period.[27] Kahle concludes, "It's a huge problem. . . . This is no way to run a culture."[28]

This research is over ten years old and an area in desperate need of attention and resources. More recently and more specifically, the Perma project at the Harvard Berkman Center has investigated web links cited in U.S. Supreme Court cases, the *Harvard Law Review*, the *Harvard Journal of Law and Technology*, and the *Harvard Human Rights Journal*.[29] Making a distinction between link rot (a link that delivers no content) and reference rot (a link that delivers information but not the referenced information), the initial study found that more than 70 percent of the URLs within the journals and 50 percent of the URLs within U.S. Supreme Court opinions did not link to the originally cited information. In response to these rates, Berkman has produced a service that provides a permanent citation link when a user creates a separate Perma link for a reference. Perma "archives a copy of the referenced content, and generates a link to an unalterable hosted instance of the site."[30] Digital preservation is recognized as a crisis by people in the forever business, and many projects and programs specialize in the area; but it is a drop in the bucket. Even these efforts have their problems. They can collect only a version of an event or a snapshot of a person, while other versions and context fall away. Even the Library of Congress's Twitter archive, which is in so many ways exhaustive, is a collection of a single platform's content and only public tweets. Additionally, digital preservation projects do not take advantage of digital manipulation. One benefit of digital content is that it can be easily updated or fixed.

Increased data discoverability is thus associated with increased data ephemerality. Easy come, easy go. "If we are to understand the dynamics of the Web as a repository of knowledge and culture, we must monitor the way in which that knowledge and culture is managed. We find that the Web in its 'native form' is a far too transitory medium," states Koehler before insisting that initiatives like the Internet Archive are vital.[31] Kahle sets out four questions related to his goal of making all published works accessible to everyone in the world: "Should we do this? Can we do this? May we do this? And will we do this?"[32] He answers all four in the affirmative and explains that he and this perspective are "very American."[33] Kahle acknowledged in his first major publication on the project in 1998 that there are serious privacy concerns with the

Internet Archive.[34] These two principles, access and privacy, have come to a head as the threat of access to harmful information is the disquiet of the day.

In the movie *The Social Network*, Mark Zuckerberg's ex-girlfriend explains to him that "the Internet isn't written in pencil, it's written in ink."[35] Google CEO Eric Schmidt quipped that "every young person . . . will be entitled automatically to change his or her name on reaching adulthood in order to disown youthful hijinks stored on their friends' social media sites."[36] The joke was taken seriously by Jonathan Zittrain, who foresees a "whole-person" reputation rating system developing and promotes a system of "reputation bankruptcy."[37] Similarly, John Hendel explains that "we live naked on the Internet . . . in a brave new world where our data lives forever."[38]

Two authors who agree on the future of forgetting but see the issue differently are Gordon Bell and Viktor Mayer-Schönberger. In *Total Recall*, Bell and his coauthor, Jim Gemmell, celebrate the e-memory revolution,[39] and Mayer-Schönberger is concerned about the chilling effects that will be created by "perfect remembering."[40] Mayer-Schönberger convincingly describes in great length the advances in storage capacity and the ease with which storage of everything could in fact be possible, and Bell and Gemmell describe their e-memory vision as inevitable. "I am a technologist, not a Luddite, so I'll leave abstract discussions about whether we should turn back the clock to others. Total Recall is inevitable regardless of such discussions."[41] Digital information is superior "because it lacks the noise problem," states Mayer-Schönberger, referring to Claude Shannon's theory of noise: decay with use, time, and reproduction.[42] Bell and Gemmell prefer digital memory because it is "objective, dispassionate, prosaic, and unforgivingly accurate."[43]

But digital content cannot be detached from its physical media; it cannot be impervious to decay. Such a quality is not, as of today, part of any record system; space, time, and energy are limitations that nothing can escape. Additionally, content on the Internet is and has been easily editable, leaving no residue from the pen or pencil—the problem described earlier by archivists and historians. In fact, the tools used in *The Social Network* to injure the ego of Zuckerberg's ex-girlfriend allowed for easy erasure.[44]

These movements have produced two camps: preservationists and deletionists. Preservationists believe we owe the entire Internet to our descendants.[45] Deletionists believe forgetting must be part of the Internet to support efficient, useful, and high-quality information practices.[46] Most people probably fall somewhere in the middle. By looking at both, we see the real issue is that *some* information lasts *longer* than the information subject, and possibly society, deems appropriate.

Although a great deal of embarrassing information may make its way online, it will not necessarily remain accessible long enough to qualify for oblivion, depending on the form the concept takes. Searching for "Kayla Laws" today does not retrieve the same results that it did when the notorious revenge-porn site IsAnybodyUp.com was in operation.[47] The site, which invited users to post "pornographic souvenirs from relationships gone sour," folded on April 19, 2012, and now redirects users to BullyVille.com, an antibullying website.[48] Laws was one of the few individuals who spoke out as a victim of the site, being interviewed by *Nightline*.[49] The only reference to the content related to her on IsAnyoneUp.com is found on the second page of Google results in one or two news stories about the site's end. JuicyCampus.com, a site that targeted college students and encouraged them to post content that was often malicious and pornographic, shut down in 2009, citing the declining economy and falling ad revenue.[50]

Whether one is a preservationist or a deletionist, the foregoing persistence research shows that intervention is necessary to promote either perspective. Based on the reasons for disappearing data, we can assume certain things about the information that will remain longer. Information will remain with entities that have the resources to and interest in maintaining access to information as it ages. We can make a few other conclusions by reflecting on these movements. They remind us that the web is very young and has transformed greatly in the past ten years and that more detailed research on content persistence is necessary to understand exactly what could and should be regulated. To determine what type of intervention should be undertaken with regard to old information, before rights or obligations can be created, a structure is needed to consider old information in a way that embraces all of the various information circumstances that arise.

Ghyslain Raza unwillingly became the Star Wars Kid in 2003 and, according to Google, still is as of 2013. Caitlin Davis was an eighteen-year-old New England Patriots cheerleader who was fired after pictures were posted online showing her posing next to a passed-out friend who was covered in Sharpie markings including a swastika.[51] Alexandra Wallace quit school and made a public apology for a racist video she posted on YouTube that spurred debate online about a university's authority to monitor or regulate student speech. In 1992, John Venables and Robert Thompson viciously murdered a two-year-old and, both at age ten, became the youngest people ever to be incarcerated for murder in English history. These stories deserve varying levels of sympathy but are all embarrassing and negative and may lead the subjects to want to disconnect their names from their past transgressions to make them less retrievable when interviewing for a job, college, or first date—oblivion. Paradoxically, the only individuals who have been offered oblivion are the two who committed the most heinous social offense: Venables and Thompson were given new identities upon their release from juvenile incarceration. In the Digital Age, it may actually be easier for two convicted murderers to get a job than it is for Alexandra Wallace.

This paradox is one of many that result from an inconsistent and distorted conception of information persistence and how to manage it in the Digital Age. The story of Julian Barnes's *Flaubert's Parrot* is informative. The protagonist is on a search for truth of the past, the life of Gustave Flaubert, an ardently private man with a protected reputation as a recluse. An acquaintance significantly underpays an unknowing woman for letters between Flaubert and a lover. The protagonist is mortified when the acquaintance explains that he destroyed the letters

at the request of the author, Flaubert, who had ended the series of letters with that instruction to his lover. Here we find an unfair transac-
tion for personal information of an individual who had explicitly stated
that the information was to be deleted; the historical information is at
the mercy of subjective judgment. Today, are we any better equipped
to address the appropriate actions of those who hold the information?
Perhaps we are.

Archeology and library ethics are certainly not undisputed or easy to
practice, but they are examples of use regulation related to maintaining
the integrity of information and the dignity of subjects in the pursuit of
knowledge. An interesting excavation practice involves leaving some of
the site untouched for future researchers who may seek different answers
or have improved methods of extracting more precise or enriched information from the site.[52] Similarly, archivists are guided by the Archival
Code of Ethics. The Society of American Archivists has drafted a Code
of Ethics that states, "[Archivists] establish procedures and policies to
protect the interests of the donors, individuals, groups, and institutions
whose public and private lives and activities are recorded in their hold-
ings. As appropriate, archivists place access restrictions on collections
to ensure that privacy and confidentiality are maintained, particularly
for individuals and groups who have no voice or role in collections' creation, retention, or public use."[53]

People once asked other people for answers. Now we ask machines,
but these machines are created by humans to meet human goals. At the
Time & Bits conference in 1998, the attendees asked, "Who is responsible?" "There are serious questions as to who will take responsibility for
making digital information persist over time."[54] I propose that everyone,
including users, take responsibility for this space as stewards of information produced, used, collected, and organized online. Extending this
ethic is a maternal, as opposed to paternal, form of privacy protection.
It does not prescribe specific behavior that is best for users or prohibit
any specific behavior but encourages users to nurture the space for long-

term benefits and emphasizes the web as a whole and as part of our social existence.

Data managers have long been stewards of the information they have been entrusted with, maintaining the timeliness, accuracy, and control of access to the data.[55] These information stewards manage data over its life cycle by accounting for the changing value of information from conception to disposition.[56] These basic principles underscore widespread information stewardship, which can be addressed and promoted through a number of mechanisms including markets, norms, computer code, and laws.[57] These mechanisms may simply allow for personal information to be less accessible over time or may actively limit access to or edit personal information in an attempt to minimize harm while retaining valuable substance.

Digital information does not naturally last forever, nor does it last long in anthropological or historical terms. Looking back on all the formats used to preserve information that later became important historical anecdotes or markers, those built in binary, interpreted by constantly updated code, maintained by decentralized users, and organized by institutions able to preserve a tiny portion of the web are not the most reliable. "Right or wrong, the Internet is a cruel historian."[58] But content persistence in fact proves that the Internet is a lazy historian with no principled practices of preserving or protecting knowledge. If digital information is not more thoughtfully maintained as a collection, neither goal of privacy or preservation will be met in the future.

Widespread acceptance of information stewardship, currently practiced only by certain information professionals, may provide the necessary framework to achieve more effective preservation and privacy online. In order to construct a right to be forgotten that embraces information stewardship, we must have a better sense of the *digital* landscape, how it is used, and how it is different.

What does it mean for information to be "irrelevant" or "inadequate," and how do we measure "newsworthiness" or the "public interest" in a digital world? The discourse surrounding these terms is from a paper world with daily newspapers, diaries, letters, and filing cabinets. Digital information is different. The ways we use it, rely on it, create it, attach meaning to it, attach other content to it, share it, organize it, keep it, and destroy it are all somewhat different and still changing. Determining whether harms to the dynamic self or a lack of control over the flow of personal information somehow outweigh the value of the information requires a closer look at the social life of digital information and how digital information changes over time.

All information is not created equal, and even if it is, it does not remain equal. Different information has different value, and that value changes as time passes. The desire to move forward without being shackled to one's past may result in information disputes with the information creator, storer, and intermediaries. All information disputes weigh competing rights, values, and/or interests to determine the best course of action for a specific type of information (true, false, newsworthy, owned, private, etc.). When confronted with an old piece of personal information, the question "why should this information be retained?" needs to be asked and answered, but we need the tools and vocabulary to do so. Disputes related to old information are no different from disputes related to new information, but they require a reassessment of information characteristics and valuation under the conditions of passed time. As information ages, it takes on new characteristics relevant to its role in meeting the needs of society. These nuances matter to crafting appropriately tailored policy. In order to find nuance, it may be helpful to think about information as a single file—a representation or piece of communication. The value of a single piece of information can be analyzed as it meets the needs of the present and the future. In other words, an information life cycle can be described and assessed.

There are a number of scenarios to which a right to be forgotten may apply, too many, in fact. The right to be forgotten is an incredibly daunting concept to implement. The following scenarios are variations from the matrix presented in chapter 3. The difference in the scenarios should not be ignored, because providing different treatment for different scenarios may prevent opportunities to achieve the goals of privacy and preservation—stewardship. In order to assess contested aspects of obstruction, the options presented in chapter 3 are discussed in terms of eight hypothetical scenarios:

1. A Facebook image from a user's college days five years before, portraying a camping trip where he or she went skinny-dipping (actively created and posted by the subject him- or herself on the original site—internal, content, initial)

2. A rape victim whose name was included in a news story from ten years before about the rape allegations and conviction (actively created content by someone other than the subject, on the initial site—external, content, initial)

3. Information on the child support owed by a father that washes downstream to a "deadbeat dad" site and resides there years after all payments have been made and a relationship has been built with the child (actively created content by another external source that has moved from the initial site—external, content, downstream)

4. A young user's racist tweet about her favorite young-adult movie adaptation that has been retweeted throughout the Twittersphere and that is now seven years old (actively created content by the subject that has been moved downstream from the initial site— internal, content, downstream)

5. Amazon clickstream (passively created data, subject derived, held by the initial site—internal, data, initial)

6. Amazon clickstream traded to another party, for example, Acxiom (passively created, subject derived, downstream—data, internal, downstream)

7. Google data on a subject's family, such as how many children the user has or a user's interest in firearms, available in a dashboard feature that is derived from predictive analytics (data passively cre-

ated by someone other than the data subject residing on the initial site—external, data, initial)

8. The same Google predictive data sold to another data broker (data passively created by someone other than the data subject moved beyond the initial site—external, data, downstream)

As "data," scenarios 7 and 8 will follow a similar information life cycle to scenarios 5 and 6 and, for the most part, will be condensed into those scenarios for the purposes of assessing value associated with a particular piece of data. These four scenarios all suffer from implementation challenges—namely, the data subject's difficulties in knowing about and locating the personal data held about him or her by initial but particularly by downstream data controllers. Feasibility, implementation, and enforcement are discussed further in chapter 6, but for the purposes of assessing the changing value of information as it continues to harm individuals, they will be discussed in terms of scenarios 5 and 6. Scenarios 1 through 4, on the other hand, involve content and the public in a way scenarios 5 and 6 do not. Content may be easier to track down but harder to remove.

The right to be forgotten could cover all of these scenarios, which vary dramatically in almost every way (resides on initial or downstream location, created by the subject or another, created passively or actively). If the right does not impact actively created content, it would not reach scenarios 1 through 4 because they are authored as opposed to passively collected data (a blurry distinction). If the right applies only to information that the subject creates either passively or actively, it would apply to the information held by Amazon, Acxiom, Facebook, and possibly Twitter but not the news or deadbeat-dad sites. If the right does not extend beyond its limited reach to criminal information, only the deadbeat-dad site would be restricted in publishing the information. Categorizing information in terms of life-cycle phases assists in addressing how information should be managed as it ages to meet a number of demands.

"Information," like "privacy" and any other closely analyzed term, suffers from a contentious definition. Claude Shannon's work spawned the field of information theory and a less axiomatic definition of the term "information."[59] Information in the formal, engineering sense, developed by Shannon, is a quantitative description of the output of an information source.[60] Shannon ignores the meaning held by the information or, as Leon Brillouin states, he ignores "the human value of the information."[61] The right to be forgotten, however, must consider information as having meaning, because it deals with competing human values associated with the human-created/processed information. The rich debate on the definition of "information" is beyond the scope of this book; however, the information scientist Gernot Wersig offers six types of information: structures of the world are information; knowledge developed from perception is information; message is information; meaning assigned to data is information; effect on a specific process is information; and process or transfer is information.[62] For the purposes of the information life cycle, information has two broad meanings, a condensed version of Wersig's set. The first uses "information" as an action word: to inform or communicate. The second uses it as a noun, that which represents something in the world—an opinion, fact, or idea represented by language, image, numbers, and so on. These simplified definitions become useful when assessing the value of information at each phase of its life cycle.

Within the IT community, management of information life cycle is "the policy-driven management of information as it changes value through the full range of its life cycle from conception to disposition."[63] Information takes on different values over its life cycle depending on whether the information need is immediate or remote. Information for immediate purposes includes that which is relevant to immediate decisions based on the current state of the world. Information for remote purposes is that which is relevant to uncovering previously unknown insight into the past or future. These categories of information needs help us to better assess our competing demands for aged information and remind us that management principles from other disciplines have provided groundwork for these issues.

Though the value of information is subjective, value can be assigned when there is an action potentially influenced by the information and the consequences of the action also can be measured.[64] Immediate need includes the need for information to make decisions, and the value of information is its role in maximizing expected utility.[65] Information, then, is assessed based on its utility value. An IT professional manages information over its life cycle for the utility purpose of a single entity.

There are certain principles of information that make its valuation a unique assessment for immediate information needs. Unlike almost all other resources or properties, which have characteristics of divisibility, appropriability, scarcity, and decreasing returns on use, information functions in an opposite way.[66] Information is infinitely shareable—I can possess it while you possess it and a million others possess it. In fact, sharing information, or increasing its use, increases its value. Unused information is arguably not information at all. Information requires human interaction and more people utilizing it to maximize its value. The more information is used, the more information is created—it is self-generative, a concept that squarely contradicts general principles of other resources. New or consequential information is produced from many individuals processing information. The value of information, therefore, also increases when combined with other information.

Similar to other resources, however, information is perishable. Its value depreciates over time.[67] Different types of information depreciate in value more quickly than others do. The speed of depreciation generally correlates to the relevance and accuracy of content. Information, as a representation of something in the world, will not be relevant or accurate forever and maybe not for long. The shape of Earth, stock prices, lyrics to a song, and addresses all have different rates at which their relevancy and accuracy will diminish. In turn, the value of the information record will diminish.

Finally, while the value of information increases upon combination, it does not necessarily increase upon accumulation. That is, more information does not always support its utilization. Humans seek more information beyond the threshold of optimal cognitive processing. Information behavior studies show that individuals gain increased confidence and satisfaction in decisions made with excess information but have poorer performance rates.[68]

The immediate needs of the eight scenarios include decision-making needs related to the individual, on the basis of the current state of the subject and information currently representing the individual. When the skinny-dipping image was created, it may have been very relevant to hiring or dating decisions as well as news reporting. The rape-victim story may have been relevant to many immediate decisions, such as which neighborhoods to avoid. The inclusion of the victim's name may have been relevant to many decisions made about her, such as employment or relationships, but allowing use of this information for immediate decisions is not socially desirable. The information about the deadbeat dad was likely to be relevant to the school his child attended in its effort to meet his or her educational needs or to a woman deciding whether to say yes to his marriage proposal. The racist tweets may have been very relevant to immediate decisions that involve the teen's character, intelligence, and maturity, such as college admissions, dating, befriending, and employment. The data scenarios (those passively created and derived from the data subject) may have immediate information needs related to how to meet the needs of the customer, like mailing a product to the correct address or providing desired services. Access to information for immediate needs is imperative to completing specific tasks of a particular entity, but information may meet the needs of nonspecific tasks as well.

Beyond immediate decision-making needs, aged information not only helps us learn from and about our past but also helps us make better decisions about the future. While the benefits of targeted advertising may be disputable outside the marketing industry, predictive analytics also claim a benefit to fraud prevention, data security, health care, and machine learning—that we can better understand our world by analyzing all of this information.[69] Remote informational needs have a long history of safeguards elsewhere. For instance, academic researchers involved with human subjects are guided by a set of ethical principles enforced by internal review boards (IRBs), referred to as the Common Rule. The basic tenets are (1) that people who participate as subjects are selected equitably and give fully informed, fully voluntary, written consent, (2) that the proposed research be reviewed by an IRB, and (3) that projects are approved only if risks are minimized and are reasonable in relation to anticipated benefits to the subject, as well as to the importance of the knowledge that is reasonably expected to be gained. Although the issues are difficult to navigate in light of hacking, reidentification, and a murky understanding of harm and risk, modern university review boards determine whether subjects' privacy is sufficiently protected.[70]

Predictive analysis and experimentation may be less universally valued when compared to the value placed on cultural history. The information involving the skinny-dipping college student may be important to a collection of images representing the first generation of digital natives in college, sociological research on expressions of sexuality, or predictions on future courses of action when included with other information. The rape-victim content may be important to statistics on the reporting of sexual violence or the commentary on such crimes, as well as the prediction and prevention of such acts. Information regarding the nonpayment of child support is relevant to determining reasons for nonpayment to help improve the system as well as to impacts on the child over the course of his or her lifetime. The racist tweet could be very relevant to assessing social progress. Information will change in relation to immediate and remote needs over the course of its life cycle; this breakdown provides policy makers with a structure for balancing the demands of contested discoverability of old information.

Having outlined two categories of information needs, I also outline the way in which information meets those demands as it ages. The following organizes the phases of an information life cycle in a descriptive fashion. The principles of information perishability and unpredictable value are the centerpieces for the following analysis, but other considerations are important to the assessment or measurement of information value over time. Focusing on information as a form of communication and representation helps to distinguish its use and value over time into phases.

Upon release, information holds a unique status. It is novel, contributes to the knowledge base, and is heavily sought after, shared, and used. Internet memes and news are examples. Information at the distribution phase is an accurate representation of *something* in the world and held within the context it was created. At that moment, the piece of information, sentence, data, figure, or image symbolizes something—an address, an opinion, a reaction, the best way to dice an onion, how many planets are in the solar system, that the world is flat. These expressions represent someone's interpretation of an aspect of the world as it stands. The information is also a reliable communication from the speaker. At the moment of release, the speaker intends to communicate the message held in the information. The information communicated may not be valuable, but the act of communicating is valuable.

There is also a sense of justice in the priority of speech over privacy at this point. The information subject should be accountable for his or her actions and interactions. The existence of the information online and the limitations it may impose on the subject will act as a deterrent to others. Exposure as a deterrent is very powerful, but as a society, we have not collectively established those behaviors that should be deterred and those that should be protected against our most salacious interests.

Immediate value is at its highest at the distribution phase. New information is the most accurate representation of the state of the world and communication from the speaker. Therefore, current information allows us to make the best decisions. For companies, this information is operational and necessary to functioning efficiently. A company wants your current address to ship your order. For companies wanting to hire an employee, the skinny-dipping image may not reflect the maturity or other traits desired in an employee. The nonpayment of child support may have a similar impact on decisions; someone dodging child support may not be an ideal date or employee. An employer making a decision about an applicant may want past information, but the old information may lead to poor decisions because it overshadows the current state of the applicant. A city determining how much funding should go to a sexual-violence clinic may have an immediate need for the information that a rape has occurred and the details of the victim. The racist comments from a teenager may be used by the school system to ramp up diversity education in the school. These are immediate needs that factor into operational decisions. Acxiom may have no operational needs for the subject. Amazon needs your information to mail you the correct product but may also need it to make recommendations to you. Recommendations are lower needs than is the correct address. Remote value is low at this point. The information is readily available, its value to historical or predictive research may be difficult to ascertain, and it may need to be combined with other information that is not yet available.

What happens to information when it is no longer newsworthy? Information becomes stale and subsequently may need verification and is not sought out by the general public, a stage I call the record phase. For instance, GoogleTrends shows that interest in all but the most popular "viral" content exists only for a few weeks or months at best. This information has been absorbed into the knowledge base, and its finer details may no longer be passed on.

Records often are reduced for manageability and efficiency. Information, as a representation of something, generally becomes less accurate over time. The "something" that it represents may have changed, but the piece of information stays the same; and so it requires effort to verify its accuracy. Wikipedia can be quite a bit more useful than a traditional encyclopedia because it can be updated with current information.

Information also becomes less reliable as a communication from the speaker. Few of us continue to talk about the same thing over time or talk about it in the same way. We may no longer feel the need to communicate information found on our blogs or other formats, but the information remains. Many of us stop caring about the things we cared about a few years ago or see things differently as we learn and experience more. If our communications are not managed, that information can cause problems for both the communicator and the subject of the communication. How many users delete blogs, pictures, or other content without considering whether valuable information may be destroyed? How many users go through old content to update or edit it? How many users consider whether the information may have very low value but significant harms?

Information loses context over time. It becomes displaced from its original setting. For instance, pictures stored on personal computers without tags, dates, or organizing file may be discarded because they do not contribute to a story or sentimental moment. Information without context not only decreases in value but can be frustrating and dangerous. It is common to experience moments of judgment or assessment by another person who has missed the whole story. Print publications solely reporting on those who have been arrested in a local area have spawned free websites that include mug shots, names, and charges that are fully indexed by search engines. These arrests may lead to convictions or acquittals or may be simple cases of mistaken identity—the rest of the story is not told. Context offers a much more informed citizenry but is not a consistent part of the web.

Immediate and remote needs for information at the record phase are difficult to assess. Verification of continued accuracy or other resources may be necessary to record information in order to make the best decisions for immediate information needs. It may be difficult to determine whether the information is relevant, contextualized, or accurate or should be used in decision making. When was that skinny-dipping picture taken and under what circumstances? Did the father ever make or try to make any child-support payments? Were the racist tweets made in response to some other conversation? How has the rape victim coped with the crime? Has a user dramatically changed interests since the last time data was collected? These questions put speed bumps in the decision-making process. For remote needs, capturing the information while situated in its original context may become problematic at the record stage, and it may not be clear that the information should be captured or processed.

Expired information is that which is no longer an accurate representation of the state of the subject or communication. The expiration phase occurs when the substance of the content changes but the information stays the same or the communication is no longer being actively expressed—the world or speaker has moved on, but the data record is stuck in time. The older a traditional print encyclopedia, the more likely the information within has expired. Blogs may communicate an idea from years ago that the author no longer stands by or cares about. Context, such as time markers or updates, can help maintain information in the expiration phase, but without context, this information may require intervention to prevent harms and retain value.

Immediate information needs are not benefited by incorporating information at the expiration stage. When the skinny-dipper is no longer engaging in such activities, the rape victim has moved on, the deadbeat dad becomes a good father, and the teenager is no longer racist, acting on old information may not meet immediate needs that would be better served with current information regarding the character of the information subjects. Information will eventually no longer represent the state of the world or the communication of the speaker. For instance, information that says that the world is flat is no longer helpful for making decisions when the information that the world is round has been disclosed. A company is not benefited by your old address if it is trying to send you a package. But your old address may be relevant for historical or predictive needs. If a company is tracking the migration of its largest market from New York to Arizona, it may better predict the needs of an aging customer base. Remote information value is at its highest when things start to change, because understanding change is vital to prediction and history.

On the basis of the foregoing considerations, users of all types alter access to information through action or inaction at some point. Information may be deindexed to quarantine it from everyday engagement and still preserve its existence. It may be anonymized to limit liability or harm to identified individuals and still retain much of its value. It may be archived in a separate space specifically designed to manage old information. It may be reduced and organized to retain some context without increased resources. It may be deleted simply to get it out of the way. Nothing may be done, and the information is buried or, through neglect, loses its access point and dies. Or the information may be associated with something painful, and access is manipulated to limit exposure to those feelings.

This assessment of old information supports and opposes oblivion and erasure, but it also explains *why* the web is quite ephemeral on its own. The web is a human communication system; its content is for humans, and it is maintained by humans. We do not always care to continually communicate the same thing as our interests move forward. Information as representation loses value over time because it does not support operational decisions as well as new information does. Of course, communicated information will decay and be buried. While some people may choose to communicate the same thing over a long period of time, a new information life cycle begins for each information contribution over that continuation. We are left with those who value the information as something that was communicated or that represented some aspect of the past. These values are generally handled through the regulation of use or access, as opposed to deletion.

The difficult task inherent in information stewardship is determining what information may have future value. All eight of our scenarios involve information with immediate value that may decay as remote value ripens. When immediate needs are no longer being met, it may be "fair" to dissociate the individual from the information, which may also protect the decision maker from making poor decisions. Though a complete history of an individual may lead to unfair and poor decisions, there are certain roles in some locales for which the public has tradition-ally been entitled to a complete history, such as political office. Voting is an immediate need that, correctly or incorrectly, relies on old informa-tion. Most people do not run for political office, a role that is particu-larly exposed by special information practices and standards,[71] but any of the individuals from the eight scenarios could run for office. Deleting associations between individuals and their past is dangerous, but main-taining the association with access and use restrictions may prevent the disappearance of personal pasts with the ability to reestablish full access and use upon the presentation of a new immediate need, such as voting.

In a few years, Alexandra Wallace may still be making racist videos, or she may be running for political office. Which of these is true will help to determine the value of her name being associated with a piece of negative information. Preserved information may still be very accurate (if she is still creating racist media) or relevant (if she is running for office)—it could retain or regain much of its value. More likely, she will try to dissociate herself from the content as best she can so that she can pursue a normal job and maintain normal relationships.[72] When her name is searched, she will be exposed to the employer or prospective friend. Wallace is hardly the most sympathetic of online reputation vic-tims, and her video sparked a large amount of interesting debate. Ques-tions for the right-to-be-forgotten debate, however, should be whether her name adds to the value of the content, whether the information remains accurate, and whether the information does more harm than good after a period of time. Determining whether information will have future value is an exercise that is much more calculable and insightful at the expiration phase than at the distribution phase. More time means more perspective on discoverability decisions.

Upon the release of information, the heightened protection from the First Amendment protects it over other rights, values, and interests. When freedom of expression is pitted against privacy at this stage, newly distributed information claims many more wins than losses. Courts de-fine prior restraint as "a predetermined judicial prohibition restraining specific expression."[73] A heavy presumption of invalidity follows any requirement of judicial approval prior to publication. The presumption originated in 1931 in *Near v. Minnesota* when Chief Justice Charles Evans Hughes reversed a trial court's injunction on the *Saturday Press* pursuant to a Minnesota law based on public nuisance: "The fact that the liberty of the press may be abused by miscreant purveyors of scandal does not make any the less necessary the immunity of the press from previous restraint in dealing with official misconduct. Subsequent punishment for such abuses as may exist is the appropriate remedy, consistent with constitutional privilege."[74] Thus, the government "carries a heavy burden of showing justification for the imposition of such a restraint."[75] The Pentagon Papers case fumbled over the exceptions described in *Near* when the Supreme Court rejected an executive-sought injunction to prevent the *New York Times* and *Washington Post* from publishing classified information related to the Vietnam War—information previously undisclosed, despite being very dated.[76] Justices Hugo Black and William Douglas made no exception for national security, Justice William Brennan allowed for injunctions only during war time, Justices Potter Stewart and Byron White required proof that the nation would suffer "direct, immediate, and irreparable damage,"[77] and Justice Thurgood Marshall stressed the absence of legislation guiding the Court.[78] Even in the consideration of old information, the presumption against prior restraints even when extreme danger to national security or some overriding governmental interest is at stake remains strong.

Under Swiss law, the media is not entitled to identify an individual with his or her criminal past after sentencing has occurred—it is no longer newsworthy.[79] Countries with this type of formalized expiration phase have determined that immediate information needs are not or should not be supported by old information. The social and individual value of rehabilitation outweighs the public's right to the name of the individual involved in the prior criminal conduct. "The truth of the facts could no longer justify the infringement of the plaintiff's right to have his honor and his private life respected."[80]

The Second Circuit Court of Appeals protected the publication of information that is legally available even when it rehashes the past.[81] Recall that in *Sidis v. F-R Pub. Corporation*, the details of a child prodigy's adult reclusive life were protected as "newsworthy" over the privacy rights of the information subject.[82] Similar to *Sidis*, the information-life-cycle approach would conflict with the European form of forgetting, because a single piece of information would be assessed in a way similar to a file. Old information that is newly distributed gains a new life cycle—a new file is created. Information is assessed at its point of distribution, not at the original point in time when the substance of the information occurred, and a willingness to continue to redistribute suggests high value.

The ECtHR has heard a spattering of related cases, many that address the changing value of information over time. In *Schwabe v. Austria*, a case decided by the ECtHR in 1992, the conviction for defamation and reproaching an individual with a previous criminal offense in a letter to the editor was overturned.[83] The Austrian court held the applicant liable for statements regarding a politician's multiple traffic-accident arrests because he failed to prove they were true. It seems odd not to be able to prove whether someone was arrested twice for traffic accidents, but "truth" in information disputes means two different things in European courts and U.S. courts.[84] The ECtHR determined that the point of the press release was to present sufficient justifications for the resignation of the politician, which is a "value judgment" that cannot be proven true. The court found that the context of the reference to old criminal offenses concerned political morality and that such reference might be relevant to assessing fitness to exercise political functions. In light of these various interpretations, the ECtHR determined that the Austrian holding was a violation of article 10 of the ECHR, because the applicant did not "exceed the limits of freedom of expression." Here the ECtHR is grappling with information in the record phase—it is not clear how accurate or relevant it is, and the details of the incidents are not entirely clear; but because the issue revolves around politics and concerns an immediate decision regarding political functions, the court errs on the side of caution, allowing this type of information to be brought back into this type of conversation without punishment.

In 2008, a Turkish national, Cemalettin Canli, complained that during pending criminal proceedings in 2003, police reports were submitted to the court and published in the national press that detailed two sets of criminal proceedings from 1990 regarding his alleged membership in illegal organizations.[85] The old police reports did not note that he was never convicted. Failure to keep the records up-to-date before submitting them to the public violated his right to respect for private and family life in article 8. In essence, the ECtHR found the retention and disclosure of this snapshot of the past that was no longer accurate and now misleading (an expired piece of information) to be a privacy violation.

In 2012, M.M. successfully appealed the indefinite retention and disclosure of information about her formal caution for child abduction, and the ECtHR found a violation of article 8.[86] M.M. was a grandmother who took her grandson away for two days in the hope that her son and his girlfriend could work out some relationship problems without affecting the boy. Instead of pursuing charges, the director of public prosecution administered a caution, accepted and signed by the grandmother, who was told it would remain on her record for five years, but six years later, she was denied employment on the basis of a background check that revealed her kidnapping past. When she challenged her acceptance of the caution, she received a letter explaining that the old policy had changed: "The current policy is that all convictions and cautions, where the injured party is a child, are kept on the record system for life."[87] Notably, in the end, the ECtHR found that the safeguards of the system were insufficient to ensure that the retention and disclosure of the applicant's data had not and would not violate her right to privacy. There is in this case a reference to a need for systematic information stewardship and, without it, an assumed violation of privacy.

Today the policy makers have to ask slightly different questions. The DP Directive addressed the differences of information throughout its life cycle, albeit briefly, vaguely, and somewhat indirectly. Article 6(1)(e) directs personal data to be kept in such a way that identifying data subjects is permitted for no longer than necessary for the purposes for which the data was collected or further processed, and safeguards should be put in place for stored personal data held longer for historical, statistical, or scientific use.[88] Article 12(b) guarantees that a data subject may rectify, erase, or block the processing of data if it is incomplete or inaccurate.[89] In *Google v. AEPD*, the CJEU interpreted the language of the Directive that seems to point to some kind of information life cycle, stating that the articles provided for oblivion (removal of links with personal information about data subjects) when personal data is inaccurate, inadequate, irrelevant, or excessive.[90] The proposed DP Regulation includes explicit safeguards for remote users in the exceptions of article 17(3) for the retention of data where it is "necessary for historical, statistical and scientific research purposes, for reasons of public interest in the area of public health, for exercising the right of freedom of expression, when required by law or where there is a reason to restrict the processing of the data instead of erasing them."[91]

Without more guidance, the DP Regulation will not quell fears about rewriting history. It also does not protect against unwanted deletion. It alludes to an information life cycle but in reality provides no way of determining which personal data is irrelevant, inaccurate, inadequate, or excessive, under what circumstances, and when obstruction is and is not justified. Even inaccuracy is not something that is universally agreed on; comparative defamation law reveals differences in who bears the burden of proving truth (or substantial truth) or falsity (when provable). Assume that a data subject contacts a data controller to erase personal content available to the public. The data controller may be able to keep it for historical purposes but may erase it because it is simply easier and less dangerous considering the uncertainty of the claim. Preservation efforts are already insufficient. Obstruction and use restrictions are better than deletion for protecting information in the expiration phase for future information needs. But without some approach or approaches for determining when and why information is inadequate, irrelevant, or excessive, these seemingly more mild responses may lead to the loss of more information in the end.

An information life cycle allows countries to break down the circumstances of and interests in data and content and make tailored decisions about how to move forward in addressing discoverability. It allows for the ad hoc approach more popular in Europe and the definitional approach used in the U.S. The legal scholar Melville Nimmer distinguishes ad hoc and definitional approaches to balancing speech rights with other interests by explaining that ad hoc balancing involves weighing competing interests under the particular circumstances presented, whereas a definitional approach asks only "which forms of speech are to be regarded as 'speech' within the meaning of the first amendment."[92] In *New York Times Company v. Sullivan*, the U.S. Supreme Court answered whether libel laws constituted an abridgement of speech in violation of the First Amendment by defining the type of defamatory speech protected by the Constitution.[93] The Court still performed a balance, but it was categorical, not circumstantial. Similarly, a German appellate court in Koblenz (Third Civil Senate of Superior District Court of Koblenz) recently upheld a lower court that ruled that intimate photographs should be deleted upon the end of a relation if either person requests such deletion.[94] Under the ruling, private enjoyment of nude photographs is not protected when a party has rescinded consent.[95] Put differently, the Koblenz court decided that when a relationship expires, intimate photos from the relationship must also expire. By contrast, the CJEU explains that generally the data subject's rights override the interests of Internet users, but this balance depends on case-specific circumstances, the nature of the information at issue, sensitivity toward the data subject's private life, and the interest of the public.[96] The information life cycle provides tools for decision makers to weigh the particulars of a situation, as well as to categorize old information as speech that receives less protection.

When an employer searches a possible candidate, a parent searches a child who is away at college, a new acquaintance searches for a bio, or a targeted marketing technology seeks to provide enticing ads to a user, the searchers are probably interested in everything, but that does not mean they have a right to or legitimate interest in discovering all of the personal information attached to an individual. A personal search or the processing of personal information does not necessarily serve the public interest. For instance, GoogleTrends results for "Caitlin Davis"[97] and "Alexandra Wallace"[98] show spikes of interest that only last a matter of months immediately after the event. There are individuals who are much more innocent, whose stories have somehow caught the attention of a well-read blog, site, or Twitter feed. Much more common are the many individuals who may want to move beyond personal information that has never been "trending" and may never get more than a few hits that dwindle in number over the years.

Wikipedia's Biographies of Living Persons Policy draws a distinction between general public interest in the individual and interest in the event or topic of an entry: "Caution should be applied when identifying individuals who are discussed primarily in terms of a single event. When the name of a private individual has not been widely disseminated or has been intentionally concealed, such as in certain court cases or occupations, it is often preferable to omit it, especially when doing so does not result in a significant loss of context. . . . Consider whether the inclusion of names of private living individuals who are not directly involved in an article's topic adds significant value."[99] On the basis of this policy, Ghyslain Raza was not named in the entry on the Star Wars Kid the first time I viewed it, but he has since been identified in the first line of the entry.[100] Wikipedia has a deletion policy that results in five thousand pages being deleted each day, one reasoning being a lack of "notability," which requires significant coverage, reliability, sources, independence from the subject, and a presumption that the subject is suitable for inclusion.[101] Articles with questionable notability should not resort to deletion; but those that are clearly not notable should be deleted, and useful material should be preserved on the talk pages,[102] which are not indexed by Google.[103]

Like Wikipedia, the right to be forgotten could examine the difference between public interest and private searches in order to determine the right course of action when a user seeks to have personal information "forgotten," as opposed to quick deletion or automatic First Amendment preservation. This is similar to assessing the information needs over time. An individual may be a public fixation for a time but not relevant to the story once it has been collected for historical purposes. Or like Ghyslain Raza, an individual may remain actively of interest, even as the event or meme passes.

When the German Federal Court of Justice heard the first lawsuits initiated by Manfred Lauber and Wolfgang Werlé, it was to determine whether the storage of old news stories in online archives was the equivalent of a current dissemination of the story; in other words, is providing continual access to online content essentially the same as publishing a new story? Disseminating information that associates an individual with his or her criminal past may violate the personality rights of those who are reintegrating into society after serving time in a criminal system, depending on how much time has passed since the offense, the harm to the offender, and whether new coverage has been triggered by some act of the offender. In deciding cases of archived Internet content, the German Federal Court of Justice devised a two-part test to settle inconsistencies among lower courts. Some found the online archive the same as a current, and therefore new, dissemination of the story, and others found the online archive comparable to traditional archives. The Court of Justice asked both how the report was disseminated and how the reader will perceive it. Dissemination of information that is deemed minor, such as a listing in a website calendar or teasers that lead to pay-to-view archives, will not violate personality rights. The court compared actively searching for the specific information online to prime-time television coverage. If the content must be actively searched, as the Lauber and Werlé content was, the publication is not a violation, but if it is pushed onto the reader or brought to the attention of a reader through links from current content, the publication might constitute a violation. The second part of the test requires that the archived information not give the impression that the content is current or a fresh publication.[104]

Whether online archives are a new or current publication is not precisely the issue raised by the digital right to be forgotten. But this type of interpretation of personality rights has traditionally granted a right to be forgotten, and therefore, the court's analysis is relevant. Neither the traditional nor the new German interpretation of the right to have one's criminal past forgotten aligns with the life-cycles approach. This is because the fresh dissemination of content resets the information life cycle. The creation of new content about a criminal past holds high value to the communicator and potential users in the distribution phase and would not be restricted under a life-cycle analysis. However, once the content is born online, its life cycle begins, and its harm to the subject can be assessed against other information needs. The analysis of the German Federal Court of Justice does not address the value of the information; the court determines that if a user must actively search for the content, it does not violate the personality rights of the plaintiff. This aspect of the decision does not account for current information behavior; active online searching is a gateway to all media today, including television documentaries. What online information is actually pushed on a user? Almost all content is actively obtained. The second prong of the test requires that a reader will perceive the information as dated. This certainly falls in line with a life-cycle approach, because it presents an accurate time to the user and any technical system inclined to recognize the date. The life-cycle approach seeks to enhance the overall value of content on the web by measuring the interests of the communicator, immediate users, and remote users in light of the harm to the individual.

A similar case came to the New York Court of Appeals, the state's highest court, in *Firth v. New York*. A New York State employee attempted to bring a defamation claim for a report criticizing him on a state agency's website, but the report had been posted online for more than a year; the statute of limitations had run out on the claim.[105] Firth argued that because the page had changed within the year, it constituted a republication.[106] Because the page could be altered at any time, Firth argued that the defamation statute of limitations "should not be applied verbatim to defamatory publications posted on the Internet in light of significant differences between Internet publications and traditional mass media."[107] The court disagreed, choosing to treat online archives the same as traditional print archives.[108] The single-publication rule emphasized by *Firth* does not follow a life-cycle approach because it looks at a piece of information only once, in the distribution phase.

Expired information has very low value—though it is not valueless[109]—and potentially significant harms. Easy discoverability of expired information for immediate and remote information users can be harmful to all parties, because it generally does not support information stewardship. The harms to the subject as well as to immediate and remote users created by expired information are rarely justified under a life-cycle approach. Particularly with a medium that may so easily be corrected, maintaining accuracy, context, and utility are the priority of the approach.

Ctrl + Z in Legal Cultures

Even as we create and make sense of a digital reality, making choices among the many options on the matrix and determinations along the information life cycle will need to fit within the socio-technical legal cultures. This is particularly true of laws that revolve around forgiveness, privacy, and speech—all of which are laden with different meanings and deeply rooted in cultural norms of justice, utility, and human flourishing. It is clear that the EU version of a right to be forgotten will not be transported into the U.S., because it defines and gives weight to public interest in different ways, relies on intermediary liability, and limits access to such a significant amount of content. That does not mean that the U.S. should not think about digital redemption within its own borders. Many observers completely disregard the possibility of a right to be forgotten in the U.S. because of the weight given to the First Amendment when balanced against other interests. However, Justice Anthony Kennedy stated at a speaking engagement with civics and history teachers in his hometown of Sacramento, "I think problems that arise out of the Internet [will be addressed by the Court in the coming years]. There is a law in Europe that there is a right to be forgotten. . . . Do you have that right?"[1] Being able to wriggle free from one's past to strive for something better still resounds with some Americans. Included in the findings of the federal Do Not Track Kids bill, 94 percent of U.S. adults and parents believe that individuals should have the ability to request the deletion of personal information stored by a search engine, social networking site, or marketing company after a specific period of time.[2] These figures are similar to findings across the EU, but the institutional and legal capacities to implement and enforce digital redemption are very different than in the U.S. The protection of one's personal information privacy is a fundamental right in the EU and more easily accommodates a digital right to be forgotten, no matter its form. The EU will continue to provide digital redemption on a country-by-country basis until the DP Regulation attempts to converge the different approaches.

Each country should be having a conversation about how its own legal culture addresses the socio-technical issues presented by information as it moves through its life cycle, information stewardship choices, and the balance of interests triggered in the numerous and varied disputes over the right to be forgotten. Earlier chapters have emphasized the importance of recognizing cultural specificity wrapped up in digital redemption and questioned the need and wisdom of harmonizing the right to be forgotten. The strong protection of freedom of speech in the U.S. makes it the most challenging place to imagine a legal mechanism for digital redemption. The Supreme Court has stated that restrictions on the publication of information to the public would "invite timidity and self-censorship and very likely lead to suppression of many items that would otherwise be published and that should be available to the public."[3] Timidity and self-censorship are, of course, the same concerns associated with the retention of and easy access to old information, but U.S. law has not developed a system for weighing the competing values at issue throughout the information life cycle. Under the right circumstances, it may be compelled to do so.

The U.S. has an interesting intersection of laws, interests, and values related to a right to be forgotten. Part of patriotic lore is the notion that the country was built by people seeking a second chance and hoping for reinvention. The United States—the presumed "land of opportunity"—is itself the product of second chances and has allowed individuals and groups to break free from their past to prosper. Those who were negatively labeled in Europe came to America to start a new life, and later, similarly motivated midwesterners and easterners migrated and settled the West. Today, however, U.S. society appears harsh, at least in terms of criminal treatment and criminalizing behavior. As detailed in James Whitman's *Harsh Justice*, the European emphasis on dignity has created an environment that is more supportive of second chances, whereas the United States has the highest per capita rate of incarceration in the world, nearly ten times the rate in western Europe.[4] For the past twenty-five years, the United States has been in the midst of a "get-tough" movement; we have started to criminalize schoolchildren drawing on their desks, put people in jail for smoking on the subway or not wearing a seatbelt, and revitalized the death penalty and public shaming.[5] This sharp movement has left us isolated from our Western sister nations and established common ground with Afghanistan (where public shaming was also reintroduced), Yemen and Nigeria (where those who commit crimes as minors can be executed), and China and Russia (where incarceration rates rival those in the United States).[6] The U.S. system is more degrading (makes the punished person feel diminished, lessened, and inferior) than European systems. While the U.S. has moved toward harsher and more demeaning forms of punishment, other Western societies have developed principles to support dignity and rehabilitation, "characterized by a large variety of practices intended to prevent the symbolic degradation of prison inmates," such as the elimination of prison uniforms.[7] In Germany, "the principle of normalcy" seeks to achieve a lifestyle in prison that approximates life outside prison as much as possible, with *real jobs* and the removal of barred doors.[8] Unlike U.S. inmates, French and German prisoners are encouraged to vote.[9]

A long history of "heading west" has resulted in appreciation for loosening the shackles of one's past. But perhaps we are no longer a land of second chances but now, instead, a land of choices. Americans advocate more strongly than Europeans for reliance on choice in defining privacy, but second chances and reinvention have served us so well that perhaps we would be willing to reconsider the hard lines taken. As the law professor Samantha Barbas notes, "At any given time, a society calls on privacy law to do certain kinds of work—to validate particular social structures, practices, and ethics."[10] This book calls on privacy law to validate the important role that forgetting plays in the value of forgiveness and to do so in a manner that respects and references existing legal regimes in this country. In many ways, it calls for the U.S. to reflect on this aspect of our national identity and recent shifts away from reinvention. While U.S. law may not be prepared to address old, truthful, public information, it has some experience with legal reinvention that involves the suppression of information. Just as Warren and Brandeis did not attempt to create a right out of thin air and instead drew on related, established legal doctrines in place to protect personal privacy in order to propose an extension of remedies, digital redemption should fit within existing forgiveness laws. By looking to other U.S. forgiveness laws, a few possibilities present themselves to meet the demand for digital redemption within the confines of the U.S. Constitution.

The U.S. legal approach to forgiveness can be uncovered by analyzing the circumstances under which individual and social benefits have compelled us to legally forgive and forget in two key contexts: restoration (financial, criminal, and immunity from suit) and protection from the disclosure of information (criminal, credit, government records). By investigating the Fair Credit Reporting Act (FCRA), pardons, expungement of records, statutes of limitations, the Freedom of Information Act (FOIA), and bankruptcy law in the U.S., a style of legal reinvention is revealed. Extracting overlapping themes informs the development of a U.S. approach to digital redemption.[11]

Three key factors must be present before existing U.S. laws offer forgiveness: (1) a "forgivable" offense, (2) specific harms, and (3) social benefit. Each area of law carves out exemptions—some offenses are unforgivable. None of the described legal forgiveness measures extend to all circumstances. There are financial decisions one can make that will preclude filing for bankruptcy. Some criminal activities will never be considered for informational forgiveness, particularly ones with high recidivism rates and of great public concern (e.g., the sex offender list). Statutes of limitations do not exist for murder or manslaughter. Some things are simply too terrible to forget or forgive. Digital redemption, then, should be no different. Certain information about an individual, no matter how reformed, should not be blotted out.

Legal forgiveness is not offered lightly in the U.S. The harms from old information that an individual seeks to remedy must be of similar degree and kind to those recognized by other forgiveness efforts. When an individual does not deserve punishment, pardons can end negative consequences and certify good character. Unfair prejudices are softened by forgiveness laws that address financial limitations or denial of access to services created by information. When inaccurate information related to an individual may limit opportunities, pardons and the Fair Credit Reporting Act offer solutions. Much of the writing on these laws also addresses the psychological and relational harms that create more hurdles for the individual. And although social stigma may be severe, overriding public interests may not allow mitigating legal intervention.

The amount of content that resides on the web and the data stored, processed, and shared may both well be sufficiently damaging to warrant legal intervention. Content is heavily relied on by many social actors. Searching an individual's name using Google to size him or her up is increasingly common—so much so that expectant parents now consider how search results for their future child's name will impact the child's life.[12] Parents search prospective names to help their kids retrieve top search results, and only a few rare parents want their children to be "lost in a virtual crowd."[13] With 92 percent of U.S. children under the age of two holding an online presence, "life, it seems, begins not at birth but with online conception. And a child's name is the link to that permanent record."[14] Searching for an individual is done for many different reasons, and more and more information is freely disclosed. But though the harm from content that resides online is severe, this harm is not necessarily pervasive. The number of takedown requests from EU citizens suggests that the harm is quite pervasive, but those numbers do not represent Americans. Not everyone has his or her ill-fated relationship, prior arrests, or embarrassing photo posted online. Big data leads both to the same concern as web content and to the same skepticism regarding its harms, because it is definitely pervasive but not necessarily severe. Data is captured, collected, and created at absurd rates; big data has captured our imagination. It is difficult even to discuss governing this aspect of the Digital Age because the harms associated with big data are not yet well understood. Though we can imagine reidentification risks, possible discrimination, and complete surveillance, the severity of these harms is not easy to act on.

In considering the institution of a forgiveness policy and choosing among the options in the matrix presented in chapter 3, it is necessary that the harms to be addressed exhibit a level of both severity and pervasiveness. Finally, legal forgiveness depends on some social benefit in addition to supporting a harmed individual. We see a weighing of interests and the requirement of social benefit in a variety of contexts. Bankruptcy offers a fresh start for those who file for it, but it also benefits creditors. Juveniles who accumulate a criminal record are often granted forgiveness not just to protect the youth population but also to cultivate and protect society's future, to decrease recidivism, and to limit costs of committing individuals essentially for lifetimes. The social benefits of offering people credit to purchase everything from homes to electronics are primarily economic, but credit forgiveness inhibits credit evaluators from using any and all data to predict future payment. Although some people are disadvantaged by these laws, the social benefits trump their interests.

It is also essential to evaluate and articulate the benefit to society as a whole when considering legal approaches to redemption.[15] Forgiveness laws in general offer great comfort. We as a population let out a sigh of relief knowing that certain violations do not remain on our record forever or that bankruptcy is an option when debt leaves us in ruin. In fact, Americans lead the developed world in bankruptcies "because for more than a century, we've worked hard to build the best—and, not coincidentally, the most generous—bankruptcy code in existence."[16] Though bankruptcy and debt are certainly polarizing topics, other countries are looking to create a more "free-and-easy, all-is-forgiven model" and to move away from "harshly punitive treatment of insolvent debtors."[17] A way to prevent being forever branded by a piece of negative information would probably quell some fears about the Digital Age and perhaps make us freer individuals, more willing to participate in open public discourse. Addressing expired information can also benefit the searcher and data controllers. When old information reaches an expiration phase (no longer represents a person), it is inaccurate and less valuable, particularly when it is presented out of context. Increasing information quality benefits the subject, the many users, and society as a whole.

When the prerequisites to legal forgiveness have been satisfied, analysis reveals three key elements of legal approaches to forgiveness: (1) time, (2) oversight, and (3) relief from accountability. Time is an important aspect of each of the existing legal forgiveness measures. It helps to ensure that any relief is appropriate and has been earned. For instance, sealing and expunging a juvenile criminal record occurs upon the juvenile's entry into the adult world. Pardon or parole boards consider certification of good behavior after a set amount of time. Similarly, when negative information is more than seven years old, the FCRA prevents its consideration, with exceptions for certain bankruptcy issues and criminal records. Immunity from suit attaches only after the statutorily prescribed period of limitations, which correlates with the severity of the offense. The element of time adds reassurance that relief is both deserved and appropriate.

Thus, restoring an individual who is the subject of negative information must account for time. Outside the legal context, the time it takes to forgive an indiscretion depends on the indiscretion. From an information-life-cycle perspective, information will lose or gain value at different rates based on the immediate and remote needs it fulfills. In the legal context, it appears more suitable to require standardized sets of time before allowing for categories of information forgiveness to be considered.

In addition to incorporating time, a legal approach to forgiveness in the U.S. must incorporate the correct level of oversight by a decision maker. The level of oversight necessary depends on the underlying offenses, harms, and societal interests. With the FCRA, relief is applied automatically, but disputes may be heard by the judiciary. Statutes of limitations apply broadly to categories of offenses, but courts make determinations with respect to when the period of limitations begins and whether the facts of a particular case warrant tolling (pause or delay) or exemptions. Bankruptcy, pardons, and expungement require a decision maker to make case-by-case determinations of whether forgiveness is appropriate. Without organized oversight, any structure for the right to be forgotten will be highly susceptible to manipulation. When forgiveness or forgetfulness is sought with respect to information that has been legally disclosed, a legal approach must consider the public's right to access that information, and any legal mechanism for forgetting information will require the correct level of oversight by a decision maker to account for the effects on the individual subject, the speaker (and/or data controller), and society as a whole.

Analysis of existing laws reveals a final common element: relief from accountability. The U.S. legal system acknowledges that punishment should not necessarily be eternal and that limiting the use of information about an individual can be a form of relief. In a sense, limiting the use of information can determine which sectors of society must not hold an individual accountable. This determination depends on the severity of the harm and its directed impact. Bankruptcy, the FCRA, and state employment-discrimination statutes limit what and how information can be used to judge someone in certain situations. For instance, filing for bankruptcy relieves the individual of debt and also ensures that public and private employers cannot discriminate based on the filing. Relief in the form of an expunged or sealed record, if not otherwise disclosed, limits access to information about an individual's offense and offers the individual relief from legal and social stigma. Importantly, none of the existing legal schemes limit all use of the information by all parties.

Existing laws also offer relief from accountability by adjusting information. Appropriate information adjustment must be nuanced. Data can be added to the existing body of information related to an individual to provide a broader context for the individual represented in the information. For example, certifications of rehabilitation or good behavior provided by state entities in the case of pardons and parole supplement existing information. The old information does not go away; it is simply contextualized as part of an individual's past.

One must earn relief from accountability in the U.S. Bankruptcy offers relief but at the price of social scrutiny. Sealed records require the price of punishment, time, and good behavior. Statutes of limitations require a period of time without continued bad conduct as evidence of self-rehabilitation. Existing relief from accountability is narrowly tailored to situations where the price paid (whether it be time, money, or imprisonment) by the individual compensates for the wrong committed.

These types of relief from accountability can inform the development of new legal approaches to reinvention. Relief could take the form of limiting how, by whom, and for what purpose information can be used. It could also involve the adjustment or obstruction of information. In the case of past personal information found online, an individual seeking relief from accountability likely will be required to pay some price to obtain it. The punishment of days or years of social scrutiny may be enough, but in instances when social norms have been harshly violated, such as violent criminal actions, or when social utility still exists, such as consumer protection, special rules may be required on top of time.

Additionally or alternatively, one could earn relief through proven rehabilitation, which could also be considered proof of the information's expiration.

With the foregoing set of prerequisites in mind, a number of possible directions are available to the U.S. legal system to deal with pervasive, lingering personal information online that causes individuals to be significantly hindered in life. On the basis of the elements extracted from existing forgiveness laws, a few possibilities can be assessed, though some deserve more attention and others can easily be discarded. As described in chapter 3, content is created by individuals about themselves or about other individuals. It is inherently expressive, and any kind of legal claim that limits or punishes it will receive strict scrutiny. If one were to construct a claim against a party who provides access to information in the expiration phase, likely to be the only phase in which oblivion would be contemplated, a considerable number of customs and doctrine would need to change. Deletion of data, on the other hand, may not even need to reach an expiration phase in order to achieve legal support.

The first possibility to consider is a radical right to be forgotten that allows for decreased discoverability of content. U.S. courts could take a page from the mid-twentieth-century civil law judges and attempt to expand the privacy torts to protect a right to dignity of some sort that includes a right to be forgotten. The challenge is tying that right to some strong source. The closest thing to a right to "development of personality" may be the inherent and inalienable rights to the preservation of "life, & liberty, & the pursuit of happiness" found in the Declaration of Independence, which serves only as an intermittently consulted source for interpreting the Constitution.[18] Just as unlikely is creating an exception to rights that prevent effectively obstructing content. Expression is generally and feverishly protected in the U.S., though categories of speech have been exempted from protection because of their low value—they are considered to be undeserving of protection.[19] These categories are obscenities, threatening words, fighting words, incitement, fraud, and child pornography.[20] While these kinds of speech may be of public interest to some extent, they also harm the public in ways that overpower, as a rule, the speaker's interest in expression as well as the public's interest in hearing it. Expired content could be added to this list, but these categories are so much more offensive, dangerous, and harmful than truthful, old information and not likely to be categorized together as exceptions to expression.

Another option would allow U.S. data subjects to object to the inclusion of information that easily identifies them, like names and photos. Some courts have scrutinized specific private facts disclosed and offered plaintiffs anonymity. In *Barber v. Time, Inc.*, the court explained, "While plaintiff's ailment may have been a matter of some public interest because it was unusual, certainly the identity of the person who suffered this ailment was not."[21] The Tenth Circuit adopted a "substantial relevance" test, meaning that the individual must be substantially relevant to the published content. In *Gilbert v. Medical Economics Co.*, the court stated that some facts are indeed beyond the sphere of legitimate public interest: "Even where certain matters are clearly within the protected sphere of legitimate public interest, some private facts about an individual may lie outside that sphere. . . . To properly balance freedom of the press against the right of privacy, every private fact disclosed in an otherwise truthful, newsworthy publication must have some substantial relevance to a matter of legitimate public interest."[22] The newsworthiness test established by these courts reinforces the notion that just because a story is of legitimate public concern does not mean that the plaintiff's identity is necessary to disclose. A more common judicial response is reflected in *Shulman v. Group W. Productions, Inc.*, in which the court refused to make this determination regarding a woman who was identified by the news in association with a horrendous car crash. The court stated, "That the broadcast *could* have been edited to exclude some of Ruth's words and images and still excite a minimum degree of viewer interest is not determinative. Nor is the possibility that the members of this or another court, or a jury, might find a differently edited broadcast

more to their taste or even more interesting. The courts do not, and constitutionally could not, sit as superior editors of the press."[23] Obstruction
offers means for promoting information stewardship, but it also requires
a reconceptualization of American newsworthiness, which may be too
great a shift within the legal culture to be viable in the U.S.

A different possibility is to limit the use of personal information. Leg-
islatures could enact laws that limit potential employers' ability to search
for or to consider online information about a potential applicant that is
older than a designated period.[24] An employer may have an interest in
how an employee reflects on the company to the world through a search
engine but less of an interest in how he or she reflects on the company to
a smaller group of connected people on Facebook. An employer digging
around in applicants' social media profiles that are not publicly available
is different from an employer searching for public information easily
retrievable through a Google search. Thus, laws might distinguish between searching publicly available information and seeking to obtain
information that is available only through social networks or other
more private spheres. Similarly, a law could distinguish between data
and content and prevent old privately held data from being processed
to predict employability or admissibility, a system not unlike the FCRA.
While numerous entities like banks, employers, and universities could
be prevented from using data or content after a certain point, there are
implementation problems. Of course, it is difficult to tell if certain information is used by prohibited parties, but the information at play in these
debates has lost its context, meaning it may be difficult to tell whether
it is information in the record or expiration phase or whether it is even
old at all.

Situating digital oblivion within a remix of false-light and retraction
laws is perhaps the most viable arrangement in the U.S.—information
can be *added* to the harmful content to provide context and accuracy. Similar to the way the market has addressed online reputational
harms, adding more information can limit the weight given to negative information. This notion also fits with the marketplace of ideas, a

foundational First Amendment concept. The truth will arise from the competition of ideas, or as Thomas Jefferson explained it, "This institution will be based on the illimitable freedom of the human mind. For here we are not afraid to follow truth wherever it may lead, nor to tolerate any error so long as reason is left free to combat it."[25] In 2012, the U.S. Supreme Court struck down the Stolen Valor Act, which made it a crime to fraudulently claim having received particular military decorations and awards, finding that these false statements are protected by the First Amendment and reiterating that the "remedy for speech that is false is speech that is true."[26] Expired or even false information can be combated with more information. This solution, however, does not necessarily foster information stewardship, in much the same way that online reputation services do not. It leaves a mass of expired informational waste to sort through and adds conflicting information to the pile. Thus, contextual information should be added to the same file to attain relief from accountability and stewardship.

More in line with U.S. forgiveness and information stewardship are small additions to old information that can be recognized automatically. A time element could be incorporated into false-light claims, which offer the plaintiff the opportunity to correct old online information that causes harm. When someone suffers the financial, social, or personal harms of truthful information from his or her past, a false-light claim would ensure that the information is presented as old. The information must actually have become old, embracing the time element of U.S. forgiveness law.

While false light has been called duplicative and outdated,[27] thirty-one states allow the cause of action; ten have rejected it. However, in 2008, the Missouri Court of Appeals recognized that the tort may have new life in the Digital Age: "As a result of the accessibility of the Internet, the barriers to generating publicity are quickly and inexpensively surmounted. Moreover, the ethical standards regarding the acceptability of certain discourse have been diminished. Thus, as the ability to do harm grows, we believe so must the law's ability to protect the innocent."[28] False-light claims that offer relief to the plaintiff who is harmed by old information found online could simply require the addition of a time frame, by allowing a subject to demand that old information be marked as such so as not to further harm the subject or mislead potential viewers.

This form of injunctive relief could be offered for false-light claims under state retraction laws. A growing number of states are enacting statutes or establishing through case law retraction policies that generally require the following:

1. Individuals who believe they have been defamed must request a retraction or service notice of the allegedly libelous statements before proceeding with a legal claim.
2. The request must be made within a reasonable period of time after publication of the allegedly defamatory statement.
3. If a "frank and full" retraction of a defamatory statement is issued, defendants will be entitled to a reduction in certain types of damages (e.g., preventing punitive damages or limiting damages to out-of-pocket costs).

In order to establish a right to be forgotten within false-light claims and to utilize retraction laws, U.S. law would still need to change to treat old information that is not marked as such as a misrepresentation of an individual. False light would need to experience a resurgence within state legal systems. And retraction laws would need to alter the time element, requiring time to have passed, and to be extended beyond traditional media sources like newspapers and radio broadcasts.[29] Adding information, especially as limited an addition as a time stamp, may not be sufficient relief from accountability to fall in line with other forms of U.S. forgiveness laws.

If the U.S. wanted to limit the discoverability of content through search engines, it would need an approach different than that of the EU. Section 230 of the Communications Decency Act would need to be overhauled in order to limit access to old content through the search engine directly. The U.S. is incredibly unlikely to require intermediaries to obstruct discoverability of personal information upon request when certain conditions are met, like the CJEU has recently required. Such a request could incorporate each of the aforementioned forgiveness law elements and serve as a means for the law to encourage the informal resolution of privacy disputes, but as discussed in chapter 3, this type of informality is not appropriate for a right that has yet to develop contours and certainly not in the U.S., where it directly impacts access to information. A takedown system inspired by the DMCA takedown-notice regime is also unsuitable for U.S. forgiveness, because it does not provide appropriate oversight.

Instead, the source of the information could prevent the indexing of the URL at issue. Going directly to the source is important because the source is in the best position to argue the state of the content in the information life cycle and associated interests. If a claim for digital oblivion were to be made against the source, information stewardship in the U.S. would likely prevent deleting the content, but obscuring the content from search-engine crawlers is possible. This scheme is particularly plausible, given that it has been voluntarily implemented by certain sites. For instance, Public.Resource.org, a site that publishes court records, also evaluates requests to remove these records from search-engine results.[30] If Public.Resource.org finds limited access appropriate, it uses a robots.txt file[31] to prevent the content stored on its server from being published in search-engine results, in order to protect the privacy of the requester. Ethical crawlers that build the index of search-engine page results will not crawl pages specified by the site in the robots.txt file.[32] The documents still exist on Public.Resource.org's server, and a researcher or journalist looking for court records can find them by going directly to the URL http://bulk.resource.org/robots.txt. All of the URLs of the search-engine-blocked cases are listed and can be easily accessed. But the documents will not be retrieved by a search-engine search for information on a certain person. Discoverability is obstructed at the source of the file, where the obstruction can easily be removed by the steward of the information if interest is revived. Thus, injunctive relief would come in the form of a signal to crawlers not to index a certain URL. This form of digital redemption may lead to the requirement of legal enforcement of crawler ethics but would certainly be a radical U.S. legal response because it prevents access to information shared by a private party to a public audience.

Requiring operators to include an accurate time stamp on content or a signal to search-engine crawlers that certain pages should not be indexed would allow technology to be layered to discourage digging around in old personal information in inappropriate circumstances. For instance, employers could be legally restricted to searching information online from the past two years only, and a search for a potential employee performed on a company computer could be technically limited to time-stamped content within the past two years. A false-light claim for identifying information that is void of the context of time in combination with retraction laws promotes the goals of information stewardship and is legally, socially, and technologically feasible.

If a U.S. right to be forgotten was established that created a new category of unprotected speech, blocked access to content, altered content, or required additions to be made to content, it would be a major shift away from the consideration of time and injunctive relief in information cases. Doctrine regarding information-related cases often focuses on the expressive consequences of the claims. As a general rule, injunctive relief is not available to information claimants, and time has little impact on information claims. These doctrines would need to be completely disregarded to obscure old content.

Although the First Amendment does not absolutely bar injunctive relief for libel, slander, invasion of privacy, and related claims, many courts refuse to grant equitable relief for these informational actions. Essentially the question comes down to whether the injunctive relief—requiring a defendant to say or not say something—is considered a prior restraint. In *Near v. Minnesota*, the newspaper successfully appealed a lower-court decision that determined its content was "chiefly devoted to malicious, scandalous and defamatory articles" and granted "perpetual" injunctive relief.[33] The Supreme Court overturned because *Near* "involved a true restraint on future speech."[34] More recently, in Pennsylvania, a doctor tried to obtain injunctive relief against the American Academy of Orthopaedic Surgeons and the American Association of Orthopaedic Surgeons, requiring them to remove an article from their website that portrayed the doctor in a false light, a claim he had earlier won and been awarded $196,000 for. After the lawsuit, the organizations did not remove the article, and the Eastern District Court of Pennsylvania agreed that they did not have to do so. Although the doctor alleged "continued tortious conduct" from the fixed false representation,[35] the court determined that the monetary award was enough under Pennsylvania law.

However, the legal scholar David Ardia has found that there has been a spike in granting injunctive relief for libel claims since 2000, even though plaintiffs have consistently sought such relief for some time.[36] When the speech at issue is part of continuous tortious content or the defendant has made it clear that he or she will continue to publish the tortious content, some courts have been willing to grant an injunction to prevent further damage.[37] For instance, in an unpublished opinion, the California Court of Appeals upheld a permanent injunction against one of Johnny Cochran's former clients, Ulysses Tory, who was picketing with signs accusing Cochran of being a fraud, among other things.[38] Cochran sued for defamation, false light, and invasion of privacy, and the Supreme Court of California declined to review the permanent injunction that prohibited Tory and his agents from picketing Cochran or his law firm, displaying signs about Cochran or his firm, and uttering statements about Cochran or his firm.[39] The U.S. Supreme Court granted certiorari; but Cochran died seven days after oral arguments, and so the Court ruled that in light of Cochran's death, the injunction would certainly be an overly broad prior restraint on free speech (Justices Antonin Scalia and Clarence Thomas found that Cochran's death made it unnecessary to rule on the case).[40] Of course, this issue is particularly relevant to content posted online. States including Kentucky, Ohio, Georgia, Minnesota, and California have adopted the "modern rule," which allows for defamatory speech to be enjoined after a determination that the speech is false, while other states have declared that their state constitutions bar injunctive relief for libel.[41] Ardia finds that some of these injunctions are probably constitutionally overbroad, but those that are "limited solely to false statements on matters of private concern that a court has found—after full adjudication—are defamatory" are constitutional.[42] Though the right to be forgotten does not meet that standard, it does suggest a possible shift toward information stewardship. Even with a possible trend away from the no-injunction rule, digital redemption for content will need its own new structure with very unique attributes—which, again, may be too drastic a shift.

Time will similarly need to be reconsidered. The single-publication rule articulated in *Firth v. New York* allows for the content to be challenged only once, and statutes of limitations require the challenge to be in the distribution phase. Statutes of limitations generally require bringing claims within a certain amount of time, but a digital-redemption claim would need to be brought *after* a certain amount of time. As discussed in chapter 2, time has not altered many U.S. information cases, but it is an important attribute to forgiveness in the U.S. At least two Supreme Court justices have argued that the passage of time may "erase" public-figure status even though public figures are fair game for later content covering their prior fame or notoriety or the event in which they were involved.[43] Additionally, within the confines of FOIA, the Supreme Court has interpreted the privacy protections in Exemption 7(C) to be strong but emphasized the distinction between government collections of information and other forms of public information. When a CBS News correspondent and the Reporters Committee for Freedom of the Press brought suit to obtain the FBI rap sheet that had been withheld for Charles Medico as part of an investigation into his family tied to organized crime, the Supreme Court upheld the FBI's denial and explained,

"In an organized society, there are few facts that are not at one time or another divulged to another."[44] And it continued, just because "an event is not wholly 'private' does not mean that an individual has no interest in limiting disclosure or dissemination of the information."[45] Relying on the decision, the Fifth Circuit stated in 1989, "That otherwise-private information may have been at one time or in some way in the 'public' domain does not mean that a person irretrievably loses his or her privacy interests in it."[46]

Each of these departures has occurred, but only in the form of the rare or rogue group of decisions. The beauty of digital content is that its persistence is nuanced and manipulable; there is no need to adhere fully to the old rules of informational relief as long as we adhere to the socio-legal constructs of forgiveness. By relying on the information life cycle, utilizing robot.txt files and/or time stamps, and combining false light with retraction laws, the U.S. *could* construct a constitutional forgiveness law that contains the elements of time, oversight, relief, a forgivable offense, specific harm, and social benefit.

Data is a bit less complicated. Accessing, correcting, or deleting digital footprints is a form of digital redemption that impacts fewer interests; namely, it does not impact the public. Wiping your digital dossier clean, even with respect to just one entity, allows for the opportunity to start anew, to be presented with information and opportunities other than nonstop diet advertisements or flight deals, to be treated as a student likely to achieve instead of fail.

This form of digital redemption receives a great deal of support because we all know how hard it is to manage one's digital footprint, and few of us use or even see these footprints. Even if one could read all of the long, complicated privacy policies that one is exposed to daily, understanding and making a choice about risks remain exceedingly challenging. Control over the data that seems to fall off of us is exceptionally hard as it changes hands and purposes. Offering a form of retroactive control is appealing because it is so difficult to provide at the point of data capture.

Beyond the computational designations and categories that our mediated actions land us in, the actions of others can redesignate us as something we are uncomfortable with. For instance, Target knows that if I buy a set of products (including a blue rug), I am likely at the early stages of pregnancy, on the basis of data collected and analyzed from other women, but perhaps I want to buy that set of products and do not want to be designated as pregnant (for any number of reasons, including that I am not). A form of digital redemption would allow me to delete the purchases from my digital footprint or to remove the designation from my digital dossier. Individuals have so little control over their digital footprints and dossiers, both increasingly powerful representations, that extending digital redemption to these categories has become more appealing.

The *American Idol* contestants in the case mentioned in the introduction attempted to use case law on initial and downstream data to justify their claims. They were unsuccessful because they were attempting to obscure content. The cases they point to are illuminating, however. In *Swafford v. Memphis Individual Practice Association*, a doctor filed a libel suit against a health maintenance organization because of allegedly false reports it sent to the National Practitioner Data Bank, which is a privately held data bank on physicians.[47] The data bank sent out reports on the doctor to three hospitals. The Tennessee Court of Appeals addressed whether defamatory material reported by the data bank gives rise to a separate cause of action each time the information is disseminated or whether it was an aggregate communication or mass publication. The court explained, "The facts in this case are analogous to the facts in the above credit report decisions. . . . The health care entities in this case, like the entities accessing credit information, requested information from the Data Bank on separate and distinct occasions. Therefore, there is no 'aggregate publication' as contemplated in cases applying the single publication rule. While information in the Data Bank may be accessed by several entities, the justification for the single publication rule, a vast multiplicity of lawsuits resulting from a mass publication, is simply not present here."[48]

Frank Pasquale argues that modern data controllers and processing are very similar to old credit schemes and should receive similar political action.[49] Neil Richards argues that data may not receive the full force of First Amendment protection as commercial speech.[50] He assesses a set of cases that address whether the sale of commercial data is free speech, focusing on the 2011 case of *Sorrell v. IMS*, in which the Supreme Court found that regulating the marketing of data about doctors' prescribing practices violated the First Amendment.[51] A number of scholars have argued that data flows are protected speech and find that *Sorrell* assumed as much.[52] Jane Bambauer, for instance, argues that "for all practical purposes, and in every context relevant to the privacy debates, data is speech. Privacy regulations are rarely (if ever) burdens to knowledge."[53] Richards encourages a more nuanced assessment: "Just because data may have expressive value in some cases does not mean that we should be afraid to experiment with legal tools in others. . . . We should reject the idea that just because some restrictions on information flows threaten free speech, they all do."[54] Expired data, whether on the initial site or downstream, is vulnerable to a digital-redemption claim, because it involves fewer of the elements of the pillars of free speech than does content, such as newsworthiness and public interest.

Although many Americans may not be convinced that most people should be given an opportunity for digital reinvention, there are a few populations that receive more consideration from skeptics. Digital redemption may be specifically carved out for those who have been born with more complicated identity issues, children, and victims of cruelty. In the U.S., these are populations that, when seen through a richer context than provided by search results, have done little wrong or are extreme victims of circumstance who are seeking to grow or reinvent themselves. Forgiveness laws, as well as privacy laws, in the U.S. are particularly good at addressing specific people with specific problems.

More than any other group I have spoken with, parents are the most enthusiastic about a right to be forgotten—not for themselves but for their children. Feeling unfamiliar with "growing up digital" and having little oversight of their children's online behavior, parents worry about their children making grave mistakes online. While children are actually much more privacy savvy than adults are (at least in terms of understanding and managing their information disclosures),[55] youths suffer from a more limited foresight about how their online content will impact their future. But this is not because of a technical misunderstanding; it is because they are experimentally building identities that will frame their future selves—because they are children.

Engaging and connecting online through status updates, picture posts, YouTube videos, comments, liking, and sharing is part of growing up. A great deal of content is created by youths over the course of their development. This is good. Rey Junco, a professor and researcher of students' use of social media, argues that developing identity is an important precursor to other developmental tasks such as constructing self-esteem, confidence, strong relationships with others, and adaptability to new social environments. In his book *Engaging Students through Social Media*, Junco explains that participating in online social spaces like social media allows youth to "try on" different facets of their identity through their online self-presentation.[56] Creative risks and identity exploration are easier to undertake online than offline, because ramifications feel virtual ("online disinhibition effect"). "The exploration of identity online not only seems safer, it *is* safer because there is less ego investment by the actor and their audience."[57] While the reduction of inhibitions provided by online spaces grants to youths a sense of safety to exercise various forms of identity, ideas, and communication, it is the instantaneous feedback by the community and adjustments by the child that are particularly valuable and unique characteristics of engaging online. This testing group moves youth toward consistency in identity across situations and settings. These behaviors are perceived by adults as follies of youth that serve no purpose beyond shallow and dangerous social activities, but this is an adult-normative view, according to Junco, and one that is oblivious to the benefits provided by online engagement.

Without the recognition of the benefits of juvenile experimentation and exploration online and with continuation of the adult-normative perspective, there can be serious future repercussions when youths make mistakes and post something cringe worthy. In an annual Kaplan survey of over four hundred college admissions officers, 35 percent checked applicants' social media profiles in 2013 (up from 31 percent in 2013 and 26 percent in 2012).[58] In an interesting development, the Kaplan survey notes that although it is becoming more commonplace to look into the social media of college applicants, college admissions officers are finding fewer things online that negatively impact decisions. According to Junco, adults are evaluating youth not on the basis of an understanding of how youths use social technologies in relation to their development but from their own adult-normative framework. "I would *never* post something like that!" gets translated into excluding potentially productive students. Adults see questionable content not as the testing ground of youths that they may have learned and grown from but as negative and stable characteristics of their personalities.

It is worth noting that even before kids are at the mercy of their peers, many parents begin their children's digital history, often before they are even born. In a 2010 study, 34 percent of U.S. mothers posted sonograms, and a third of children have photos of them posted online within two weeks of birth. Although American parents are more likely to post photos and share information than are parents in the other countries surveyed (United Kingdom, Spain, France, Germany, and Italy), the average "digital birth" happens at about six months worldwide.[59]

Arguing in support of legal recourse for at least sexual content involving minors, the law scholar Anupam Chander states, "The youth facing a fishbowl life might be tempted to adopt either of two strategies: excessive caution or foolhardy fearlessness. The first strategy might limit decisional autonomy now, constraining the choices available now. The second strategy might limit decisional autonomy later, constraining the choices available then. We should not tolerate this unnecessary choice between reduced choice set now, or reduced choice set later."[60] Protecting youth development with a right to be forgotten relies less on privacy actions like creating obstructions or privacy theory of contextual integrity and more on the idea of the dynamic self, and no self is more dynamic than the adolescent self. While youths exercise obstruction and rely on contextual integrity, often they are not hiding expression and understand its visibility. Much of the time, however, youths' expression online represents only a fleeting moment in their identity development that will hopefully be positively shaped by feedback from the community. Holding children or teens to an ignorant or cruel post may prevent their ability to try on a different hat, thereby stifling their progress to become an informed, kind adult.

The Disney Channel runs public service announcements starring the beloved cartoon characters Phineas and Ferb, reminding children to "be careful what you put online; it never goes away, ever!"[61] As part of a campaign to help keep kids safe online, children are regularly exposed to the message that what is on the Internet will be there forever. Amanda Todd's suicide is an example of the desperation that such a message can create. Digital redemption for children is an existing movement within the U.S. and can benefit from a life-cycle approach. Digital redemption for children should still address expired information related to a forgivable offense that causes a specific harm. The elements of time, oversight, and relief from accountability will vary depending on the nature of the content but should be explicitly addressed by policies trying to systematically address these concerns.

There are other times when a broader clean-slate approach is needed to meet the demands of a changing individual, such as gender changes, which are socially and legally assigned in a dichotomous (male or female) fashion. The categorization of either male or female at an early age has dramatic impacts on identity and development. Moving away from the assigned designation requires a separation from that past categorization. Outdated gender references can dramatically impede one's ability to choose a gender and create problems with successful self-presentation and unfortunate stigmatization.

Paulan Korenhof and Bert-Jaap Koops investigate this issue extensively by taking Harold Garfinkel's subject, Agnes, in his 1967 *Studies in Ethnomethodology*, into a digital world.[62] Agnes was designated male at birth on the basis of physiological characteristics but disagreed with her male assignment and sought to change it. All kinds of intersexuality (gonadal sex, chromosomal sex, genital sex) complicate the male-female gender designation—not to mention gender identity, which may often move and change along a spectrum. When Agnes began living as a woman, she recognized the need to be perceived by those around her as female, which left her with a seventeen-year gap in her past. She was convinced there was no remedy for the "punishment, degradation, loss of reputation, and loss of material advantages [that] were the matters at risk should the change be detected."[63] The threat of disillusioning an "audience" with inconsistent information that contradicts performed identity can make it impossible for the desired identity to be accepted, thereby disrupting an individual's own identity and relationships.

Agnes's gender change is not something to be forgiven or a failure to overcome, but it does represent a form of reinvention. It is something appropriate to move forward with in a way that she sees fit—here disconnecting her present as a woman from her past as a man. It is estimated that there are seven hundred thousand transgendered individuals in the U.S. For those who struggle to develop a dynamic identity within dichotomous social categories like gay or straight, male or female, the Internet is a roadblock, not a path of experimentation. The web challenges this population's happiness, dignity, and choices.

Most states already have policies and processes in place for adjusting records that include some kind of sex designation.[64] For instance, in twenty-five states, new birth certificates are issued to those who proffer proof of sex reassignment surgery, and amendments to birth certificates are offered upon proof of surgery in sixteen states. Six states and Washington, DC, do not require any proof of sex reassignment surgery, and three states will not issue or amend existing documents (Idaho, Tennessee, and Ohio). State agencies or courts use administrative or judicial discretion, depending on the state, to interpret these general statutes—some are more sensitive to the problem than others. Digital oblivion for one's prior gender may also be possible within the U.S. legal culture.

For victims, another potentially exceptional category, "privacy is like oxygen; it is a pervasive, consistent need at every step of recovery."[65] By "victims" here, I refer to those who have suffered physical or sexual violence as well as forms of bullying and sexual humiliation. While many victims choose to remain pseudonymous or anonymous, others find it important to speak out against the crime or social problem related to their victimization; others are outed by someone else. Victims who go through the proper channels to remain pseudonymous or even anonymous can easily be identified, sometimes accidentally.

At an event on the right to be forgotten, a woman told me about a friend who had been raped in college. She was a victim of a systemic sexual-misconduct problem at her school and did what we hope victims will feel comfortable doing—she came forward, followed by others. The problem, the woman explained, was that years later, her friend is still prominently identified as a rape victim when searched online—it is on the first page of her Google search results. Anyone, from potential dates and employers to family members past and present to her, knows instantly that she is a rape victim.

Details of offline assaults can move online, but today assaults take place online as well.[66] As mentioned earlier, nude or sexually explicit images or videos of people (mostly women) vindictively posted online without their consent, even if the content itself was taken with consent, often are accompanied by the victim's name, address, phone number, employer, and links to social media profiles so as to further expose victims to people in their lives and to allow other users to harass them on other platforms and using other forms of communication. Some revenge-porn websites even charge a fee to have the materials removed. Named for the spurned spouses, boyfriends, and lovers who posted on the site to get revenge for some perceived wrong, these sites are now a place where women who have found themselves in unfortunate circumstances are humiliated publicly.

Although not everyone responds the same way to the violation, generally victims of rape suffer from rape trauma syndrome, which occurs in three stages.[67] First, the acute stage involves an emotional reaction of shutting down, hysteria, or disorientation. The second stage involves outward presentations of coping like minimizing, analyzing, or fleeing from the incident. Over the final stage of renormalization, the rape is no longer the focal point of the victim's life. While victims realize they will never forget the assault, the pain and memories begin to weaken and come less frequently. Eventually the victim finds her way from victim to survivor. Revenge-porn victims not only have a difficult time getting away from their online humiliation, which frequently bombards their email and social media accounts, but also have a difficult time keeping the threats online. Many complain of threatening phone calls, house calls, mail, stalking, and other forms of harassment seeping into real life. While many states are criminalizing revenge porn, it is still very difficult to get the content removed—revenge-porn sites freeze and extend the violation. If the web prevents these victims from making important transitions from victim to survivor, there is a problem to address.

Attempting to find informational justice for victims of violent and sexual crimes is not a new crusade. For many commenters, *Florida Star v. B.J.F.* ended the conversation,[68] because if disclosure of a rape victim's identity could not be punished, what could? The case held that "where a newspaper publishes truthful information which it has lawfully obtained, punishment may lawfully be imposed, if at all, only when narrowly tailored to a state interest of the highest order."[69] But if we bring the conversation into the digital discourse, new hope for nuance comes with it.

Digital media allow for statutes to be more nuanced and tailored. Increased discoverability of information that lingers is a different harm than an initial disclosure is. Expired information that (1) can be shown to be old, (2) has little public search or click activity, (3) can still be preserved for remote needs, and (4) utilizes obstruction to decrease discoverability in terms of relief is surely worth giving legal consideration in the U.S. In sum, expired content and data could be addressed by legal mechanisms that have elements of time, oversight, and relief from accountability and extend to forgivable offenses causing specific harms, as long as a larger social benefit is realized. For expired data that is privately held, the circumstances need not be much narrower than the elements of forgiveness law. Digital redemption that decreases discoverability of expired content can likely only include narrow circumstances—limited to special populations. Digital redemption that requires the addition of information to prevent content from being expired and causing harm to both the public and the subject is the best horse to back in this race. Even in the U.S., there are ways to make the Digital Age a forgiving era, but the ways must be within the bounds of what makes Americans the most free. Europeans will find ways within the bounds of what protects their most important priorities—and these systems will not look the same.

Ctrl + Z in the
International Community

The world has a stake in the right to be forgotten for a number of reasons. First, content on the Internet is generally accessible around the world, and the removal of content affects all users.[1] Additionally, services that derive from big-data analytics have the potential to benefit all users. Second, data controllers around the globe will be obligated to address personal information on the basis of the rules of foreign jurisdictions. Third, designing systems to comply with one country's laws may result in "privacy creep," meaning that if systems and platforms are designed to provide deletion for users in one region, the opportunity for deletion will extend beyond that region to anywhere the platform or system is utilized.[2] Since Europeans have been informed of their right to have search results edited, Google has received 216,810 requests for web links to be removed, which resulted in 783,510 links being reviewed and 262,280 links being hidden.[3] This is an extraordinary amount of obstruction. Perhaps it is the appropriate amount of obstruction, but it is difficult to say since European countries have had little opportunity to determine what the right to be forgotten will mean for them. International legal interoperability is the most pressing matter. The right to be forgotten may provide manipulation that leaves gaps for individuals to change and grow, but exercising such a right in a networked world requires legal systems to be interoperable (but not the same), social systems to be accounted for, and technical systems to be coordinated.

Viviane Reding, the former European Commissioner for Justice, Fundamental Rights and Citizenship who led the changes to the EU's Data Protection Directive,[4] has made it clear that "all companies that operate in the European Union must abide by [European] high standards of data protection and privacy."[5] Reinforcing this point in 2011, Reding stated, "Privacy standards for European citizens should apply independently of the area of the world in which their data is being processed. . . . Any company operating in the E.U. market or any online product that is targeted at E.U. consumers must comply with E.U. rules."[6] While the EU may consider it wise to condense its member countries' informational and redemptive legal approaches and to outsource the development of a right to be forgotten to intermediaries, the logistics and viability of the right to be forgotten in a global context remain vital for all regions considering digital redemption.

Interoperability is simply the ability to make systems work together. First used as an engineering term to describe information technology systems that allow for information exchange, the term has recently been used more broadly. It was borrowed in 2012 by the Harvard Berkman Center's John Palfrey and Urs Gasser as a theory to decide where and at what level interconnectedness in complex systems is needed in order to achieve "better, more useful connectivity while simultaneously finding better ways to manage its inherent risks."[7] Seeking to achieve optimal interoperability levels, the authors address the adverse effects of high levels of interoperability (coordinated homogeneity) on market competition and system diversity, focusing on a loss of innovation. Legal interoperability, defined as "the process of making legal norms work together across jurisdictions,"[8] is particularly important in an increasingly interconnected world. The authors argue that policy makers should strive for higher levels of legal and policy interoperability for three reasons: compliance costs are lower, innovation and economic growth are higher, and laws that foster the development of fundamental values and rights spread. The authors recognize that total harmonization is a fantasy. I have argued that it is not only unrealistic but also undesirable. To ask that fundamental rights and values be the same is asking for cultures to be the same legally and socio-technically. The high prioritization of the First Amendment is an important aspect of U.S. culture; the way in which France treats Nazi information is important to its cultural identity. Of course, these legal cultures are not static; they are dynamic and are in the midst of acknowledged shifts to adjust to a digital and networked world. Use of law to force a universal balance of interests on various populations that have not come to such a conclusion on their own is dangerously paternalistic.

Although a number of authors have argued that the right to be forgotten would violate the First Amendment, the unconstitutionality of the right to be forgotten in the U.S. is of little consequence to Europeans. Upon receiving a right-to-be-forgotten takedown request, a data controller may simply ignore the claim, perhaps because it conflicts with the data controller's legal rights within his or her own country or because there is no way to enforce the claim. There are, of course, consequences to such neglect.

Whether EU authorities can regulate and adjudicate activities located outside the EU on the basis of their impacts within the EU is not clear. This is a very old and very complex conundrum. Jurisdiction is generally based on sovereignty (boundaries and borders), but cyberspace is (semi)borderless and therefore problematic—an "effects" standard naturally steps in to substitute for territorial sovereignty, but this approach can lead to unlimited jurisdiction and exposes intermediaries to more liability than the U.S. wishes. The U.S. relies on the "Zippo test," which is a sliding scale for deciding jurisdiction that rests on distinctions between active and passive Internet contacts with a forum state, crafted in *Zippo Mfr. Co. v. Zippo Dot Com, Inc.*[9] Passive contacts are those created when a site "does little more than make information available," and these contacts create no basis for personal jurisdiction. Conversely, active contacts result when the site involves "knowing and repeated transmission of computer files over the Internet" (e.g., doing business with a state over the Internet, entering into contracts with residents, directing content to state residents, etc.).[10]

The EU takes a different approach to jurisdiction. It applies EU law to any organization that uses means within the EU to collect or process personal data even though the DP Directive only purports to regulate EU entities.[11] The DP Regulation extends the EU's jurisdictional reach by changing the focus from "use of equipment" in article 4(1)(c) to entities that offer goods and services to or monitor the behavior of EU data subjects, which is suggested to mean "all collection and processing of personal data about Union residents."[12] It has been suggested by the Article 29 Data Protection Working Party that any online interaction with an individual residing in the EU may be enough to force compliance with EU data-protection requirements.[13]

While the EU may *say* its laws apply to non-EU entities, the countries where non-EU entities are established may say otherwise. The possibility of entities ignoring EU laws and court orders hinges on enforcement. This area of law is uncertain, due in large part to the now iconic Yahoo! Nazi-memorabilia case from 2000 and the subsequent U.S. litigation concluding in 2006, which acknowledged, "The extent of First Amendment protection of speech accessible solely by those outside the United States is a difficult and, to some degree, unresolved issue."[14] The dilemma began when the Tribunal de Grande Instance in Paris ruled against Yahoo! and its French subsidiary after being sued by two antiracist organizations, LICRA and UEJF, for allowing users in France to view and buy Nazi memorabilia on its auction site. Allowing such communication in France was determined to be a "manifestly illegal disturbance" and qualified as the distribution of Nazi paraphernalia.[15] Yahoo! servers were located in California, and the company argued that the auction site was intended for U.S. users and that it would be impossible to exclude

French users.[16] Yahoo! was ordered to exclude French users from Nazi artifacts and hate speech or suffer a penalty of ₣100,000 per day.[17] The Northern District of California found that it had personal jurisdiction over LICRA, that the claim was ripe, and that enforcement of the French order would be inconsistent with the First Amendment.[18] On appeal, the Ninth Circuit overturned and dismissed the case, but little clarity was established: three justices found no personal jurisdiction (eight found personal jurisdiction), and six found against ripeness (five in favor of ripeness), which resulted in a 6–5 majority for dismissal.[19] While the district court acknowledged that a "basic function of a sovereign state is to determine by law what forms of speech and conduct are acceptable within its borders," it refused to enforce the order on public policy grounds.[20] The Ninth Circuit noted, "Inconsistency with American law is not necessarily enough to prevent recognition and enforcement of a foreign judgment in the United States. The foreign judgment must be, in addition, repugnant to public policy."[21] The majority of the Ninth Circuit agreed that the extraterritorial reach of the First Amendment would not be decided, but the dissent did argue that the order was repugnant to U.S. public policy.[22]

"Most high-profile online businesses make a determined effort to comply with the laws of targeted States by, for example, having specially tailored sites which are compliant with local law managed by local subsidiaries, even when evasion of local law would easily be possible,"[23] by, say, avoiding physical presence in the targeted country. Google, for example, complies with DMCA takedown requests as well as orders to remove speech-related content. Between January and June 2012, Google removed 992 of the 1,026 web search results requested by French court orders.[24] Google explains, "Some requests may not be specific enough for us to know what the government wanted us to remove (for example, no URL is listed in the request), and others involve allegations of defamation through informal letters from government agencies, rather than court orders. We generally rely on courts to decide if a statement is defamatory according to local law."[25]

Some entities that receive a right-to-be-forgotten takedown notice could in theory be within the jurisdiction of a European country because the content is accessible by users in that country; others will be more squarely within the jurisdiction maintaining specifically targeted access, engaging in transactions with the country, or otherwise having a presence in the country. As Steven Bennett explains, "Indeed European case law tends to extend well beyond U.S. views of the reach of jurisdiction, based on Internet activity. . . . In addition to the *Yahoo!* case . . . and a host of other similar cases, in the recent criminal prosecution of Google executives in Italy, the Italian court held that, because at least some of the information took place in Italy, the court could properly exercise jurisdiction."[26] For those entities that do not want to ignore the right to be forgotten because it has become an important tenet of European information principles or cannot ignore the right to be forgotten because enforcement is possible, completely ignoring requests is not an option. The penalty for ignoring the new DP Regulation is up to €100 million or up to 5 percent of the company's annual worldwide income.[27]

The EU DP Directive currently in place tried to create a comprehensive approach to data transfers to the U.S. by granting safe-harbor protection to U.S. companies that met a certain self-regulatory standard. The Safe Harbor agreement was designed to give U.S. companies that import data from Europe some room to breathe. It provides an adequacy framework comprising seven basic privacy principles concerning notice, choice, onward transfer, security, data integrity, access, and enforcement. U.S. companies may meet the adequacy standard to comply with article 25 of the 1995 DP Directive. This is a self-certification process that consists of a letter that details how the company meets the standards and is signed by a corporate officer. The Department of Commerce maintains the letters and publishes a list of participants.

Current tensions suggest that this Safe Harbor approach may not have much of a future, meaning that data controllers that have European citizens' data will need to comply more strictly with EU restrictions. Backed strongly by Germany, Reding made it quite clear that the current arrangement was in jeopardy,[28] and the European Parliament even voted to suspend Safe Harbor, but the Commission has not yet done so.[29] After revelations that the U.S. National Security Agency was eavesdropping on European phone calls, the European Commission announced it would be reviewing the Safe Harbor agreement. In January 2015, Berlin Data Protection Commissioner Alexander Dix stated, "The Safe Harbor agreement is practically dead, unless some limits are being placed to the excessive surveillance by intelligence agencies."[30]

The EU and U.S. are not the only regions or countries around the world that will need to comply with noncitizens' rights to be forgotten or to consider their own potential rights to be forgotten. After the CJEU ruling was announced, governments around the world, including those of Russia, India, and Hong Kong, began considering whether a right to be forgotten was appropriate for their citizens. After winning a case involving Google search results that pointed to a Japanese man's involvement with a criminal organization, plaintiff's attorney Tomohiro Kanda told the Associated Press, "We asserted Google as a controller of the site had the duty to delete the material. . . . We are fighting the same battle as the one in Europe, and we won a similar decision."[31]

There are important questions of scope as well. After the CJEU's decision in *Google v. AEPD*, concern arose about whether blogs, news sites, social networking sites, and personal websites would be next. The European Commission responded to these concerns and others with some public-relations materials to help clarify the decision and its impact, including "Myth-Busting: The Court of Justice of the EU and the 'Right to be Forgotten.'" This document states,

> Myth 2:
> "The judgment entails the deletion of content"
> In fact
> The Court's judgment only concerns the right to be forgotten regarding search engine results involving a person's name. This means that the content remains unaffected by the request lodged with the search engine,

in its original location on the internet. It also means that the content can still be found through the same search engine based on a different query.[32]

While it is true that in *Google v. AEPD* the CJEU was asked specifically about the Directive's applicability to Google's search functions—whether Google's search engine is a data controller—the court had long ago interpreted the uploading of information to the Internet as acting as a data controller. In 2003, the CJEU's judgment in *Lindqvist* quickly became a powerful case on data-protection laws in the EU.[33] Bodil Lindqvist was prosecuted as a Swedish national for posting information about her work colleagues on her personal webpage without obtaining their consent. The court found loading personal data onto a website to be processing under article 2(b) of the Directive (any operation performed on personal data such as collection, recording, organization, storage, adaption, retrieval, use, disclosure, etc.). A more difficult question relates to social network platforms. Social networking sites are data controllers (because they determine the purposes and means of processing personal information on their online platform), but whether a user who posts to a social network site is considered a data controller is more complicated because the Directive does not apply to the processing of personal information by a natural person when done in a purely personal or household activity context.

Another of the six questions the Swedish national court posed to the CJEU was whether the act of loading information to a personal website that is publicly available is within the scope of the Directive or whether it is exempted under article 3(2). The CJEU decided, "[The] exception must therefore be interpreted as relating only to activities which are carried out in the course of private or family life of individuals, which is clearly not the case with the processing of personal data consisting in publication on the internet so that those data are made accessible to an indefinite number of people."[34] The French DPA has implemented the household exemption by advising users who create personal websites for circles of friends or family to impose access restrictions, to inform the individuals involved, and to give the data subjects the opportunity to object. The UK has uniquely focused on users as opposed to platforms, taking a hands-off approach by guiding users without addressing issues that arise when users process information of other users. The Article 29 Working Party (WP29) released an opinion on the subject in June 2009 saying that the household exemption applies when users operate within a "purely personal sphere" and that most users are considered data subject but can be considered data controllers that do not qualify for the exemption, such as when using a social network platform mainly to advance commercial, political, or charitable goals.[35] All data controllers that do not qualify for the household exemption must respect the Directive's right to access in article 12 and the right to object in article 14, which have now been interpreted as a right to be forgotten. And so the potential scope of the Directive's right to be forgotten is incredibly expansive, and the proposed Regulation does not resolve the issue differently.

Since the ruling, a number of controversial links to pages have been removed from Google's search results, though these links are not controversial to everyone. Google removed links connecting British individuals to their convictions but not those of Swiss individuals, and a district court in Amsterdam decided that Google did not need to delete the data because "negative publicity as a result of a serious crime in general is accurate permanent relevant information about a person."[36] These differences are in line with WP29's guidelines, released in November 2014, for implementing the *Google v. AEPD* ruling, which instruct interpretations to be made within existing national law.

The guidelines provide substantive direction as well. They provide a set of criteria for data-protection authorities handling right-to-be-forgotten complaints to follow:

1. Does the search result relate to a natural person—that is, an individual? And does the search result come up in a search on the data subject's name, nickname, or pseudonyms?

2. Does the data subject play a role in public life? Is the data subject a public figure?
3. Is the data subject a minor?
4. Is the data accurate?
5. Is the data relevant and not excessive? Does it relate to the working life of the data subject? Does the information constitute hate speech, slander, libel, or similar offense? Is it clear the information is a personal opinion, or does it appear to be fact?
6. Is the information sensitive within the meaning of article 8 of the Directive 95/46/EC (e.g., information about the person's health, sexuality, or religious beliefs)?
7. Is the data up-to-date? Is the data being made available for longer than is necessary for the purpose of the processing?
8. Is the data processing causing prejudice to the data subject? Does the data have a disproportionately negative privacy impact on the data subject?
9. Does the search result link to information that puts the data subject at risk (e.g., at risk of identity theft or stalking)?
10. In what context was the information published? Was the content voluntarily made public by the data subject, intended to be made public, or reasonably expected to be made public?
11. Was the original content published for journalistic purposes?
12. Does the publisher of the data have a legal power or a legal obligation to make the personal data publicly available?
13. Does the data relate to a criminal offense?

The criteria are intended to be flexible tools for DPAs to work with as they determine whether an individual's removal-request rejection by a search engine or other intermediary should be overturned. In December 2014, the Paris Civil Court ordered Google to remove two search results for press articles that detailed the plaintiff's past fraud conviction.[37] In doing so, the judge determined that the articles should be deindexed because the incidents and article covering them were from 2006, more than eight years earlier; the accessibility of the information through the search engine was impacting the plaintiff's job prospects; and the severity of the crime was categorized as relatively low in the criminal code. The judgment did not extend deindexing beyond the .fr domain, but it is not clear whether this aspect of the right is also subject to local discretion.

The WP29 guidelines conflict with the Advisory Council to Google on the Right to Be Forgotten's report on two key issues: whether links should be removed only from the national domains or from all domains, including Google.com, and whether Google should notify searchers that results may have been removed due to European data-protection law. WP29 explains,

> In order to give full effect to the data subject's rights as defined in the Court's ruling, de-listing decisions must be implemented in such a way that they guarantee the effective and complete protection of data subjects' rights and that EU law cannot be circumvented. In that sense, limiting de-listing to EU domains on the grounds that users tend to access search engines via their national domains cannot be considered a sufficient mean to satisfactorily guarantee the rights of data subjects according to the ruling. In practice, this means that in any case de-listing should also be effective on all relevant domains, including .com.[38]

Google's advisory board, on the other hand, stated,

> In considering whether to apply a delisting to versions of search targeted at users outside of Europe, including globally, we acknowledge that doing so may ensure more absolute protection of a data subject's rights. However, it is the conclusion of the majority that there are competing interests that outweigh the additional protection afforded to the data subject. There is a competing interest on the part of users outside of Europe to access information via a name-based search in accordance with the laws of their country, which may be in conflict with the delisting afforded by

the Ruling. These considerations are bolstered by the legal principle of proportionality and extraterritoriality in application of European law.[39]

Google has implemented the CJEU decision in a country-specific way, meaning it only adjusts the search results for users on the Google portal (e.g., www.google.fr, www.google.es) of which the data subject is a citizen. The company has received some push-back, and it is not clear whether the right to be forgotten will extend to all Google domains or remain restricted to certain regions.

Through an information-stewardship lens and using information-life-cycle tools, the answer depends on whether regional users are actually utilizing Google.com, whether the individual is likely to suffer harm from searchers beyond French borders, what phase the information is in, and whether searchers beyond French borders would find the personal search valuable for immediate or remote purposes. If French users do not use Google.com, the harm of preserving discoverability is relatively low. If there is a massive shift by French users to Google.com to discover personal content, there is a question of which phase the content is in and how the French data-protection agency would balance public interest at an international level with the other relevant values. Allowing for the information to be discoverable beyond national portals may be desirable because for nonpublic figures, it will likely cause little harm and supports information stewardship. However, it is unclear under what circumstances a nonpublic figure would be personally searched beyond national borders for immediate or remote information needs. This circumstance may be better addressed by geo-filtering, wherein search results are tailored to the geographic region where the search query originates. This was the eventual resolution in the Yahoo! French case. The court ordered Yahoo! to take all measures necessary to prevent French users from accessing the illicit pages.[40] While in the end the Yahoo! case relied on geolocation to prevent French citizens from having to see Nazi paraphernalia, the right to be forgotten relies on the right to object to processing and the right to withdraw consent. The difference will matter greatly to the global enforcement of the right.

Notifying the public that content has been altered is another point of controversy and seemingly important for journalists, academics, and researchers, who must understand and rely on their sources. Notifications may allow watchdogs to curb abuse by political figures or corporations and may curb individuals from frivolously seeking obstruction to public information, which seems to support information stewardship. Notifying users, as Google currently does, that "some results may have been removed under data protection law in Europe" only reveals that information has been altered. Because search results prior to the alteration were not a complete portrait of the data subject and already tailored to the searcher and geographic region, such notifications may do little to foster information stewardship. Notifying users does not add context to the information presented; it simply signals that there is more information about the individual not presented in the results, which should already be apparent. In fact, when one clicks on the "learn more" link in the notice, he or she is informed that the notification just quoted is presented "when a user searches for most names, not just pages that have been affected by a removal."[41]

In the proposed DP Regulation, paragraph 2 of article 17 provides procedures for the removal of content that has been made publicly available. As discussed, this aspect of the proposed Regulation relates to the right to oblivion—how content that is easily discoverable online impacts reputation, self-perception, second chances, and transformation. The values, rights, and interests associated with publicly available information are different from those associated with privately held data, particularly if it is commercial. The right to oblivion (the right to remove information made available to the public) will conflict with the tenets of free speech in the U.S. However, the negative consequences of significant disappearance of information would be limited by procedural changes that would mitigate abuse and uncertainty resulting from a user-initiated takedown system.

The differences between the balances of various values are embodied in different legislative, administrative, and judicial determinations. The problem is that data subjects and data controllers will be determining what should be forgotten and what qualifies as free speech under the right to be forgotten for the jurisdiction where the request originates, which may be unfamiliar and unclear. As mentioned, this has been problematic for users responding to DMCA takedown notices, which have a body of legal decisions offering at least some guidance—the right to be forgotten will not be able to offer even that. Although I have argued for different treatment of data and content because of the different rights, values, and interests associated with passively created, privately held data and actively created, publicly available content, the two can converge. For instance, the right to be forgotten interpreted in *Google v. AEPD* impacts data held by Google. Google holds this data in a privately owned index, but the information (the URL and content on the page) is not private. The information that Google holds and organizes for its search functions is publicly available content. Google also holds privately held passive data, but because it is not publicly available or actively created, interest and value considerations are significantly limited. Fiddling with Google's search results impacts the public's ability to access publicly available information and so can be categorized as a content issue.

Not only should altering search results be considered within the actively created content category, but there are real problems with handing this responsibility to intermediaries. They are far from the optimal party to be assessing oblivion claims. The parties in the best position to assess the needs of the data controller, the subject, and the public are data-protection agencies or, at a minimum, the data sources themselves. Although the source of the content knows the context and justifications for the communication far better than an intermediary like Google does, the source may still just remove the content upon request to avoid any legal issues. It is best if users request oblivion through DPAs, which may continue to make these assessments in line with their evolving domestic laws. The DPAs are in the best position to assess the many needs at issue, are engaged with the public, and are paid to develop laws. Currently, Google is suffering extreme compliance costs assessing each of the requests as the company ushers European countries' information laws into the Digital Age.

Instead, when information is made public, a court or agency order should be required for right-to-be-forgotten removal requests. For U.S. sites and services that receive CDA § 230 immunity in the U.S., dealing with liability in countries where they receive no such immunity is difficult, but as the Google Transparency Report shows, they are capable of handling these orders. Responding to user takedown requests is incredibly disruptive to operations of sites and services around the world—determination of validity, authentication, and country-specific legal interpretation of each claim will be so time-consuming, costly, and inconsistent that many will just remove content automatically. This conflicts with the European treatment of intermediaries.

The EU 2000 E-Commerce Directive provides limited liability for "mere conduits, caching and hosts," but only so far as the provider does not have actual knowledge of the defamatory activity or information and upon obtaining such knowledge expeditiously removes or limits access to the defamatory content.[42] Article 15 prevents member countries from forcing hosts to monitor for potentially illegal content, but when intermediaries have "actual knowledge" of facts and circumstances that suggest illegal content or activities, they must immediately remove it.[43] For instance, in the recent UK case of *Payam Tamiz v. Google*, the Court of Appeal ruled in Google's favor for lack of evidence as to the number of people who read the offending blog comments on its Blogger platform, but it also determined that once a platform provider has been notified of allegedly offending material, it becomes "a publisher by acquiescence" and will be held liable for failing to remove the content quickly.[44] Payam Tamiz, a former Conservative Party local council candidate, filed the claim after notifying Google of comments posted on the *London Muslim* blog in July 2011 calling him a drug dealer and a thief. Google removed the content but took five weeks to do so, which the court determined "was sufficiently long to leave room for an inference adverse to Google Inc."[45] Had Tamiz been able to show that a sufficient number of people had read the blog comments, Google would have been held liable for not removing them quickly enough. However, different countries have imparted liability on intermediaries for actual knowledge of illegal content in different ways. Finland and Lithuania, for instance, use a counternotice and put-back system, very similar to the U.S. DMCA takedown system. The content is removed, the posting user is notified and given an opportunity to dispute removal with a counternotice, and the intermediary may put the content back up without risking liability. In Germany, a rapid preliminary review process is in place to limit the damage of certain types of information. In October 2013, the ECtHR upheld an Estonian court decision against Delfi, a news portal, for libelous comments made by anonymous users. The ECtHR affirmed Delfi as a publisher and explained that Delfi was "expected to exercise a degree of caution" in monitoring controversial articles, particularly because the comments were anonymous and Delfi gained a commercial benefit.[46] In Europe, it is possible for a platform provider to be held liable for not removing (or even failing to monitor for) allegedly defamatory or other illegal comments about the news—a far cry from U.S. jurisprudence.

Digital oblivion deserves an exception to this general rule. Recall that a data controller is any person who determines the purposes for which and the manner in which any personal data are, or are to be, processed. That definition is far reaching, and in order to avoid massive loss of discoverability of content, a procedural adjustment is warranted. Requiring a court or agency order would allow a body of law to develop for each jurisdiction instead of leaving the development of the right in the hands of private companies. It would move forward the different prioritization of privacy and other interests among countries and be less disruptive to sites, services, and information that the world has come to rely on.

Although it may seem pro-speech to obstruct discoverability of personal information at the intermediary level because it preserves the content while hiding it in search results, it is not all it is cracked up to be. This system relies on a completely detached party (the intermediary) to make decisions about the importance, relevance, and adequacy of information it did not produce or preserve. Obscuring content at the source grants the data controller more expressive freedom in how to preserve the content and, most importantly, provides the controller an opportunity to challenge the obstruction, a mechanism of protecting the freedom of expression that is currently not provided. There is still no need to erase the content. The source of the information can signal to search engines—all of them, not just one at a time—not to index the page. Instead, under the current system, the data controller must hope that private companies like Google will fight in court for its decision not to obscure search results that point to the data controller's speech.

A strong appeals process is already being prepped for the new DP Regulation; it involves a specific contact at each data-protection authority, but again, these regulatory schemes are unnecessarily complex. Data-protection authorities that receive claims, presumably after a data subject has been denied by Google or other data controllers, will have a common record of decisions and a "dashboard to help identify similar cases."[47] If this database was not intended to create a uniform right across the EU, it would be a nice tool. However, the appeals process is not clear-cut. When a claim's impact can be confined to a single EU member state, decisions are left to the national DPAs. While search results can be confined to a particular country's version of Google (which will not be true for other search engines and most sites), suggesting the impact is confined, the EU has argued that search results should be edited for all of Google's results. When a claim has EU-wide impact, and arguably obstructing content on the Internet always has EU-wide impact, the matter is referred to the Data Protection Board.[48] Thus, it is not clear whether right-to-be-forgotten claims will be appealed through national DPAs and whether any domestic legal culture will survive the transition to the DP Regulation or whether claims will be considered EU-wide and need to go through Data Protection Board approval. A simpler system that still promotes the single market would entail data subjects going directly to their national DPA to make a claim, which can be investigated by the agency that will determine whether an order should be issued. For the sake of rights to be forgotten, data controllers should be able to continue to wait for an agency or court order before removing publicly available, actively created content.

Development of the right to be forgotten is best done by national legislators, regulators, and adjudicators, not by data controllers and private intermediaries. An interoperable system is already in place for other information claims, and it has not required significant compliance costs, inappropriate delegation of policy making, and a potentially inaccurate balance between information access and privacy under domestic law.

Regulatory harmonization may be possible and desirable for the regulation of passively created, privately held data (deletion). In order to harmonize this aspect of the right to be forgotten, deletion must be separated from oblivion. As I have argued previously, the DP Regulation currently condenses the two and treats them similarly, which is inappropriate because of the different interests associated with the retention of privately held versus publicly available information. If the right to deletion were to be separated, the existing article 17 would be much less problematic. Many versions of FIPPs already include the principles of data minimization and user participation,[49] and paragraph 1 of article 17 essentially grants users a right to participate in and enforce data-minimization principles, as well as the right to withdrawal of consent to retroactively cure issues of informed consent in an online environment. There may be room for a right to be forgotten in the U.S., but it is unlikely to apply to content made publicly available online anytime in the near future and will certainly not look like the takedown system in the EU. A more limited right could apply only to data that has been voluntarily submitted, and deletion would require legislative action to establish an implied-in-law covenant in contracts between data controllers and data subjects.[50] These versions of the right would not reach an individual seeking to have search results disappear from Google.

The legal interests associated with data collected through automated surveillance online are far from established, but there has been a general movement to grant users stronger rights to participate in how data about them is collected, processed, and used. Many scholars have argued that the EU DP Regulation should grant only this type of right to be forgotten: user participation in the principle of data minimization to ensure its deletion after the original purpose for collection has been fulfilled.[51] A number of data controllers and services already offer this type of user participation, including participation tools that allow users to remove content like pictures and comments they themselves post, which is why Jeffrey Rosen calls this aspect of the right to be forgotten "mostly symbolic and entirely unobjectionable."[52] The Network Advertising Initiative allows users to opt out of receiving targeted advertisements from its ninety-eight member companies,[53] Spokeo allows users to opt out of being listed,[54] and the World Wide Web Consortium is still working to develop a "Do Not Track" mechanism,[55] but often users must delete accounts in order to delete data.[56] Neither an opt-out mechanism that prevents future collection nor requiring a user to fully delete an account in order to delete data will likely meet the EU's right-to-erasure standard. It will require creating means for real user access and participation in data-processing practices, which is of course challenging but generally agreed on.[57]

However, the attorneys Eugene Volokh (also a law scholar) and Donald Falk have argued that search engines are speakers.[58] According to Volokh and Falk, speech exercises by the search engine occur when it conveys information prepared by the search engine itself, reports about others' speech by directing users to material that best suits their queries, includes select excerpts from pages, and selects and sorts results using discretion to determine the most helpful and useful information for the searcher.[59] Essentially the argument is that search engines exercise editorial judgment, similarly to newspapers, and should have the same First Amendment protection in the output of their data processing. Although the technology for information distribution has changed, Volokh and

Falk argue, "the freedom to distribute, select, and arrange such speech remains the same."[60] A highly contested claim, the extension of First Amendment protection to data, indexes, or search results would arouse many of the same censorship arguments that stem from oblivion. The issue of whether data and algorithms are speech in the U.S. is far from settled. So, while there may be some general consensus regarding user participation, the constitutionality of U.S. efforts to enforce such participation is far less clear.

As discussed earlier, market, technological, and norm-based solutions are not singular suitable responses to lingering personal digital information, but they can each support or undercut legal solutions. While the legal, the technical, and the social are intertwined, I combine technical and social aspects because they refer to norms of technical behavior. Without socio-technical support, exercised rights to be forgotten are far too easily circumvented.

The data controller should retain flexibility in the means of obstruction so as to limit infringement on expression rights. The controller should have the option to (1) remove the identifying information, (2) delete the entry completely, or (3) deindex the page. The site operator may not have received hits on old content in years, may have no interest in keeping the content, and may want to delete the content. Alternatively, the controller can choose to alter only the identification of the person, removing his or her full name. The site could also make the content inaccessible to the public but still maintain the record to avoid issues of deleting potentially useful information. A controller may be ordered to disconnect content from an individual, creating an obstruction, but that does not prevent the controller from deleting the information altogether. It is important to prevent deletion through easy and coordinated technical options and norms of stewardship.

Although Wikipedia's Biographies of Living Persons policy includes a presumption in favor of privacy and is a good rule for information stewardship, these efforts can be wasted when technical elements are not coordinated and social contextual integrity is unsettled. The "Star Wars

Kid Wikipedia Talk" page is a complete representation of the right-to-be-forgotten debate. Under the "Why Not Named" section, which appears first on the talk page, the contributor AzureFury explains, "This has been debated at great length, multiple times. There is a slim majority of editors that believe that the most important policy regarding the mention of the kid's name is WP:Biographies of Living Persons. In particular, this policy states, '. . . This is of particularly profound importance when dealing with individuals whose notability stems largely from their being victims of another's actions. Wikipedia editors must not act, intentionally or otherwise, in a way that amounts to participating in or prolonging the victimization.'"[61] After a long discussion about Wikipedia's censorship policy and the importance of Ghyslain Raza not having his own page, in 2013 the talk page takes a different turn, apparently in response to Raza, as an adult, publicly acknowledging his identity as the Star Wars Kid. The community finally agreed to explicitly name Raza in 2013, and the contributor Hamsterlopithecus added it to the page. Soon thereafter, protections were removed from the page that previously prevented easily adding Raza's name. Prior to Wikipedia's change, Google search results for Raza returned the Star Wars Kid Wikipedia page as the most relevant result, seemingly undermining the entire conversation occurring on the talk page. The discrepancy highlights the need for a more cohesive approach to old information.

Like the Wikipedia community, the archival community is faced with a competing access principle: "Archivists strive to promote open and equitable access to their services and the records in their care without discrimination or preferential treatment, and in accordance with legal requirements, cultural sensitivities, and institutional policies."[62] With more and more archives being digitized, these decisions become more important. For instance, should diaries be digitized and accessible by anyone when they contain sensitive material about a person who is still alive? Diaries typically are not meant to be read by anyone but the writer and perhaps descendants, but valuable historical and cultural information has been extracted from diaries, such as those of Anne Frank, Virginia Woolf, George Washington, Thomas Jefferson, William Bradford, and Sylvia Plath. The Internet Archive's exclusion policy follows the guidelines set forth for traditional archives and clearly lays out the appropriate response to specific types of removal requests.[63]

Data controllers like traditional newspapers have responded in less organized ways, some of them undercutting the obstruction to their content put in place upon the request of an individual named on the page. For instance, the BBC published an article titled "Google Removes 12 BBC News Links in 'Right to Be Forgotten.'"[64] The article lists (and links) to content that had been edited out of Google search results, such as "Two stories relate to the high-profile case of a British woman found guilty of running 'one of Europe's biggest prostitution rings' in 2003," which points to an article about Margaret McDonald's high-end escort service.[65] Others have highlighted decisions by Google that seemingly violate the norms of the readership. The *Manchester Evening News* covered the removal of a *Daily Mail* article detailing Ronald Castree's conviction for murder and sexual assault and the outraged reaction of the victim's father. The father, Fred Anderson, stated, "I think it's appalling. . . . He hasn't got the right to be forgotten—it's terrible. . . . We'll never get peace."[66] Categories of unforgiveable acts and behavior in the Digital Age are just beginning to be defined within various societies. While these ethics and practices are developing among various content producers, controllers, and processors, hosting data controllers (e.g., news sites) are not generally notified of the obstruction of their content, and they can do nothing about it. This leaves the entity that has found value in expressing the content out of the conversation and appeals process. Notifying hosting data controllers of altered results is important for data controllers that may begin to develop ethics and responses to obstructions.

The right must also deal technically with ubiquitous and opaque cross-platform data transfers. One could request that personal data be deleted on the initial site, but the data might have been sent downstream, perhaps without a trace on the initial site. All these potential third-party uses (or "secondary uses") are quite difficult to trace and do not necessarily take into account deletion of the primary material. Significant technical implementation issues are associated with the right.

Deleting personal data from an initial system and those downstream is no simple task. Records are overwritten because of updates and corrections, but systems can rarely distinguish between the two. Overwriting a record generally deletes the earlier version of the record. As the data moves downstream, the accountability issues travel with it and grow in complexity. Data tethering is an important design element for data moving downstream to secondary organizations. "Data tethering means when data changes at its source, the change is reflected through the entire food chain. Every copied piece of data is virtually 'tethered' to its master copy," explains Jeff Jonas, the chief scientist of the IBM Entity Analytics group.[67] A system that is not tethered will likely contain many errors, at least until the database is reloaded.[68] Centralized trust-management systems could also provide a source of participation for users across platforms and data controllers. Additionally, best practices should promote having any identifying information held or transferred also carry metadata related to what third parties the controller held arrangements with at the time. The right to be forgotten is often criticized as technologically impossible. The right is only technologically challenging when discoverability is difficult for the data subject but easy for the people and organizations that matter to him or her (e.g., for job offers, discounts, judgments). Although it is far easier for the subject to discover personal content available to the public using common platforms and search techniques than personal data hidden across a network of third-party controllers, "pretty good privacy" will always have to suffice. It is the ease of discoverability that matters, not the number of copies that exist.

In this book, I give a snapshot of a moment between international social concern and the construction of wide-reaching cyberlaw. The EU legislation proposed at the start of 2012 made it through the European Parliament in April 2014. Once the ministers resolve their views, a three-way discussion between Commission, Parliament, and member states—

known as a trilogue—will begin. Interim EU Commissioner Martine Reicherts explains, "There should be a first agreement in December [2014], because there will be a Council at the beginning of December, so we should find an agreement by then. . . . The trilogues will probably start in January."[69]

As of now, there is still time to make procedural and categorical changes to the European right that may improve its development. Additionally, the time is ripe for countries to determine their own rights to be forgotten or other approaches to digital redemption. There is a real threat that extreme, noninteroperable cyberlaw will develop in other countries with European-inspired data-protection regulations that will replicate deference to Google instead of proactively and thoughtfully moving their own information and forgiveness law into the Digital Age. The privacy scholar Paul Schwartz warns that conditions are in place to produce what Anu Bradford calls the "Brussels Effect."[70] The Brussels Effect is the EU's ability to impose its rules throughout the world and results when (1) the EU is a market that multinational companies cannot afford to avoid, (2) EU officials have strong regulatory capacity, and (3) corporations voluntarily comply with the most stringent single standard, making others obsolete.[71] The arrangement resulting from the *Google v. AEPD* case and the unified structure put forth by the DP Regulation threaten to press EU information priorities far beyond the bounds of Europe. Schwartz argues that interoperability between the EU and the U.S. to this point has been successful as a "harmonization network,"[72] a term coined by Anne-Marie Slaughter in her work on global governance in *A New World Order*.[73] The issues could also be considered "intermestic" because they involve both international and domestic affairs, like immigration and transnational pollution.[74] Intermestic issues will only increase in importance in the future, and structures for coordinated policy efforts that preserve domestic legal cultures where appropriate must be understood and developed.

In order not to fall victim to the Brussels Effect, the U.S. will need to take a hard look at its recent policy choices with regard to expression, freedom, and reinvention. These cultural aspects of U.S. society will need to be acknowledged, protected, and balanced or be considered part of history. A study conducted by Software Advice in 2014 after the *Google v. AEPD* ruling found that 39 percent of Americans believe that it is necessary for everyone to have a right to be forgotten, another 6 percent support a right to be forgotten that applies to everyone but public figures, and 39 percent of Americans think the right is either not appropriate for public information (18 percent) or too hard to implement (21 percent).[75] Others find the right appropriate only for minors (15 percent) or inappropriate only for public figures (6 percent).[76] The best place to start these conversations in the U.S. is in considering a right to be forgotten for vulnerable populations for which special information laws to mitigate social stigma and forgiveness laws to support reinvention already exist.

In sum, a right to be forgotten that establishes a harmonized balance between privacy and expression (i.e., applies the freedom-of-expression or public-interest exception in the same manner transnationally) is simply not currently possible. It ignores the particular national values that have resulted in divergent legal cultures. However, that does not mean that country-specific sites or treatment need to be created by every data controller, but data controllers must be responsive when that balance has been made by different national governments. In other words, regulatory cooperation, as opposed to harmonization, must be forged on this subject. This requires procedural changes to the user-request system so the development of the right to be forgotten is placed in the right hands.

Concluding Remarks

The web is so young in many ways, but it is old enough to have real and significant impacts on networked societies. While uncertainty still blankets the digital world, we should expect policy that aims to hold tight those values that are held most dear when innovation threatens to leave them behind. The right to be forgotten is the answer to a question about what values should be brought into the future using the force of law. This must be considered a necessary part of, not in conflict with, innovation.

In a June 2014 *New Yorker* article that took on the theory of disruptive innovation, Jill Lepore criticized modern "innovation" as aimless and uncritical:

> The eighteenth century embraced the idea of progress; the nineteenth century had evolution; the twentieth century had growth and then innovation. Our era has disruption, which, despite its futurism, is atavistic. It's a theory of history founded on a profound anxiety about financial collapse, an apocalyptic fear of global devastation, and shaky evidence. . . . In its modern usage, innovation is the idea of progress jammed into a criticism-proof jack-in-the-box. . . . Replacing "progress" with "innovation" skirts the question of whether a novelty is an improvement: the world may not be getting better and better but our devices are getting newer and newer.[77]

For some people, innovation has become a neutral word, like technology. It is neither good nor bad but what we make of it. Innovation simply means new technology. Others praise innovation, holding it in esteem as the cornerstone of economic prosperity. Still others cringe at the term, associating it with a heartless, dehumanizing force. Conversations like the one concerning the right to be forgotten do not put the brakes on new tools or progress or knowledge. They are an opportunity to be innovative about innovation—to be critical and forward thinking. They allow us to embrace uncertainty and ready ourselves to make choices that support flourishing—whatever that means. The enthusiasm for innovation should not be stifled by the protection of values like privacy and expression but animated to optimize man-machine systems to promote human flourishing. Innovation should be a question of how to have one's cake and eat it too, or at least how to maximize social gains brought by new technologies and minimize any damages or exclusions.

Digital memory is like all threats to human flourishing. A potentially powerful tool brings with it its own overlooked limitations, triggers and disrupts a number of values, and causes instant polarization. Maintaining enthusiasm for a networked world while promoting individual growth and quelling larger societal fears will not happen with an extreme or simplistic view of the interests or choices available. "Save history or delete indignity" is a false dichotomy—these are not innovative perspectives. There is nothing innovative about branding a rape victim a victim for life or a child a racist forever. There is nothing innovative about letting people hide whatever information they would like. Twenty-first-century innovation is about the flourishing networked individual. It is about the dynamic self and contextual integrity. It is about imperfect but good-enough privacy measures to limit informational harms. Socio-technical laws that support human flourishing cannot be considered anti-innovative.

The right to be forgotten is about providing some kind of recourse for information that we have tried so hard but failed to keep to ourselves, in the right hands, or out of the wrong hands—for some very good reasons and realities. Collected, shared, and analyzed information has helped so many people find, understand, and support so many other people. We are promised a future of better resource allocation and less drudgery, loneliness, and discrimination. Some of those promises have already been fulfilled, and some never will. Why not bring redemption and reinvention with us as those promises are met or broken—particularly if doing so helps us meet them?

The web is a communication and information resource—it is currently a poorly preserved one. We cannot treat it as an ongoing permanent historical record. That is not the nature of digital. The relevant attributes are twofold: (1) digital information is more decentralized and frail than paper record systems are, and (2) digital information remains more easily discoverable longer than previous communication media were. There is no systematic approach to this resource—content and data come and go from the most used information resource we have ever had. The problem is not one of information permanence but of information stewardship. Developing principles around this idea promotes use of digital information and accountability, both forms of computational innovation.

Information stewardship forces us to ask questions about what should be preserved and why. Many countries around the world are considering the right to be forgotten, including the U.S. By doing so through the lens of information stewardship, countries take an active role in categorizing the kinds of digital information that are intended to be short-lived and those that are intended to last. An Internet that is full of outdated, inaccurate information or lets go of important cultural content is not the source of innovation it could be.

In order to make good choices, the difference of digital needs an updated vocabulary and new tools for analysis. The way in which digital data is created, dispersed, and used, the way it changes and loses context as it lingers online and in databases, and the way it is or is not accessed as it ceases to represent its original substance—these attributes of digital culture matter to updating legal concepts of irrelevance, public interest, public figures, newsworthiness, and inaccuracy. Consider the Pilate Stone. A stone found in Caesarea-on-the-Sea, Israel, in 1961, it is the only archaeological find mentioning the name Pontius Pilate. Had someone "anonymized" the stone, we would have no such record. We have the same historical dilemma as the people in Pilate's day and those who followed but a new set of opportunities and solutions. Digital is different, which is what makes it valuable in new ways. We cannot assess the potential social and economic value of digital information through a new lens without also assessing the potential impacts on other types of values through a similar lens.

These important conversations involve a number of players with different interests and politics, all trying to grapple with the immense number of situations and types of information at issue while still struggling to define the problem and the goal of a right to be forgotten. Many individuals still struggle with their own stances on the issue, feeling the pull of both preservationists and deletionists, but a shift is occurring. The willingness to consider innovative information rights and protections for a new digital landscape is spreading, even in the U.S. How digital redemption fits within a particular legal culture can be assessed by looking at existing forgiveness laws. As a country that has benefited from providing opportunities for reinvention and redemption, the U.S. has some interesting choices to make about the future. Conservatively, the U.S. could institute digital redemption by providing legal mechanisms to add information to expired content that has not received much public attention, extending a right to obstruct content to a few choice groups, and join the EU in a data-participation right to delete privately held data.

The values at play are deeply rooted in cultural variation and do not need to be universal in order to be initiated. As this imaginative undertaking is performed, decision and policy makers should take care to make good cyberlaw first and foremost. Cyberlaws should be internationally interoperable in order to be effective. International interoperability relies heavily on procedures, institutions, and respect for another region's prioritization of shared values. This is not only an issue for policy makers, however. Information stewardship should be supported by law but must also be socially and technically interoperable. We must all be stewards. Before you delete your next Facebook post, tweet, blog, comment, email, set of cookies, or chat, consider whether you are destroying history or exercising your power to participate in your digital identity.

Notes

INTRODUCTION

1. Case C-131/12, Google Spain SL and Google Inc. v. Agencia Española de Protección de Datos (AEPD) and Mario Costeja González (Euro. Ct. of Justice May 13, 2014).
2. Clark v. Viacom Int'l, Inc., No. 3:12–0675, 2014 WL 1934028 (M.D. Tenn. May 13, 2014).
3. Lateef Mungin, *Bullied Canadian Teen Leaves Behind Chilling YouTube Video*, CNN (Oct. 12, 2012), http://www.cnn.com/2012/10/12/world/americas/canada-teen-bullying/.
4. Amanda Todd, *My Story: Struggling, Bullying, Suicide, Self Harm*, YOUTUBE (2012), https://www.youtube.com/watch?v=ej7afkypUsc.
5. *Id.*
6. Max Mosley v. News Group Newspapers Limited, [2008] EWHC 1777 (QB), available at http://news.bbc.co.uk/2/shared/bsp/hi/pdfs/24_07_08mosleyvnewsgroup.pdf.
7. Josh Halliday, *Max Mosley Sues Google in France and Germany over "Orgy" Search Results*, GUARDIAN (Feb. 25, 2011), http://www.theguardian.com/media/2011/nov/25/max-mosley-google-france-germany.
8. *Google Launches Challenges to Max Mosley's Privacy Bid*, BBC NEWS (Jan. 14, 2015), http://www.bbc.com/news/uk-30816523.
9. Editorial Board, *Wrong Responses to Charlie Hebdo*, N.Y. TIMES (Jan. 15, 2015).

10. Neil Spencer, *How Much Data Is Created Every Minute?*, VISUAL NEWS (June 9, 2012), http://www.visualnews.com/2012/06/19/how-much-data-created-every-minute/?view=infographic (sources include http://news.investors.com/, http://royal.pingdom.com, http://blog.grovo.com, http://blog.hubspot.com, http://simplyzesty.com, http://pcworld.com, http://bitztechmagazine.com, http://digby.com); *World Internet Users Statistics Usage and World Population Stats*, INTERNET WORLD STATS, http://www.internetworldstats.com/stats.htm (accessed June 23, 2015).

11. Reputation.com, *The Real-World Effect of Online Reputation Management*, http://www.reputation.com/reputationwatch/articles/the-real-world-effects-of-online-reputation-management (accessed June 28, 2015); Paulina Firozi, *Law School Admissions Use Facebook, Google to Screen Applicants, Study Finds*, DAILY NW. (Oct. 30, 2011), http://dailynorthwestern.com/2011/10/30/blogs/oncampus/law-school-admissions-use-facebook-google-to-screen-applicants-study-finds.

12. Jeffrey Rosen, *The Web Means the End of Forgetting*, N.Y. TIMES MAGAZINE (July 21, 2010), http://www.nytimes.com/2010/07/25/magazine/25privacy-t2.html?pagewanted=all.

13. These are so common that "Top 10" lists are regularly assembled. *See* Shawn Paul Wood, *Top 10 Social Media Fails of 2013*, MEDIABISTRO (Dec. 16, 2013), http://www.mediabistro.com/prnewser/pr-newsers-top-10-social-media-fails-of-2013_b80443; Natalie Umansky, *10 Outrageous Tweets That Got People Fired*, ODDEE (Feb. 21, 2014), http://www.oddee.com/item_98873.aspx; Christina Warren, *10 People Who Lost Jobs over Social Media Mistakes*, MASHABLE (June 16, 2011), http://mashable.com/2011/06/16/weinergate-social-media-job-loss/; Dan Fastenberg, *Facebook Firings: Top 10 Cases and the NLRB's New Guidelines*, AOL JOBS (Sept. 2, 2011), http://jobs.aol.com/articles/2011/09/02/facebook-firings-top-ten-cases-and-the-nlrbs-new-guidelines/.

14. Zosia Bielski, *If a Teacher's Decades-Old Erotic Films Can Resurface Online, What Rights Should We Have to Digital Privacy?*, GLOBE AND MAIL (Oct. 22, 2014), http://www.theglobeandmail.com/life/relationships/if-a-teachers-decades-old-erotic-films-can-resurface-online-what-rights-should-we-have-to-digital-privacy/article21218588/.

15. *Id.*

16. Laura M. Holson, *The New Court of Shame Is Online*, N.Y. TIMES (Dec. 23, 2010), http://www.nytimes.com/2010/12/26/fashion/26shaming.html?ref=todayspaper&_r=0.

17. Tracie Egan Morrissey, *Racist Teens Forced to Answer for Tweets about the "N*****" President*, JEZEBEL (Nov. 9, 2012), http://jezebel.com/5958993/racist-teens-forced-to-answer-for-tweets-about-the-nigger-president.

18. Cross Tab, *Online Reputation in a Connected World* (Jan. 2010), http://www.job-hunt.org/guides/DPD_Online-Reputation-Research_overview.pdf (accessed Aug. 1, 2015) (75 percent of human resource departments are expected to research

candidates online; 89 percent of hiring managers and recruiters review candidates' professional online data; 86 percent of employers believe a positive online reputation influences their hiring decisions); Natasha Singer, *They Loved Your G.P.A. Then They Saw Your Tweets*, N.Y. TIMES (Nov. 9, 2013), http://www.nytimes.com/2013/11/10/business/they-loved-your-gpa-then-they-saw-your-tweets.html?_r=0; Paulina Firozi, *Law School Admissions Use Facebook, Google to Screen Applicants, Study Finds*, DAILY NW. (Oct. 30, 2011), http://dailynorthwestern.com/2011/10/30/blogs/oncampus/law-school-admissions-use-facebook-google-to-screen-applicants-study-finds.

19. *Match.com Presents Singles in America 2012*, UP TO DATE (blog), Match.com, http://blog.match.com/SIA/ (accessed June 23, 2015).

20. Alex Mooris, *Hunter Moore: The Most Hated Man on the Internet*, ROLLING STONE (Oct. 11, 2012), http://www.rollingstone.com/culture/news/the-most-hated-man-on-the-Internet-20121113.

21. *Cyberbullying-Linked Suicides Rising, Study Says*, CBC NEWS (Oct. 20, 2012), http://www.cbc.ca/news/technology/story/2012/10/19/cyberbullying-suicide-study.html.

22. Bullying Statistics, *Bullying and Suicide*, http://www.bullyingstatistics.org/content/bullying-and-suicide.html (accessed June 23, 2015).

23. VIKTOR MAYER-SCHÖNBERGER, DELETE: THE VIRTUE OF FORGETTING IN THE DIGITAL AGE 272 (2009).

24. Google, *Company Overview* (Mar. 1, 2012), http://www.google.com/about/company/.

25. ELI PARISER, THE FILTER BUBBLE 1–3 (2011).

26. Mark Frauenfelder details the exchange between John Battelle and contacts at Google in his book RULE THE WEB: HOW TO DO ANYTHING AND EVERYTHING ON THE INTERNET—BETTER, FASTER, EASIER 361–362 (2007). *See also* JOHN BATTELLE, THE SEARCH: HOW GOOGLE AND ITS RIVALS REWROTE THE RULES OF BUSINESS AND TRANSFORMED OUR CULTURE (2006).

27. Michael Zimmer, *The Externalities of Search 2.0: The Emerging Privacy Threats When the Drive for the Perfect Search Engine Meets Web 2.0*, 13:3 FIRST MONDAY (Mar. 2008), http://www.uic.edu/htbin/cgiwrap/bin/ojs/index.php/fm/article/view/2136/1944.

28. Google, *Privacy Policy* (Mar. 1, 2012), http://www.google.com/intl/en/policies/privacy/.

29. Julia Angwin, *The Web's New Gold Mine: Your Secrets*, WALL ST. J. (July 30, 2010), http://online.wsj.com/article/SB10001424052748703940090457539507351298 9404.html.

30. *Id.*

31. Woody Leonhard, *"Zombie Cookies" Won't Die: Microsoft Admits Use, HTML 5 Looms as New Vector*, INFOWORLD (Aug. 22, 2011), http://www.infoworld.com/t/

Internet-privacy/zombie-cookies-wont-die-microsoft-admits-use-and-html5
-looms-new-vector-170511.

32. Ciaran O'Kane, *BlueKai Explain Their Data Exchange Platform and Hint at
European Move*, EXCHANGEWIRE (blog) (Aug. 10, 2009), http://www.
exchangewire.com/blog/2009/08/10/
bluekai-explain-their-data-exchange-platform-and-hint-at-european-move/.

33. JULIAN BARNES, FLAUBERT'S PARROT 38 (1984).

34. Jim Gray and Catharine van Ingen, *Empirical Measurements of Disk Failure Rates
and Error Rates*, MICROSOFT RESEARCH TECHNICAL REPORT MSR-TR-
2005–166 (Dec. 2005).

35. Jonathan Zittrain, Kendra Albert, and Lawrence Lessig, *Perma: Scoping and
Addressing the Problem of Link and Reference Rot in Legal Citations*, 14:2 LEGAL
INFO. MANAGEMENT 88 (2014).

36. Giorgio Pino, *The Right to Personal Identity in Italian Private Law: Constitutional
Interpretation and Judge-Made Rights*, in THE HARMONIZATION OF PRIVATE
LAW IN EUROPE 225, 237 (Mark Van Hoecke and François Ost eds., 2000).

37. DP Directive 95/46.

38. European Commission, *Data Protection Reform—Frequently Asked Questions*,
press release, MEMO/10/542 (Nov. 4, 2010), http://europa.eu/rapid/
press-release_MEMO-10-542_en.htm?locale=fr.

39. European Commission, *Proposal for a Regulation of the European Parliament
and of the Council*, COM(2012) 11 final (Jan. 25, 2012) (DP Regulation), http://
ec.europa.eu/justice/data-protection/document/review2012/
com_2012_11_en.pdf.

40. European Parliament, Committee on Civil Liberties, Justice and Home Affairs,
Report on Draft European Parliament Legislative Resolution, A7–0402/001–207
(Mar. 6, 2014) (DP Regulation, LIBE edits), http://www.europarl.europa.eu/sides/
getDoc.do?pubRef=-//EP//NONSGML+AMD+A7-2013-0402+001–
207+DOC+PDF+V0//EN.

41. Edmond Cahn, *The Firstness of the First Amendment*, 65 YALE L.J. 464 (1956).

42. VIKTOR MAYER-SCHÖNBERGER, DELETE: THE VIRTUE OF FORGETTING
IN THE DIGITAL AGE 2 (2011).

43. *Id.* at 126.

44. *Id.* at 113.

45. Jeffrey Rosen, *Free Speech, Privacy, and the Web That Never Forgets*, 9 J. ON
TELECOMM. & HIGH TECH. L. 345 (2011).

46. Julie Juola Exline, Everett L. Worthington Jr., Peter Hill, and Michael E.
McCullough, *Forgiveness and Justice: A Research Agenda for Social and Personality
Psychology*, 7 PERSONALITY & SOC. PSYCHOL. REV. 337 (2003).

47. *See generally* Robert D. Enright, Suzanne Freedman, and Julio Rique, *The
Psychology of Interpersonal Forgiveness*, in EXPLORING FORGIVENESS 46
(Robert D. Enright and Joanna North eds., 1998). Whether forgiveness requires

positive feelings toward an offender or whether the absence of negative feelings alone is sufficient is a definitional debate had by social psychologists. *Id.* The authors consider the absence of negative feelings the most important aspect of a definition of forgiveness related to this topic. *Id.* at 50.

48. ROBERT JEFFRESS, WHEN FORGIVENESS DOESN'T MAKE SENSE 221 (2001) (32 percent found the statement very accurate, and 34 percent found it somewhat accurate).

49. *Id.* at 218. When asked about the accuracy of the statement "If you really forgive someone, you would want the person to be released from the consequences of their actions," 28 percent answered that the statement was very accurate, and 32 percent answered that is was somewhat accurate.

50. *Id.* at 220. When asked about the accuracy of the statement "If you genuinely forgive someone, you should rebuild your relationship with that person," 35 percent found it very accurate, and 38 percent found it somewhat accurate.

51. Julie Juola Exline, Everett L. Worthington Jr., Peter Hill, and Michael E. McCullough, *Forgiveness and Justice: A Research Agenda for Social and Personality Psychology*, 7 PERSONALITY & SOC. PSYCHOL. REV. 337, 340 (2003).

52. *Id.*

53. *Id.* at 338.

54. MARK S. UMBREIT, THE HANDBOOK OF VICTIM OFFENDER MEDIATION: AN ESSENTIAL GUIDE TO PRACTICE AND RESEARCH 183 (2002).

55. *See generally* Jonathan R. Cohen, *Apology and Organizations: Exploring an Example from Medical Practice*, 27 FORDHAM URB. L.J. 1447 (2000).

56. *See* Brad R. C. Kelln and John H. Ellard, *An Equity Theory Analysis of the Impact of Forgiveness and Retribution on Transgressor Compliance*, 25 PERSONALITY & SOC. PSYCHOL. BULL. 864, 871 (1999). For example, following an ostensible transgression, an experimenter reacted in one of four ways: forgiveness only; forgiveness and retribution; retribution only; or neither forgiveness nor retribution. *Id.* at 865. Those transgressors who were forgiven without any form of retribution complied with experimenters' requests more than any other group did. *Id.* at 869.

57. Frederick Luskin, *The Stanford Forgiveness Projects, in* FORGIVENESS: A SAMPLING OF RESEARCH RESULTS 14, 15 (American Psychological Association, 2006), http://www.apa.org/international/resources/publications/forgiveness.pdf.

58. Mayo Clinic, *Forgiveness: Letting Go of Grudges and Bitterness* (Nov. 11, 2014), http://www.mayoclinic.org/healthy-living/adult-health/in-depth/forgiveness/art-20047692.

59. Loren Toussaint and Jon R. Webb, *Theoretical and Empirical Connections between Forgiveness, Mental Health, and Well-Being, in* HANDBOOK OF FORGIVENESS 349 (Everett L. Worthington Jr. ed., 2005).

60. Charlotte van Oyen Witvliet, *Traumatic Intrusive Imagery as an Emotional Memory Phenomenon: A Review of Research and Explanatory Information Processing Theories*, 17 CLIN. PSYCHOL. REV. 509 (1997).

61. *See generally* Roy F. Baumeister, Julie Juola Exline, and Kristin L. Sommer, *The Victim Role, Grudge Theory, and Two Dimensions of Forgiveness, in* DIMENSIONS OF FORGIVENESS: PSYCHOLOGICAL RESEARCH & THEOLOGICAL PERSPECTIVES 79 (Everett L. Worthington Jr. ed., 1998).

62. *Id.* at 98.

63. Charlotte van Oyen Witvliet, Thomas E. Ludwig, and Kelly L. Vander Laan, *Granting Forgiveness or Harboring Grudges: Implications for Emotion, Physiology, and Health*, 12 PSYCHOL. SCI. 117, 118 (2001); *see also* Everett L. Worthington Jr., *Empirical Research in Forgiveness: Looking Backward, Looking Forward, in* DIMENSIONS OF FORGIVENESS: PSYCHOLOGICAL RESEARCH AND THEOLOGICAL PERSPECTIVES 321 (Everett L. Worthington Jr. ed., 1998).

64. Charlotte van Oyen Witvliet, Thomas E. Ludwig, and Kelly L. Vander Laan, *Granting Forgiveness or Harboring Grudges: Implications for Emotion, Physiology, and Health*, 12 PSYCHOL. SCI. 117 (2001).

65. *Id.* at 120.

66. *Id.* at 121 (measured by corrugator electromyograms).

67. *Id.* at 122.

68. Caryl E. Rusbult, Peggy A. Hannon, Sevaun L. Stocker, and Eli J. Finkel, *Forgiveness and Relational Repair, in* HANDBOOK OF FORGIVENESS 185, 194 (Everett L. Worthington Jr. ed., 2005).

69. *Id.*

70. Frank D. Fincham, Julie H. Hall, and Steven R. H. Beach, *Til Lack of Forgiveness Doth Us Part: Forgiveness in Marriage, in* HANDBOOK OF FORGIVENESS 207 (Everett L. Worthington Jr. ed. 2005).

71. Robert Enright, *Forgiveness Education with Children in Areas of Violence and Poverty, in* FORGIVENESS: A SAMPLING OF RESEARCH RESULTS 11, 12 (American Psychological Association, 2006), http://www.apa.org/international/resources/forgiveness.pdf.

72. Cynthia L. Battle and Ivan W. Miller, *Families and Forgiveness, in* HANDBOOK OF FORGIVENESS 233, 234 (Everett L. Worthington Jr. ed., 2005).

73. Frank D. Fincham, Steven R. H. Beach, and Joanne Davila, *Forgiveness and Conflict Resolution in Marriage*, 18 J. FAM. PSYCHOL. 72 (2004).

74. *See, e.g.,* Eileen R. Borris, *Forgiveness and the Healing of Nations, in* PARALLEL EVENT OF THE 55TH COMMISSION ON THE STATUS OF WOMEN, UNIVERSAL PEACE FEDERATION (2011), http://www.upf.org/education/speeches/3464-eileen-r-borris-forgiveness-and-the-healing-of-nations (presentation at the Parallel Event of the 55th Commission on the Status of Women "Women and the World at a Turning Point," Mission of Nigeria to the UN, New

York, an example of the United Nations' relationship with the Universal Peace Federation and their efforts and funding for fostering forgiveness).

75. Robert Enright, Jeanette Knutson, Anthony Holter, Casey Knutson, and Padraig Twomey, *Forgiveness Education with Children in Areas of Violence and Poverty, in* FORGIVENESS: A SAMPLING OF RESEARCH RESULTS 11, 13 (American Psychological Association, 2006), http://www.apa.org/international/resources/forgiveness.pdf.

76. Frederick Luskin, *The Stanford Forgiveness Projects, in* FORGIVENESS: A SAMPLING OF RESEARCH RESULTS 14, 15 (American Psychological Association, 2006), http://www.apa.org/international/resources/publications/forgiveness.pdf.

77. Michael J. A. Wohl and Nyla R. Branscombe, *Forgiving the Ingroup or the Outgroup for Harm Doing, in* FORGIVENESS: A SAMPLING OF RESEARCH RESULTS 23, 24 (American Psychological Association, 2006), http://www.apa.org/international/resources/forgiveness.pdf.

78. Ervin Staub and Laurie Anne Pearlman, *Promoting Reconciliation and Forgiveness after Mass Violence: Rwanda and Other Settings, in* FORGIVENESS: A SAMPLING OF RESEARCH RESULTS 31 (American Psychological Association, 2006), http://www.apa.org/international/resources/forgiveness.pdf.

79. Stephanos Bibas, *Forgiveness in Criminal Procedure*, 4 OHIO ST. J. CRIM. L. 329, 334 (2007).

80. *Id.* at 334.

81. *Id.* at 335. "As twelve-step programs such as Alcoholics Anonymous emphasize, admitting guilt is an essential step along the road to reform."

82. *Id.*

83. *Id.* at 334–335.

84. *See* Paul A. Mauger, J. F. Perry, T. Freeman, D. C. Grove, A. G. McBride, and K. E. McKinney, *The Measurement of Forgiveness: Preliminary Research*, 11 J. PSYCHOL. CHRIST. 170 (1992).

85. Jeanne S. Zechmeister and Catherine Romero, *Victim and Offender Accounts of Interpersonal Conflict: Autobiographical Narratives of Forgiveness and Unforgiveness*, 82 J. PERSONALITY & SOC. PSYCHOL. 675, 681 (2002).

86. O. Carter Snead, *Memory and Punishment*, 64 VAND. L. REV. 1195, 1233 (2011).

87. *Id.* at 1233–1234; *see also* AVISHAI MARGALIT, THE ETHICS OF MEMORY 205 (2002) ("as long as the offended one retains any scars from the injury, the forgiveness is not complete").

88. Caryl E. Rusbult, Peggy A. Hannon, Sevaun L. Stocker, and Eli J. Finkel, *Forgiveness and Relational Repair, in* HANDBOOK OF FORGIVENESS 185, 195 (Everett L. Worthington Jr. ed., 2005).

89. O. Carter Snead, *Memory and Punishment*, 64 VAND. L. REV. 1195, 1234 (2011).

90. Kashmir Hill, *How the Past Haunts Us in the Digital Age*, FORBES (Oct. 4, 2011), http://www.forbes.com/sites/kashmirhill/2011/10/04/how-the-past-haunts-us-in-the-digital-age/.

91. Johan C. Karremans, Paul A. M. Van Lange, and Rob W. Holland, *Forgiveness and Its Associations with Prosocial Thinking, Feeling, and Doing beyond the Relationship with the Offender*, 31 PERSONALITY & SOC. PSYCHOL. BULL. 1315 (2005).

92. *See* Marilyn McCord Adams, *Forgiveness: A Christian Model*, 8 FAITH & PHIL. 277 (1991); Margaret R. Holmgren, *Forgiveness and the Intrinsic Value of Persons*, 30 AM. PHIL. Q. 341 (1993); Herbert Morris, *Murphy on Forgiveness*, 7 CRIM. JUST. ETHICS 15 (1988), http://dx.doi.org/10.1080/0731129X.1988.9991836; Joanna North, *The "Ideal" of Forgiveness: A Philosopher's Exploration, in* EXPLORING FORGIVENESS 15 (Robert D. Enright and Joanna North eds., 1998); Joanna North, *Wrongdoing and Forgiveness*, 62 PHILOSOPHY 499 (1987).

93. *See, e.g.,* PETER A. FRENCH, THE VIRTUES OF VENGEANCE (2001); Jeffrie G. Murphy, *Two Cheers for Vindictiveness*, 2 PUNISHM. & SOC'Y 131 (2000); Michael Moore, *The Moral Worth of Retribution, in* RESPONSIBILITY, CHARACTER, AND THE EMOTIONS 179 (Ferdinand Schoeman ed., 1987).

94. *See* Jeffrie G. Murphy, *Forgiveness in Counseling: A Philosophical Perspective, in* BEFORE FORGIVING: CAUTIONARY VIEWS OF FORGIVENESS IN PSYCHOTHERAPY 41 (Sharon Lamb and Jeffrie G. Murphy eds., 2002).

95. *See generally* Jeffrie G. Murphy, *Forgiveness, Mercy, and the Retributive Emotions*, 7:2 CRIM. JUST. ETHICS 3 (1988).

96. Jeffrie G. Murphy, *Forgiveness in Counseling: A Philosophical Perspective, in* BEFORE FORGIVING: CAUTIONARY VIEWS OF FORGIVENESS IN PSYCHOTHERAPY 41 (Sharon Lamb and Jeffrie G. Murphy eds., 2002); Jeffrie G. Murphy, *Forgiveness, Mercy, and the Retributive Emotions*, 7:2 CRIM. JUST. ETHICS 3 (1988).

97. Jeffrie G. Murphy, *Forgiveness, Self-Respect, and the Value of Resentment, in* HANDBOOK OF FORGIVENESS 33, 33 (Everett L. Worthington Jr. ed., 2005).

98. ABRAHAM L. NEWMAN, PROTECTORS OF PRIVACY 6 (2008). For a discussion of the difference between the "functional approach" in social sciences and comparative law, see Ralf Michaels, *The Functional Method of Comparative Law, in* THE OXFORD HANDBOOK OF COMPARATIVE LAW 339 (Mathias Reimann and Reinhard Zimmermann eds., 2006).

99. LAWRENCE M. FRIEDMAN, PRIVATE LIVES: FAMILIES, INDIVIDUALS, AND LAW 17 (2005).

100. Sheila Jasanoff, *Ordering Knowledge, Ordering Society, in* STATES OF KNOWLEDGE 13, 14 (Sheila Jasanoff ed. 2004).

101. For a discussion of STS debates in the information and communication technologies contexts, see MEDIA TECHNOLOGIES: ESSAYS ON COMMUNICATION, MATERIALITY, AND SOCIETY (Tarleton Gillespie, Pablo J. Boczkowski, and Kirsten A. Foot eds., 2014). *See also* THE SOCIAL CONSTRUCTION OF

TECHNOLOGICAL SYSTEMS: NEW DIRECTIONS IN THE SOCIOLOGY AND HISTORY OF TECHNOLOGY (Wiebe E. Bijker, Thomas P. Hughes, Trevor Pinch, and Deborah G. Douglas eds., 2012); and STATES OF KNOWLEDGE (Sheila Jasanoff ed. 2004).

102. THE SOCIAL CONSTRUCTION OF TECHNOLOGICAL SYSTEMS: NEW DIRECTIONS IN THE SOCIOLOGY AND HISTORY OF TECHNOLOGY (Wiebe E. Bijker, Thomas P. Hughes, Trevor Pinch, and Deborah G. Douglas eds., 2012); STATES OF KNOWLEDGE (Sheila Jasanoff ed. 2004).

103. James Q. Whitman, *The Two Western Cultures of Privacy: Dignity versus Liberty*, 113 YALE L.J. 1151, 1160 (2004).

104. Irwin Altman, *Privacy Regulation: Culturally Universal or Culturally Specific?*, 33 J. SOC. ISSUES 66 (1977).

105. James Q. Whitman, *The Two Western Cultures of Privacy: Dignity versus Liberty*, 113 YALE L.J. 1151, 1163 (2004).

106. *Id.*

107. *Id.*

108. *Id.*

109. *Id.* at 1172.

110. *Id.* at 1171–1179.

111. *Id.* at 1180, citing EDWARD J. EBERLE, DIGNITY AND LIBERTY: CONSTITUTIONAL VISIONS IN GERMANY AND THE UNITED STATES 85 (2002) (quoting the Microcensus Case, 27 Entscheidungen des Bundesverfassungsgerichts [BVerfGE] [Federal Constitutional Court] July 16, 1969, 1(7) (F.R.G.)).

112. *Id.* at 1190–1193.

113. *Id.* at 1193.

114. By "legal culture," I mean "the ideas, attitudes, and values that people hold with regard to the legal system." LAWRENCE M. FRIEDMAN, GUARDING LIFE'S DARK SECRETS 5 (2007).

115. YOCHAI BENKLER, THE WEALTH OF NETWORKS: HOW SOCIAL PRODUCTION TRANSFORMS MARKETS AND FREEDOM (2007).

116. David R. Johnson and David Post, *Law and Borders: The Rise of Law in Cyberspace*, 48 STAN. L. REV. 1367 (1996).

117. Bernie Hogan, *Pseudonyms and the Rise of the Real-Name Web, in* A COMPANION TO NEW MEDIA DYNAMICS 290 (John Hartley, Jean Burgess, and Alex Bruns eds., 2013); *see also* Danielle Keats Citron, *Cyber Civil Rights*, 89 B.U. L. REV. 61 (2009); Daegon Cho, Soodong Kim, and Alessandro Acquisti, *Empirical Analysis and User Behaviors: The Impact of Real Name Policy, in* PROC. OF 45TH HAWAII INTERNATIONAL CONFERENCE ON SYSTEM SCIENCE (HICSS 2012).

118. VIKTOR MAYER-SCHÖNBERGER, DELETE: THE VIRTUE OF FORGETTING IN THE DIGITAL AGE 109 (2009) (quoting Eric Schmidt, interviewed by

Thomas Friedman at the Google Personal Democracy Forum 2007 event (Mar. 23, 2007), available at https://www.youtube.com/watch?v=ut3yjR7HNLU).

119. For a discussion of three structural conditions for human flourishing in network societies (access to knowledge, operational transparency, and semantic disconti- nuity), see JULIE COHEN, CONFIGURING THE NETWORKED SELF: LAW, CODE, AND THE PLAY OF EVERYDAY PRACTICE 223–266 (2012). For a discussion of cultural specificity in the reconstruction of rights in times of techno-scientific advancements, see SHEILA JASANOFF, DESIGNS OF NATURE (2005).

1. FORGETTING MADE EASY

1. GLORIA GONZÁLEZ FUSTER, THE EMERGENCE OF PERSONAL DATA PROTECTION AS A FUNDAMENTAL RIGHT OF THE EU (2014).

2. COLIN J. BENNETT AND CHARLES RAAB, THE GOVERNANCE OF PRIVACY: POLICY INSTRUMENTS IN GLOBAL PERSPECTIVE (2006).

3. Axel Springer AG v. Germany (2012) 55 EHRR 6 (ECtHR).

4. ABRAHAM NEWMAN, PROTECTORS OF PRIVACY 23–29 (2008).

5. Jeanne M. Hauch, *Protecting Private Facts in France: The Warren & Brandeis Tort Is Alive and Well and Flourishing in Paris*, 68 TUL. L. REV. 1219 (1994).

6. Neil M. Richards and Daniel J. Solove, *Privacy's Other Path: Recovering the Law of Confidentiality*, 96 GEO. L.J. 123 (2007).

7. *Id.*

8. See Douglas v. Hello!, Ltd. [2001] Q.B. 967 (wherein Michael Douglas and Catherine Zeta-Jones initially won injunctive relief as well as damages but on appeal were granted only damages). Lord Justice Sedley of the Court of Appeals explained the judicial circumstances: "Courts have done what they can, using such legal tools as were on hand, to stop the more outrageous invasions of individuals' privacy; but they have felt unable to articulate their measures as a discrete principle of law. . . . Nevertheless, we have reached a point at which it may be said with confidence that the law recognizes and will appropriately protect a right to personal privacy." Douglas v. Hello!, Ltd. [2001] Q.B. 967 at 997. *See also* Campbell v. Mirror Group Newspaper Ltd. [2004] UKHL 22 (supermodel Naomi Campbell sued publishers over photo- graphs taken when she was leaving a Narcotics Anonymous meeting). After a series of appeals, the declaration that there was no free-standing right to privacy under English law was made, but the House of Lords (then called the Law Lords) had to recognize the private information and fit it within a breach of confidence claim, explaining, "The continuing use of the phrase 'duty of confidence' and the description of the information as 'confidential' is not altogether comfortable. Information about an individual's private life would not, in ordinary usage, be called 'confidential.' The more natural description today is that such information is private. The essence of the tort is better

encapsulated now as misuse of private information." Campbell v. Mirror Group Newspaper Ltd. [2004] UKHL 22 at 14.

9. James E. Stanley, *Max Mosley and the English Right to Privacy*, 10 WASH. U. GLOBAL STUD. L. REV. 641 (2011).

10. *Id.*

11. *Id.*

12. *Id.*

13. *Id.*; *see also* Raymond Wacks, *Why There Will Never Be an English Common Law Privacy Tort, in* NEW DIMENSIONS IN PRIVACY LAW: INTERNATIONAL AND COMPARATIVE PERSPECTIVES 154 (Andrew T. Kenyon and Megan Richardson eds., 2010).

14. Michael Tugendhat, *The Data Protection Act of 1998 and the Media, in* THE YEARBOOK OF COPYRIGHT AND MEDIA LAW: VOLUME V: 2000 115, 120 (Eric M. Barendt, Alison Firth, Stephen Bate, Julia Palca, John Enser, and Thomas Gibbons eds., 2001).

15. HOUSE OF LORDS, EU DATA PROTECTION LAW: "RIGHT TO BE FORGOTTEN"?, EUROPEAN UNION COMMITTEE, 2ND REPORT OF SESSION 2014–15 (July 30, 2014), http://www.publications.parliament.uk/pa/ld201415/ldselect/ldeucom/40/40.pdf.

16. Wolfgang Kilian, *Germany, in* GLOBAL PRIVACY PROTECTION: THE FIRST GENERATION 80 (James B. Rule and Graham Greenleaf eds., 2008).

17. Paul M. Schwartz and Karl-Nikolaus Peifer, *Prosser's Privacy and the German Right of Personality: Are Four Privacy Torts Better than One Unitary Concept?*, 98 CAL. L. REV. 1925 (2010).

18. BGHZ 13, 334 = 7 NJW 1404 (1954).

19. BVerfGE 34, 269 = 26 NJW 1221 (1973).

20. *Id.* at 281.

21. BVerfGE 65, 1 at para. 154 of 15 (1983).

22. *Id.*

23. Wolfgang Kilian, *Germany, in* GLOBAL PRIVACY PROTECTION: THE FIRST GENERATION 80, 80–81 (James B. Rule and Graham Greenleaf eds., 2008).

24. BVerfGE 1 BvR 653/96 (1999).

25. *Id.*

26. C. von Hannover v. Germany [2004] ECHR no. 59320/00 (June 24, 2004).

27. Von Hannover v. Germany (no. 2) 40660/08 [2012] ECHR 228 (Feb. 7, 2012).

28. John Schwartz, *Two German Killers Demanding Anonymity Sue Wikipedia's Parent*, N.Y. TIMES (Nov. 12, 2009).

29. Lawrence Siry and Sandra Schmitz, *A Right to Be Forgotten? How Recent Developments in Germany May Affect the Internet Publishers in the US*, 3:1 EUR. J. L. & TECH. (2012), http://ejlt.org/article/viewFile/141/222%3E.

30. *Id.* (citing BGH, Decision of 10 Nov. 2009—VI ZR 217/08 (rainbow.at); Decisions of 15 Dec. 2009—VI ZR 227/08 and 228/08 (Deutschlandradio); Decisions of 9

Feb. 2010—VI ZR 243/08 and 244/08 (Spiegel online); Decisions of 20 Apr. 2010—VI ZR 245/08 and 246/08 (morgenweb.de)).

31. Franz Werro, *The Right to Inform v. the Right to Be Forgotten: A Transatlantic Clash, in* LIABILITY IN THE THIRD MILLENNIUM 285 (Aurelia Colombi Ciacchi, Christine Godt, Peter Rott, and Leslie Jane Smith eds., 2009).

32. *Id.*

33. Related ECtHR cases like Schwabe v. Austria, ECHR, 28/8/1992, and M.M. v. The United Kingdom, ECHR, 29/04/2013, are discussed in chapter 4.

34. AG v. W., BGE 122 III 449 (1996).

35. A. v. Journal de Genève et Gazette de Lausanne, 23 10/2003, 5C156/2003 (2003).

36. X. v. Société Suisse de Radio et de Télévision, BGE 109 II 353 (1983).

37. Jeanne M. Hauch, *Protecting Private Facts in France: The Warren & Brandeis Tort Is Alive and Well and Flourishing in Paris,* 68 TUL. L. REV. 1219, 1231 (1994).

38. Judgment of June 16, 1858, Trib. pr. inst. de la Seine, 1858 D.P. III 62 (Fr.) (*affaire Rachel*).

39. Jeanne M. Hauch, *Protecting Private Facts in France: The Warren & Brandeis Tort Is Alive and Well and Flourishing in Paris,* 68 TUL. L. REV. 1219, 1233–1235 (1994).

40. *Id.* at 1233.

41. James Q. Whitman, *The Two Western Cultures of Privacy: Dignity versus Liberty,* YALE L.J. 1151 (2004) (citing Dumas c. Liébert, CA Paris, May 25, 1867, 13 A.P.I.A.L. 247 (1867)).

42. *Id.* at 1171–1179.

43. Dumas, 13 A.P.I.A.L. at 249–250.

44. *Id.* at 250.

45. Judgment of July 12, 1966, Cass. civ. 2e, 1967 D.S. Jur. 181 (Fr.).

46. Statute No. 70–643 of July 17, 1970, J.O., July 10, 1970, at 6751 (Fr.)

47. Loi 78–17 du 6 janvier 1978 relative à l'informatique, aux fichiers et aux libertés (version consolidée au 27 août 2011) [Law 78–17 of January 6, 1978, on Information Technologies, Data Files, and Civil Liberties (consolidated version as of Aug. 27, 2011)], English version available on the CNIL website, at http://www.cnil.fr/fileadmin/documents/en/Act78–17VA.pdf.

48. MARIO VIOLA DE AZEVEDO CUNHA, MARKET INTEGRATION THROUGH DATA PROTECTION: AN ANALYSIS OF THE INSURANCE AND FINANCIAL INDUSTRIES IN THE EU 89 (2013).

49. Court of First Instance Paris, Feb. 15, 2012, Diana Z. / Google.

50. Elizabeth Flock, *Should We Have a Right to Be Forgotten Online?,* WASH. POST (Apr. 20, 2011), http://www.washingtonpost.com/blogs/blogpost/post/should-we-have-a-right-to-be-forgotten-online/2011/04/20/AF2iOPCE_blog.html.

51. Loi no. 2004–801 du 6 août 2004 relative à la protection des personnes physiques à l'égard des traîtements de données à carctère personnel physiques et modifiant la loi no. 78/17 du 6 janvier 1978.

52. BEUC (European Consumers' Organisation), *A Comprehensive Approach on Personal Data Protection in the European Union: European Commission's Communication* (Jan. 24, 2011), http://ec.europa.eu/justice/news/consulting_public/0006/contributions/organisations/beuc_en.pdf.

53. Giorgio Pino, *The Right to Personal Identity in Italian Private Law: Constitutional Interpretation and Judge-Made Rights*, in THE HARMONIZATION OF PRIVATE LAW IN EUROPE 225 (Mark Van Hoecke and Francois Ost eds., 2000).

54. *Id.*

55. Pangrazi e Silvetti c. Comitato Referendum (in Giur it. 1975, I, 2, 514).

56. Giorgio Pino, *The Right to Personal Identity in Italian Private Law: Constitutional Interpretation and Judge-Made Rights*, in THE HARMONIZATION OF PRIVATE LAW IN EUROPE 225, 235–236 (Mark Van Hoecke and Francois Ost eds., 2000).

57. Corte di Cassazione, I. Civ., n. 5259 (Oct. 18, 1984).

58. *Id.*

59. *Id.*

60. Pere Simón Castellano, *The Right to Be Forgotten under European Law: A Constitutional Debate*, 16 LEX ELECTRONICA (2012) (citing Reti telematiche a garantire il c.d. "diritto all'oblio" (Nov. 10, 2004), http://www.garanteprivacy.it/garante/doc.jsp?ID=1116068).

61. Italian Data Protection Authority, *Oblivion Rights*, doc. Web n. 1336892 (Nov. 9, 2005).

62. *Id.*

63. *Id.*

64. Corte di Cassazione, III Civ., n. 5525 (Apr. 5, 2012).

65. *Id.*

66. *Id.*

67. *Id.*

68. *Id.*

69. AEPD Decision procedure no. TD/00463/2007; procedure no. TD/01335/2008; and procedure no. TD/00627/2009.

70. Suzanne Daley, *On Its Own, Europe Backs Web Privacy Fights*, N.Y. TIMES (Aug. 9, 2011), http://www.nytimes.com/2011/08/10/world/europe/10spain.html?pagewanted=all&_r=0.

71. *Id.*

72. *Id.*

73. Elizabeth Flock, *Should We Have a Right to Be Forgotten Online?*, WASH. POST (Aug. 20, 2011), http://www.washingtonpost.com/blogs/blogpost/post/should-we-have-a-right-to-be-forgotten-online/2011/04/20/AF2iOPCE_blog.html.

74. Claire Davenport, *Spain Refers Google Privacy Complaints to EU's Top Court*, REUTERS (Mar. 2, 2012), http://www.reuters.com/article/2012/03/02/us-eu-google-idUSTRE8211DP20120302.

75. *Id.*

76. European Commission, *European Commission Sets Out Strategy to Strengthen EU Data Protection Rules*, press release, IP/10/1462 (Nov. 4, 2010).

77. European Commission, *Proposal for a Regulation of the European Parliament and of the Council*, COM(2012) 11 final (Jan. 25, 2012) (DP Regulation), http://ec.europa.eu/justice/data-protection/document/review2012/com_2012_11_en.pdf.

78. Case C-131/12, Google Spain SL and Google Inc. v. Agencia Española de Protección de Datos (AEPD) and Mario Costeja González (Euro. Ct. of Justice May 13, 2014).

79. *Id.* at para. 4 (citing Art. 2 of Directive 95/46).

80. *Id.* at para. 95.

81. *Id.* at para. 88.

82. *Id.* at para. 90.

83. *Id.* at para. 97.

84. *Id.* at para. 90.

85. *Id.* at para. 65.

86. *Id.* at paras. 36–37.

87. Jennifer Urban and Laura Quilter, *Efficient Process or "Chilling Effects"? Takedown Notices under Section 512 of the Digital Millennium Copyright Act*, 22 SANTA CLARA COMPUTER & HIGH TECH. L.J. 621 (2006).

88. The database only included seven counternotices, which is not an accurate representation of responses to the takedown notices, as these are automatically contributed to the Chilling Effect database.

89. DANIEL J. SOLOVE, THE FUTURE OF REPUTATION: GOSSIP, RUMOR, AND PRIVACY ON THE INTERNET 122 (2007).

90. Case C-131/12, Opinion of Advocate General Jääskinen, para. 78 (June 25, 2013).

91. *Id.* at para. 79.

92. *Id.* at para. 81.

93. *Id.* at para. 108.

94. At that point in 2010, the closest approximation was defined as "the right of individuals to have their data fully removed when they are no longer needed for the purposes for which they were collected or when he or she withdraws consent or when the storage period consented to has expired." *Comprehensive Approach on Personal Data Protection*, COM (2010) 609, Brussels (Nov. 4, 2010).

95. Dave Lee, *Google Removing BBC Link Was "Not a Good Judgement,"* BBC NEWS (July 3, 2014), http://www.bbc.com/news/technology-28144406.

96. *Google Sets Up "Right to Be Forgotten" Form after EU Ruling*, BBC NEWS (May 30, 2014), http://www.bbc.com/news/technology-27631001.

97. For a complete overview of the European Commission's work, see European Commission, *Commission Proposes a Comprehensive Reform of the Data Protection Rules* (Jan. 25, 2012), http://ec.europa.eu/justice/newsroom/data-protection/news/120125_en.htm.

98. Viviane Reding, *Speech at New Frontiers for Social Media Marketing Conference, EU Data Protection Reform and Social Media: Encouraging Citizens' Trust and Creating New Opportunities* (Nov. 29, 2011) (transcript available at http://europa.eu/rapid/press-release_SPEECH-11–827_en.htm).

99. DP Regulation, LIBE edits.

100. The Proposal (Recitals 47–48) also requires that data subjects are informed of their right to erasure and that modalities should be provided to exercise it.

101. *See also* Recital 54, which is almost identical.

102. Such laws should, however, "meet an objective of public interest, respect the essence of the right to the protection of personal data and be proportionate to the legitimate aim pursued" (Art. 17(3)(d)).

103. Use, in these cases, should be restricted to processing "for purposes of proof, or with the data subject's consent, or for the protection of the rights of another natural or legal person or for an objective of public interest" (Art. 17, paras. 4–5).

104. OECD Doc. (C 58 final) (Oct. 1, 1980).

105. Council of Europe, *Convention for the Protection of Individuals with Regard to Automatic Processing of Personal Data* (1981), http://www.conventions.coe.int/Treaty/en/Treaties/Html/108.htm.

106. OECD Doc. (C 58 final) (Oct. 1, 1980).

107. White House, National Strategy for Trusted Identities in Cyberspace, Enhancing Online Choice, Efficiency, Security, and Privacy appendix A (2011), http://www.whitehouse.gov/sites/default/files/rss_viewer/NSTICstrategy_041511.pdf.

108. UN General Assembly resolution 2200A (XXI) (Dec. 16, 1966), implemented Mar. 23, 1976.

109. Human Rights Committee, *General Comment 16* (23rd sess., 1988), Compilation of General Comments and General Recommendations Adopted by Human Rights Treaty Bodies, U.N. Doc. HRI/GEN/1/Rev.1 at 21 (1994), n. 208, para.10 (emphasis added).

2. FORGETTING MADE IMPOSSIBLE

1. Cease-and-desist letter to the Wikimedia Foundation, Inc. (Oct. 27, 2009), available at http://www.wired.com/images_blogs/threatlevel/2009/11/stopp.pdf.

2. Jennifer Granick, *Convicted Murderer to Wikipedia: Shhh!*, Electronic Frontier Foundation (Nov. 10, 2009), https://www.eff.org/deep-links/2009/11/murderer-wikipedia-shhh.

3. Griswold v. Connecticut, 381 U.S. 479, 484 (1965).

4. Rex D. Glensy, *The Right to Dignity*, 43 Colum. Hum. Rts. L. Rev. 65, 86 (2011).

5. Samuel D. Warren and Louis D. Brandeis, *The Right to Privacy*, 4 Harv. L. Rev. 193, 207 (1890).

6. William Prosser, *Privacy*, 48 Cal. L. Rev. 383 (1960).

7. Paul M. Schwartz and Karl-Nikolaus Peifer, *Prosser's Privacy and the German Right of Personality: Are Four Privacy Torts Better than One Unitary Concept?*, 98 CAL. L. REV. 1925, 1942 (2010).

8. Frank Easterbrook, *Approaches to Judicial Review, in* POLITICS AND THE CONSTITUTION: THE NATURE OF AND EXTENT OF INTERPRETATION 17, 29 (Judith A. Baer ed., 1990).

9. New York Times Co. v. Sullivan, 376 U.S. 254 (1964).

10. Curtis Publishing Co. v. Butts, 388 U.S. 130 (1967); Associated Press v. Walker, 388 U.S. 130 (1967).

11. Rosenbloom v. Metromedia, Inc., 403 U.S. 29 (1971).

12. Wendy Seltzer, *Free Speech Unmoored in Copyright's Safe Harbor: Chilling Effects of the DMCA on the First Amendment*, 24 HARV. J. L. & TECH. 171, 177 (2010).

13. Jennifer Urban and Laura Quilter, *Efficient Process or "Chilling Effects"? Takedown Notices under Section 512 of the Digital Millennium Copyright Act*, 22 SANTA CLARA COMPUTER & HIGH TECH. L.J. 621 (2006).

14. Restatement (Second) of Torts § 652D cmt. d (2012).

15. Melvin v. Reid, 112 Cal. App. 285, 292 (Cal. App. 1931).

16. Briscoe v. Reader's Digest Assoc., 483 P.2d 34 (Cal. 1971).

17. HAROLD L. NELSON AND DWIGHT L. TEETER JR., LAW OF MASS COMMUNICATIONS 199 (2d ed. 1973).

18. New York Times Co. v. Sullivan, 376 U.S. 254 (1964).

19. Brewer v. Memphis Publishing Co., 626 F.2d 1238 (5th Cir. 1980), *cert. denied*, 452 U.S. 962 (1981).

20. Street v. National Broadcasting Co., 512 F. Supp. 398 (E.D. Tenn. 1977), *aff'd*, 645 F.2d 1227 (6th Cir.), *cert. dismissed*, 102 S. Ct. 667 (1981).

21. Street v. National Broadcasting Co., 645 F. 2d 1227 (6th Cir. 1981), *cert. dismissed*, 102 S. Ct. 667 (1981).

22. Sidis v. F-R Pub. Corporation, 113 F.2d 806, 809 (2nd Cir. 1940).

23. Estill v. Hearst Publishing Co., 186 F.2d 1017, 1020 (7th Cir. 1951).

24. Perry v. Columbia Broadcasting Sys., 499 F.2d 797, 799 (7th Cir. 1974), *cert. denied*, 419 U.S. 883 (1974).

25. Doe v. Methodist Hosp., 690 N.E.2d 681 (Ind. 1997).

26. Cox Broadcasting Corp. v. Cohn, 420 U.S. 469 (1975).

27. Florida Star v. B.J.F., 491 U.S. 524 (1989).

28. Cox Broadcasting Corp. v. Cohn, 420 U.S. 469, 487 (1975).

29. Thornhill v. Alabama, 310 U.S. 88, 102 (1940).

30. Time, Inc. v. Hill, 385 U.S. 374, 388 (1967).

31. Bartnicki v. Vopper, 532 U.S. 514, 534 (2001).

32. Harvey Purtz v. Rajesh Srinivasan, No. 10CESC02211 (Fresno Co. Small Cl. Ct. Jan. 11, 2011), available at http://banweb.co.fresno.ca.us/cprodsnp/ck_public_qry_doct.
cp_dktrpt_frames?backto=P&case_id=10CESC02211&begin_date=&end_date=

(text of the Statement of Decision, including the judge's personal comments, can be found in the docket entry listed for Jan. 11, 2011).

33. Martin v. Hearst Corp., Case 13–3315, 5 (2nd Cir., Jan. 28, 2015).

34. *Id.* at 10.

35. G.D. v. Kenny, 15 A.3d 275, 302 (N.J. 2011).

36. Doe v. MySpace, Inc., 474 F. Supp. 2d 843 (W.D. Tex. 2007).

37. Priscilla Regan, *The United States, in* GLOBAL PRIVACY PROTECTION: THE FIRST GENERATION 50, 51 (James B. Rule and Graham Greenleaf eds., 2008).

38. *Id.* 50–78.

39. *Id.* at 78.

40. Jeffrey Rosen, *The Delete Squad,* NEW REPUBLIC (Apr. 29, 2013).

41. These workarounds are often performed by parents helping their children create social media accounts. danah boyd, Eszter Hargittai, Jason Schultz, and John Palfrey, *Why Parents Help Their Children Lie to Facebook about Age: Unintended Consequences of the "Children's Online Privacy Protection Act,"* 16 FIRST MONDAY (2011), http://firstmonday.org/ojs/index.php/fm/article/view/3850.

42. Cal. Bus. & Prof. Code, §§ 22580–22582.

43. Oklahoma Publishing Co. v. District Court, Oklahoma Cty., 430 U.S. 308 (1977).

44. Smith v. Daily Mail Publishing Co., 443 U.S. 97 (1979).

45. Hubbard v. Journal Publishing Co., 368 P.2d 147 (N.M. 1962).

46. *See* stopbullying.gov for organizations, policies, laws, and outreach.

47. Walter Olson, *Facebook Opens Takedown Hotline for Public School Officials,* CATO INSTITUTE (Oct. 3, 2013), http://www.cato.org/blog/ facebook-opens-takedown-hotline-public-school-officials.

48. Albany County Local Law No. 11 of 2010, § 1.

49. People v. Marquan M., 24 N.Y.3d 1, 9 (N.Y. 2014).

50. *Id.* at 12–15.

51. Danielle Keats Citron and Mary Anne Franks, *Criminalizing Revenge Porn,* 49 WAKE FOREST L. REV. 345 (2014); *see* EndRevengePorn.org for up-to-date statistics and initiatives.

52. N.J. Stat. Ann. § 2C:14–9 (West 2010).

53. Star-Ledger Staff, *Dharun Ravi Sentenced to Jail in Tyler Clementi Webcam Spying Case,* NJ.COM (May 21, 2012), http://www.nj.com/news/index.ssf/2012/05/ dharun_ravi_sentenced_to_jail.html.

54. Antigone Books v. Horne, ACLU Compl. (filed Sept. 23, 2014), available at https:// www.aclu.org/sites/default/files/assets/az_nude_picture_complaint_0.pdf.

55. David Segal, *Mugged by a Mug Shot Online,* N.Y. TIMES (Oct. 5, 2013).

56. Oregon HB 3467.

57. European Commission, *Safer Internet Day 2009: Commission Starts Campaign against Cyber-Bullying,* press release, MEMO/09/58 (Feb. 10, 2009).

58. Law Reform Commission, Ireland, *Issues Paper on Cyber-Crime Affecting Personal Safety, Privacy and Reputation Including Cyber-Bullying,* LRC IP 6–2014 (2014).

59. Ministry of Justice and the Rt. Hon. Chris Grayling MP, *New Law to Tackle Revenge Porn*, press release (Oct. 12, 2014).

60. Tribunal de Commerce de Paris, 28 Jan. 2014, X v. Google Inc.

61. Lawrence Lessig, Code: Version 2.0 124, 125 (2006).

62. Lauren B. Movius and Nathalie Krup, *U.S. and EU Privacy Policy: Comparison of Regulatory Approaches*, 3 Int'l J. Comm. 169, 171–172 (2009).

63. Reputation.com, *Suppress Negative Content Online: ReputationDefender*, https://www.reputation.com/reputationdefender (accessed June 28, 2015).

64. Reputation systems compute a reputation score for a set of objects on the basis of opinions expressed by other people on the objects. Kristiina Karvonen, Sanna Shibasaki, Sofia Nunes, Puneet Kaur, and Olli Immonen, *Visual Nudges for Enhancing the Use and Produce of Reputation Information, in* Proc. CEUR Workshop (2010), http://ceur-ws.org/Vol-612/paper1.pdf.

65. *See, e.g.*, Reputation.com, *A Bad Online Reputation Could Cost You the Election*, http://www.reputation.com/reputationwatch/articles/a-bad-online-reputation-could-cost-you-the-election (accessed June 28, 2015).

66. *See generally* David Brin, The Transparent Society: Will Technology Force Us to Choose between Privacy and Freedom? (1999).

67. For example, "In Japan, social networking accounts are almost always pseudonymous. People rarely use their real names, so if your real friend is someone who is not a fake friend, you share your pseudonym. That way, your real friends have access to the whole account, but employers and strangers never do, and you can always walk away from your pseudonym." Jeffrey Rosen, *Free Speech, Privacy, and the Web That Never Forgets*, 9 J. on Telecomm. & High Tech. L. 345, 353–354 (2011) (quoting and citing Hiroko Tabuchi, *Facebook Wins Relatively Few Friends in Japan*, N.Y. Times B1 (Jan. 10, 2011), who finds that in a "survey of 2,130 Japanese mobile Web users . . . , 89 percent of respondents said they were reluctant to disclose their real names on the Web").

68. Quoted in Viktor Mayer-Schönberger, Delete: The Virtue of Forgetting in the Digital Age 154 (2009).

69. Quoted in Jessica Winter, *The Advantages of Amnesia*, Boston.com (Sept. 23, 2007), http://www.boston.com/news/education/higher/articles/2007/09/23/the_advantages_of_amnesia/?page=full.

70. Jeffrey Rosen, *Free Speech, Privacy, and the Web That Never Forgets*, 9 J. on Telecomm. & High Tech. L. 345, 354 (2011).

71. Viktor Mayer-Schönberger, Delete: The Virtue of Forgetting in the Digital Age 155 (2009).

72. Jeffrey H. Reiman, *Driving to the Panopticon: A Philosophical Exploration of the Risks to Privacy Posed by the Highway Technology of the Future*, 11 Santa Clara Computer & High Tech. L.J. 27, 36 (1995).

73. Ruth Gavison, *Privacy and the Limits of Law*, 89 Yale L.J. 421, 454 (1980).

74. Viktor Mayer-Schönberger, Delete: The Virtue of Forgetting in the Digital Age 155 (2009).

75. *Id.*

76. Roy F. Baumeister, Ellen Bratslavsky, Catrin Finkenauer, and Kathleen D. Vohs, *Bad Is Stronger than Good*, 5 Rev. Gen. Psychol. 323 (2001).

77. Hara Estroff Marano, *Our Brain's Negative Bias*, Psychology Today (June 20, 2003), http://www.psychologytoday.com/articles/200306/our-brains-negative-bias.

78. Laura Brandimarte, *Discounting the Past: Bad Weighs Heavier than Good* (2010), unpublished manuscript, available at http://heinz.cmu.edu/research/384full.pdf (addressing how information related to past events and retrieved today is discounted and evaluated by the reader).

79. Although this research area is still producing unclear and conflicting findings, questions surrounding online self-censorship have increased dramatically. For an example of recent research on self-censorship, see Sauvik Das and Adam Kramer, *Self-Censorship on Facebook*, Proc. of Seventh International AAAI Conference on Weblogs and Social Media (2013) (finding that 71 percent of Facebook users engage in self-censorship); Keith Hampton, Lee Rainie, Weixu Lu, Maria Dwyer, Inyoung Shin, and Kristen Purcell, *Social Media and the "Spiral of Silence,"* Pew Research Center (Aug. 26, 2014), http://www.pewinternet.org/files/2014/08/PI_Social-networks-and-debate_082614.pdf. (finding that users were twice as likely to join discussions surrounding the Snowden-NSA controversy if they perceived that their network agreed with their opinion and that while 86 percent of Americans were willing to discuss the controversy in person, only 42 percent were willing to do so on Facebook or Twitter).

80. Elisabeth Noelle Neumann, *The Spiral of Silence: A Theory of Public Opinion*, 24 J. Commun. 43 (1974).

81. Liam J. Bannon, *Forgetting as a Feature, Not a Bug: The Duality of Memory and Implications for Ubiquitous Computing*, 2 CoDesign 3, 11 (2006).

82. *Id.*

83. Ann Cavoukian and Jeff Jonas, *Privacy by Design in the Age of Big Data*, Privacy by Design (2012), http://privacybydesign.ca/content/uploads/2012/06/pbd-big_data.pdf.

84. Gillian Tan, Douglas MacMillan, and Jack Marshall, *News and Ads to Debut on Snapchat*, Wall St. J. (Aug. 19, 2014), http://online.wsj.com/articles/snapchat-discussing-new-content-service-with-advertisers-and-media-firms-1408486739.

85. Franziska Roesner, Brian T. Gill, and Tadayoshi Kohno, *Sex, Lies, or Kittens? Investigating the Use of Snapchat's Self-Destructing Messages*, 8437 Financial Cryptography and Data Security 64 (2014).

86. *Id.*

87. Asimina Vasalou and Jeremy Pitt, *Reinventing Forgiveness: A Formal Investigation of Moral Facilitation*, in TRUST MANAGEMENT, THIRD INTERNATIONAL CONFERENCE, ITRUST 2005 146 (Peter Herrmann, Valérie Issarny, and Simon Shiu eds., 2005).

88. *Id.* at 147–149, 156.

89. *Id.* at 150, 151.

90. *Id.* at 151.

91. *Id.* at 151–153.

92. *Id.* at 154.

93. Stephen Marsh and Pamela Briggs, *Examining Trust, Forgiveness and Regret as Computational Concepts*, in COMPUTING WITH SOCIAL TRUST 9 (Jennifer Golbeck ed., 2009).

94. *Id.* at 31–37.

95. VIKTOR MAYER-SCHÖNBERGER, DELETE: THE VIRTUE OF FORGETTING IN THE DIGITAL AGE 171–173 (2009).

3. INNOVATING PRIVACY

1. ALAN F. WESTIN, PRIVACY AND FREEDOM 7 (1967).

2. Samuel D. Warren and Louis D. Brandeis, *The Right to Privacy*, 4 HARV. L. REV. 193 (1890).

3. JUDITH WAGNER DECEW, IN PURSUIT OF PRIVACY (1997).

4. Olmstead v. U.S., 277 U.S. 438, 478 (1928) (dissent).

5. Polly Sprenger, *Sun on Privacy: "Get Over It,"* WIRED (Jan. 26, 1999).

6. Alan F. Westin, *Science, Privacy, and Freedom: Issues and Proposals for the 1970's*, 66 COLUMBIA L. REV. 1205, 1214 (1966).

7. *Id.*

8. danah boyd, *Why Youth (Heart) Social Network Sites: The Role of Networked Publics in Teenage Social Life*, in MACARTHUR FOUNDATION SERIES ON DIGITAL LEARNING—YOUTH, IDENTITY, AND DIGITAL MEDIA 119, 132 (David Buckingham ed., 2008).

9. George Doe, *With Genetic Testing, I Gave My Parents the Gift of Divorce*, VOX (Sept. 9, 2014), http://www.vox.com/2014/9/9/5975653/with-genetic-testing-i-gave-my-parents-the-gift-of-divorce-23andme.

10. *Id.*

11. Paul Ohm, *Broken Promises of Privacy: Responding to the Surprising Failure of Anonymization*, 57 UCLA L. REV. 1701 (2010).

12. Ellen Nakashima, *Feeling Betrayed, Facebook Users Force Site to Honor Their Privacy*, WASH. POST (Nov. 30, 2007), http://www.washingtonpost.com/wp-dyn/content/article/2007/11/29/AR2007112902503.html.

13. Alessandro Acquisti and Jens Grossklags, *Privacy Attitudes and Privacy Behavior*, in ECONOMICS OF INFORMATION SECURITY 165, 174–175 (L. Jean Camp and Stephen Lewis eds., 2004).

14. Daniel J. Solove, *Privacy Self-Management and the Consent Dilemma*, 126 HARV. L. REV. 1880 (2013).
15. Zoe Ruderman, *The First Ever Live-Tweeted Breakup*, COSMOPOLITAN (Nov. 9, 2011).
16. Charles Duhigg, *How Companies Learn Your Secrets*, N.Y. TIMES (Feb. 16, 2012).
17. Patricia A. Norberg, *The Privacy Paradox: Personal Information Disclosure Intentions versus Behaviors*, 41 J. CONSUMER AFF. 100 (2007).
18. Aleecia M. McDonald and Lorrie Faith Cranor, *The Cost of Reading Privacy Policies*, 4 ISJLP 543 (2008).
19. Helen Nissenbaum, *A Contextual Approach to Privacy Online*, 140 DAEDALUS 32 (2011), http://www.amacad.org/publications/daedalus/11_fall_nissenbaum.pdf.
20. Alessandro Acquisti and Jens Grossklags, *Privacy Attitudes and Privacy Behavior*, *in* ECONOMICS OF INFORMATION SECURITY 165 (L. Jean Camp and Stephen Lewis eds., 2004).
21. Robert C. Post, *The Social Foundations of Privacy: Community and Self in the Common Law Tort*, 77 CALIF. L. REV. 957, 959 (1989).
22. PRISCILLA M. REGAN, LEGISLATING PRIVACY: TECHNOLOGY, SOCIAL VALUES, AND PUBLIC POLICY 23 (1995).
23. Samuel D. Warren and Louis D. Brandeis, *The Right to Privacy*, 4 HARV. L. REV. 193 (1890).
24. Ruth Gavison, *Privacy and the Limits of Law*, 89 YALE L.J. 421, 423 (1980).
25. ALAN F. WESTIN, PRIVACY AND FREEDOM 33–34 (1967).
26. Neil M. Richards, *Intellectual Privacy*, 87 TEX. L. REV. 387 (2008).
27. Charles Fried, *Privacy*, 77 YALE L.J. 475, 482 (1968).
28. DANIEL J. SOLOVE, UNDERSTANDING PRIVACY (2008).
29. Helen Nissenbaum, *Privacy as Contextual Integrity*, 79 WASH. L. REV. 119 (2004).
30. *Id.* at 129–157.
31. Noëmi Manders-Huits and Jeroen van den Hoven, *Moral Identification in Identity Management Systems*, *in* THE FUTURE OF IDENTITY IN THE INFORMATION SOCIETY 77, 86 (Simone Fischer-Hübner, Penny Duquenoy, Albin Zuccato, and Leonardo Martuc eds., 2008).
32. Bruce Cockburn, *The Trouble with Normal*, *on* THE TROUBLE WITH NORMAL (True North 1983).
33. JEFFREY ROSEN, THE UNWANTED GAZE: THE DESTRUCTION OF PRIVACY IN AMERICA 210 (2000).
34. J. David Velleman, *The Genesis of Shame*, 30 PHIL. & PUB. AFF. 27, 37 (2001).
35. Paul Freund, *Address to the American Law Institute*, *in* PROCEEDINGS OF THE 52ND ANNUAL MEETING OF THE AMERICAN LAW INSTITUTE 42–43 (1975).
36. Stanley I. Benn, *Privacy, Freedom, and Respect for Persons*, *in* PRIVACY, NOMOS XIII: YEARBOOK OF THE AMERICAN SOCIETY FOR POLITICAL AND

LEGAL PHILOSOPHY 1, 24 (J. Ronald Pennock and John W. Chapman eds., 1971).

37. IRWIN ALTMAN, THE ENVIRONMENT AND SOCIAL BEHAVIOR: PRIVACY, PERSONAL SPACE, TERRITORY, AND CROWDING 50 (1975).

38. Julie E. Cohen, *What Privacy Is For*, 126 HARV. L. REV. 1904, 1906 (2013).

39. JULIE E. COHEN, CONFIGURING THE NETWORKED SELF: LAW, CODE, AND THE PLAY OF EVERYDAY PRACTICE 239 (2012).

40. Woodrow Hartzog and Frederic Stutzman, *The Case for Online Obscurity*, 101 CAL. L. REV. 1 (2013).

41. Paul Ohm, *Good Enough Privacy*, 2008 U. CHI. LEGAL F. 1 (2008).

42. Rolf H. Weber, *The Right to Be Forgotten: More than a Pandora's Box?*, 2 JIPITEC 120, 121 (2011), http://www.jipitec.eu/issues/jipitec-2-2-2011/3084/jipitec%202%20-%20a%20-%20weber.pdf.

43. For a discussion of the difference, see Antoinette Rouvroy and Yves Poullet, *The Right to Informational Self-Determination and the Value of Self-Development: Reassessing the Importance of Privacy for Democracy, in* REINVENTING DATA PROTECTION? 45 (Serge Gutwirth, Yves Poullet, Paul de Hert, Cécile de Terwangne, and Sjaak Nouwt eds., 2009).

44. Bert-Jaap Koops, *Forgetting Footprints, Shunning Shadows: A Critical Analysis of the "Right to Be Forgotten" in Big Data Practice*, 8:3 SCRIPTED 1 (2011).

45. Paul A. Bernal, *A Right to Delete?*, 2:2 EUR. J. L. & TECH. (2011), http://ejlt.org/article/view/75/144.

46. Jef Ausloos, *The "Right to Be Forgotten"—Worth Remembering?*, 28 COMPUTER L. & SEC. REV. 143 (2012).

47. Paul A. Bernal, *A Right to Delete?*, 2:2 EUR. J. L. & TECH. (2011), http://ejlt.org/article/view/75/144.

48. Jef Ausloos, *The "Right to Be Forgotten"—Worth Remembering?*, 28 COMPUTER L. & SEC. REV. 143, 143 (2012).

49. Napoleon Xanthoulis, *Conceptualising a Right to Oblivion in the Digital World: A Human Rights–Based Approach*, SSRN WORKING PAPER SERIES (2012), http://ssrn.com/abstract=2064503 or http://dx.doi.org/10.2139/ssrn.2064503.

50. Norberto Nuno Gomes de Andrade, *Oblivion: The Right to Be Different . . . from Oneself—Reproposing the Right to Be Forgotten*, 13 IDP 122, 131 (2012).

51. Napoleon Xanthoulis, *Conceptualising a Right to Oblivion in the Digital World: A Human Rights-Based Approach*, SSRN WORKING PAPER SERIES (2012), http://ssrn.com/abstract=2064503 or http://dx.doi.org/10.2139/ssrn.2064503 (citing James Griffin, *First Steps in an Account of Human Rights*, 9 EUR. J. PHIL. 306 (2001)).

52. Norberto Nuno Gomes de Andrade, *Oblivion: The Right to Be Different . . . from Oneself—Reproposing the Right to Be Forgotten*, 13 IDP 122, 125 (2012), http://ssrn.com/abstract=2064503 or http://dx.doi.org/10.2139/ssrn.2064503.

53. *Id.* at 126.
54. Quinton v. Peirce & Anor [2009] EWHC 912 (QB), para. 92.
55. *Id.* at para. 93.
56. Law Society, Hine Solicitors & Kevin McGrath v. Rick Kordowski [2011] EWHC 3185 (QB), para. 96.
57. *Id.* at para. 100.

4. DIGITAL INFORMATION STEWARDSHIP

1. Jeffrey Rosen, *The Web Means the End of Forgetting*, N.Y. TIMES MAGAZINE (July 21, 2010), http://www.nytimes.com/2010/07/25/magazine/25privacy-t2.html?pagewanted=all.
2. Bill Barnes, *Nothing but Net*, SLATE (Feb. 28, 1997), http://www.slate.com/articles/technology/webhead/1997/02/nothing_but_net.html.
3. ROY ROSENZWEIG, CLIO WIRED: THE FUTURE OF THE PAST IN THE DIGITAL AGE 8 (2011).
4. JEFF ROTHENBERG, AVOIDING TECHNOLOGICAL QUICKSAND 2 (1998).
5. ROY ROSENZWEIG, CLIO WIRED: THE FUTURE OF THE PAST IN THE DIGITAL AGE 9 (2011).
6. *Public Session: Panel Discussion, in* TIME & BITS: MANAGING DIGITAL CONTINUITY 36, 47 (Margaret MacLean and Ben H. Davis eds., 1998).
7. Brewster Kahle, *Preserving the Internet*, SCIENTIFIC AMERICAN (July 27, 1998), http://web.archive.org/web/19980627072808/http://www.sciam.com/0397issue/0397kahle.html; Lisa Rein, *Brewster Kahle on the Internet Archive and People's Technology*, O'REILLY P2P.COM (Jan. 22, 2004), http://openp2p.com/pub/a/p2p/2004/01/22/kahle.html; Internet Archive, *Wayback Machine: Frequently Asked Questions*, https://www.archive.org/about/faqs.php (accessed June 6, 2015).
8. Wallace Koehler, *A Longitudinal Study of Web Pages Continued: A Consideration of Document Persistence*, 9:2 INFO. RESEARCH paper 174 (2004), http://informationr.net/ir/9-2/paper174.html.
9. Carol Anne Germain, *URLs: Uniform Resource Locators or Unreliable Resource Locators*, 60 C. AND RESEARCH LIBR. 359 (2000); Mei Kobayashi and Koichi Takeda, *Information Retrieval on the Web*, 32 ACM COMPUTING SURVEYS 144 (2000); Mary K. Taylor and Diane Hudson, *"Linkrot" and the Usefulness of Web Site Bibliographies*, 39 REF. & USER SERV. Q. 273 (2000).
10. S. Mary P. Benhow, *File Not Found: The Problem of Changing URLs for the World Wide Web*, 8 INTERNET RESEARCH: NETWORK APPLICATIONS & POL'Y 247, 248 (1998).
11. Mary Rumsey, *Runaway Train: Problems of Permanence, Accessibility, and Stability in the Use of Web Resources in Law Review Citations*, 94 LAW LIBR. J. 27, 35 (2002).

12. Wallace Koehler, *A Longitudinal Study of Web Pages Continued: A Consideration of Document Persistence*, 9:2 INFO. RESEARCH paper 174 (2004), http://informationr.net/ir/9-2/paper174.html.

13. *Id.*

14. *Id.*

15. Junghoo Cho and Hector Garcia-Molina, *The Evolution of the Web and Implications for an Incremental Crawler, in* PROC. OF THE 26TH INT'L CONF. ON VERY LARGE DATA BASES 200 (2000).

16. *Id.* at 205.

17. *Id.* at 208.

18. Brian E. Brewington and George Cybenko, *How Dynamic Is the Web?*, 33 COMPUTER NETWORKS 257, 258–259, 261 (2000).

19. Dennis Fetterly, Mark Manasse, Marc Najork, and Janet L. Wiener, *A Large-Scale Study of the Evolution of Web Pages*, 34 SOFTWARE PRAC. & EXPERIENCE 213 (2004).

20. Daniel Gomes and Mario J. Silva, *Modelling Information Persistence on the Web, in* PROC. OF THE 6TH INT'L CONF. ON WEB ENGINEERING 193, 193 (2006).

21. *Id.*

22. *Id.* at 195.

23. *Id.* at 194–195.

24. *Id.* at 196–197.

25. *Id.*

26. *Id.* at 199.

27. Jinyoung Kim and Viktor R. Carvalho, *An Analysis of Time Stability in Web Search Results, in* PROC. OF THE 33RD EUROPEAN CONF. ON ADVANCES IN INFO. RETRIEVAL 466 (2011).

28. Rick Weiss, *On the Web, Research Work Proves Ephemeral*, WASH. POST (Nov. 24, 2003), http://faculty.missouri.edu/glaserr/205fo3/Article_WebPub.html.

29. Jonathan Zittrain, Kendra Albert, and Lawrence Lessig, *Perma: Scoping and Addressing the Problem of Link and Reference Rot in Legal Citations*, 14:2 LEGAL INFO. MANAGEMENT 88 (2014).

30. Perma, *About*, https://perma.cc/about (accessed June 12, 2015).

31. Wallace Koehler, *A Longitudinal Study of Web Pages Continued: A Consideration of Document Persistence*, 9:2 INFO. RESEARCH paper 174 (2004), http://informationr.net/ir/9-2/paper174.html.

32. Stuart I. Feldman, *A Conversation with Brewster Kahle*, 2 QUEUE 24, 26 (June 2004), http://queue.acm.org/detail.cfm?id=1016993.

33. *Id.*

34. Brewster Kahle, *Preserving the Internet*, SCIENTIFIC AMERICAN (July 27, 1998), http://web.archive.org/web/19980627072808/http://www.sciam.com/0397issue/0397kahle.html ("To address these worries, we let authors exclude their works from the archive. We are also considering allowing researchers to

obtain broad censuses of the archive data instead of individual documents—one could count the total number of references to pachyderms on the Web, for instance, but not look at a specific elephant home page. These measures, we hope, will suffice to allay immediate concerns about privacy and intellectual-property rights. Over time, the issues addressed in setting up the Internet Archive might help resolve the larger policy debates on intellectual property and privacy by testing concepts such as fair use on the Internet.").

35. *The Social Network* (Columbia Pictures 2010).

36. Holman W. Jenkins Jr., *Google and the Search for the Future*, WALL ST. J. (Aug. 14, 2010), http://online.wsj.com/article/SB1000142405274870490110457542329409 9527212.html.

37. JONATHAN ZITTRAIN, THE FUTURE OF THE INTERNET . . . AND HOW TO STOP IT 228 (2009).

38. John Hendel, *In Europe, a Right to Be Forgotten Trumps the Memory of the Internet*, ATLANTIC (Feb. 3, 2011).

39. GORDON BELL AND JIM GEMMELL, TOTAL RECALL: HOW THE E-MEMORY REVOLUTION WILL CHANGE EVERYTHING (2009).

40. VIKTOR MAYER-SCHÖNBERGER, DELETE: THE VIRTUE OF FORGETTING IN THE DIGITAL AGE 5 (2009).

41. GORDON BELL AND JIM GEMMELL, TOTAL RECALL: HOW THE E-MEMORY REVOLUTION WILL CHANGE EVERYTHING 159 (2009).

42. VIKTOR MAYER-SCHÖNBERGER, DELETE: THE VIRTUE OF FORGETTING IN THE DIGITAL AGE 57 (2009).

43. GORDON BELL AND JIM GEMMELL, TOTAL RECALL: HOW THE E-MEMORY REVOLUTION WILL CHANGE EVERYTHING 56 (2009).

44. The old "online diary" was similar to a blogging program with a file system that allowed for edits and deletions. It must be noted that after the movie's success, it was dug up and can be found at http://www.scribd.com/doc/538697/Mark-Zuckerbergs-Online-Diary.

45. Sumit Paul-Choudhury, *Digital Legacy: The Fate of Your Online Soul*, NEW SCIENTIST (May 15, 2012), http://www.newscientist.com/article/mg21028091.400-digital-legacy-the-fate-of-your-online-soul.html.

46. *Id.*

47. Lee Moran and Beth Stebner, *Now FBI Launch Investigation into Founder of "Revenge Porn" Site Is Anyone Up?*, DAILY MAIL (May 23, 2012), http://www.dailymail.co.uk/news/article-2148522/Hunter-Moore-founder-revenge-porn-site-Is-Anyone-Up-investigated-FBI.html.

48. *Id.*

49. *Id.*

50. *College Gossip Website Shuts Down, Citing Economy*, USA TODAY (Feb. 5, 2009), http://www.usatoday.com/tech/webguide/Internetlife/2009–02–05-juicycampus_N.htm.

51. Gayle Fee and Laura Raposa, *Caitlin Davis' Life Is Not So Cheery Now*, BOSTON HERALD (Nov. 5, 2008), http://bostonherald.com/track/inside_track/view/2008_11_05_Caitlin_Davis_booted_from_Patriots__cheering_squad.

52. David Frankel, *The Excavator: Creator or Destroyer?*, 67 ANTIQUITY 875 (Dec. 1993).

53. Society of American Archivists, *Code of Ethics for Archivists*, SAA Council Approval/Endorsement (Feb. 2005), http://www2.archivists.org/statements/saa-core-values-statement-and-code-of-ethics.

54. Peter Lyman and Howard Besser, *Defining the Problem of Our Vanishing Memory: Background, Current Status, Models for Resolution, in* TIME & BITS: MANAGING DIGITAL CONTINUITY 11, 19 (Margaret MacLean and Ben H. Davis eds., 1998).

55. RICHARD A. SPINELLO, CASE STUDIES IN INFORMATION AND COMPUTER ETHICS 7 (1997).

56. DAVID G. HILL, DATA PROTECTION: GOVERNANCE, RISK MANAGEMENT, AND COMPLIANCE 57 (2009).

57. These are the mechanisms set forth by Lawrence Lessig in CODE: VERSION 2.0 (2006).

58. DANIEL SOLOVE, THE FUTURE OF REPUTATION: GOSSIP, RUMOR, AND PRIVACY ON THE INTERNET 11 (2007) (citing a comment to a blog post about the Korean responses to "Dog Poop Girl," a girl who refused to pick up after her dog in a subway car, which resulted in an online shaming campaign).

59. Rafael Capurro and Birger Hjorland, *The Concept of Information*, 37 ANN. REV. INFO. SCI. & TECH. 343, 358–359 (2003).

60. *Id.* at 360–361.

61. LEON BRILLOUIN, SCIENCE AND INFORMATION THEORY x–xi (2d ed. 1962).

62. Gernot Wersig, *Information Theory, in* INTERNATIONAL ENCYCLOPEDIA OF INFORMATION AND LIBRARY SCIENCE 312–313 (John Feather and Paul Sturges eds., 2003).

63. DAVID G. HILL, DATA PROTECTION: GOVERNANCE, RISK MANAGEMENT, AND COMPLIANCE 57 (2009).

64. DAVID G. LUENBERGER, INFORMATION SCIENCE 130 (2006).

65. *Id.*

66. Rashi H. Glazer, *Measuring the Value of Information: The Information-Intensive Organization*, 32 IBM SYSTEMS J. 99, 101 (1993).

67. *Id.*

68. *See* Michael J. Driver and Theodore J. Mock, *Human Information Processing Decision Style Theory, and Accounting Information Systems*, 50 ACCOUNTING REV. 490 (1975); Jacob Jakoby, Donald E. Speller, and Carol A. Kohn, *Brand Choice as a Function of Information Overload: Replication and Extension*, 1:1 J. CONSUM. RESEARCH 33 (1974); Charles A. O'Reilly, *Individuals and Information Overload in Organisations: Is More Necessarily Better?*, 23 ACADEMY OF MANAGEMENT J. 684 (1980).

69. Paul M. Schwartz, *Data Protection Law and the Ethical Use of Analytics*, Centre for Information Policy Leadership (2010), http://www.huntonfiles.com/files/webupload/CIPL_Ethical_Undperinnings_of_Analytics_Paper.pdf.

70. Patricia Cohen, *Questioning Privacy Protections in Research*, N.Y. Times (Oct. 23, 2011), http://www.nytimes.com/2011/10/24/arts/rules-meant-to-protect-human-research-subjects-cause-concern.html?pagewanted=all.

71. The public-figure doctrine announced by the Supreme Court in *Curtis Publishing Co. v. Butts*, 388 U.S. 130, 173 (1967), held that a prominent public person has to prove actual malice, knowledge of falsity, or reckless disregard of whether a statement is true or false.

72. Wallace has already removed videos using DMCA takedown notices. *Student in Asian Tirade Video Quits University after "Death Threats and Harassment,"* Daily Mail (Mar. 19, 2011), http://www.dailymail.co.uk/news/article-1367923/Alexandra-Wallace-YouTube-video-Student-Asian-race-row-quits-Californian-university.html.

73. Chi. Council of Lawyers v. Bauer, 522 F.2d 242, 248 (7th Cir. 1975).

74. Near v. Minnesota, 283 U.S. 697, 720 (1931).

75. Org. for a Better Austin v. Keefe, 402 U.S. 415, 419 (1971).

76. *See* N.Y. Times Co. v. United States, 403 U.S. 713, 714, 724 (1971).

77. *Id*. at 730.

78. *Id*. at 733.

79. Franz Werro, *The Right to Inform v. the Right to Be Forgotten: A Transatlantic Clash, in* Liability in the Third Millennium 285 (Aurelia Colombi Ciacchi, Christine Godt, Peter Rott, and Leslie Jane Smith eds., 2009).

80. *Id*. at 290.

81. Sidis v. F-R Pub. Corporation, 113 F.2d 806 (2d Cir. 1940), *cert. denied*, 311 U.S. 711 (1940).

82. *Id*.

83. Schwabe v. Austria, Application no. 13704/88 (Aug. 28, 1992).

84. This is a recent divergence. In previous generations, substantial truth within context was required in the U.S. as well. *See* Randall P. Bezanson, *The Libel Tort Today*, 45 Wash. & Lee L. Rev. 535 (1988).

85. Cemalettin Canli v Turkey, Application no. 22427/04 (Nov. 18, 2008).

86. M.M. v. The United Kingdom, Application no. 24029/07 (Nov. 13, 2012).

87. *Id*. at para. 13.

88. DP Directive 95/46, Art. 6(1)(e).

89. DP Directive 95/46, Art. 12(b).

90. Case C-131/12, Google Spain SL and Google Inc. v. Agencia Española de Protección de Datos (AEPD) and Mario Costeja González (Euro. Ct. of Justice May 13, 2014), at para. 93.

91. DP Regulation, Art. 17(3)(a)–(d), at 52.

92. Melville B. Nimmer, *The Right to Speak from Time to Time: First Amendment Theory Applied to Libel and Misapplied to Privacy*, 56 CAL. L. REV. 935, 942 (1967).

93. New York Times Co. v. Sullivan, 376 U.S. 254 (1964).

94. Az 3 U 1288/13 (May 20, 2014). For English reporting on the case, see Philip Oltermann, *"Revenge Porn" Victims Receive Boost from German Court*, GUARDIAN (May 22, 2014).

95. Az 3 U 1288/13 (May 20, 2014).

96. Case C-131/12, Google Spain SL and Google Inc. v. Agencia Española de Protección de Datos (AEPD) and Mario Costeja González (Euro. Ct. of Justice May 13, 2014).

97. Gayle Fee and Laura Raposa, *Caitlin Davis' Life Is Not So Cheery Now*, BOSTON HERALD (Nov. 5, 2008), http://bostonherald.com/track/inside_track/view/2008_11_05_Caitlin_Davis_booted_from_Patriots__cheering_squad.

98. *Alexandra Wallace, Student in Anti-Asian Rant, Says She'll Leave UCLA*, THE HUFFINGTON POST (Mar. 19, 2011), http://www.huffingtonpost.com/2011/03/19/alexandra-wallace-student_n_837925.html.

99. Wikipedia, "Biographies of Living Persons," http://en.wikipedia.org/wiki/Wikipedia:Biographies_of_living_persons#Presumption_in_favor_of_privacy (last modified Feb. 3, 2013).

100. Wikipedia, *Talk: Star Wars Kid*, http://en.wikipedia.org/wiki/Talk:Star_Wars_Kid (last modified Jan. 9, 2013).

101. Wikipedia, *Wikipedia: Notability*, http://en.wikipedia.org/wiki/Wikipedia:Notability (last modified July 5, 2015).

102. *Id.*

103. Wikipedia, *Wikipedia Talk: Talk Pages Not Indexed by Google*, http://en.wikipedia.org/wiki/Wikipedia_talk:Talk_pages_not_indexed_by_Google (last modified Aug. 22, 2014).

104. BGH, Decisions of 15 Dec. 2009—VI ZR 217/08 (rainbow.at); Decisions of 15 Dec. 2009—VI ZR 227/08 and 228/08 (Deutschlandradio); Decisions of 9 Feb. 2010—VI ZR 243/08 and 244/08 (Spiegel online); Decisions of 20 Apr. 2010—VI ZR 245/08 and 246/08 (morgenweb.de).

105. Firth v. New York, 98 N.Y. 2d 365, 368–369 (2002).

106. *Id.* at 369.

107. *Id.*

108. *Id.* at 370.

109. United States v. Alvarez, 132 S. Ct. 2537, 2551 (2012) (plurality opinion) (U.S. Supreme Court struck down the Stolen Valor Act, which made it a crime to lie about receiving a Medal of Honor, finding that these false statements are protected by the First Amendment and that the statute was overbroad because violations of the law did not result in cognizable harm).

5. CTRL + Z IN LEGAL CULTURES

1. Dan Morain, *Anthony Kennedy Speaks about History, Civics, Flag Burning, and Emerging Issues*, SACRAMENTO BEE (June 29, 2014), http://www.sacbee.com/2014/06/29/6512694/anthony-kennedy-speaks-about-history.html#storylink=cpy.

2. Do Not Track Kids Act, 685, § 2(17).

3. Cox Broadcasting Corp. v. Cohn, 420 U.S. 469, 496 (1975).

4. JAMES Q. WHITMAN, HARSH JUSTICE: CRIMINAL PUNISHMENT AND THE WIDENING DIVIDE BETWEEN AMERICA AND EUROPE (2003).

5. *Id.* at 41–68.

6. *Id.* at 4.

7. *Id.* at 8.

8. *Id.* at 86–87.

9. *Id.* at 65.

10. Samantha Barbas, *The Death of the Public Disclosure Tort: A Historical Perspective*, 22 YALE J. L. & HUMAN. 171, 171 (2010).

11. A full analysis of U.S. forgiveness laws was performed in *Seeking Digital Redemption: The Future of Forgiveness in the Internet Age*, 29 SANTA CLARA COMPUTER & HIGH TECH. L.J. 99 (2012), authored by myself (then Ambrose), Nicole Day (then Friess) and Jill Dupre (then Van Matre). It provides a detailed assessment of which the results are presented here.

12. Allen Salkin, *What's in a Name? Ask Google*, N.Y. TIMES (Nov. 25, 2011), http://www.nytimes.com/2011/11/27/fashion/google-searches-help-parents-narrow-down-baby-names.html?_r=2&ref=technology.

13. *Id.*

14. *Id.*

15. *See generally* PRISCILLA M. REGAN, LEGISLATING PRIVACY: TECHNOLOGY, SOCIAL VALUES, AND PUBLIC POLICY (1995) (discussing the social importance of privacy and arguing the necessity of addressing its benefits in policy debate).

16. Megan McArdle, *Sink and Swim*, ATLANTIC (June 1, 2009).

17. *Id.*

18. See Charles H. Cosgrove, *The Declaration of Independence in Constitutional Interpretation: A Selective History and Analysis*, 32 U. RICH. L. REV. 107 (1998) (particularly Cosgrove's discussion of the ways in which the abolitionist movement utilized the Declaration of Independence to undermine the inclusion of slavery in the Constitution).

19. Cass R. Sunstein, *Low Value Speech Revisited*, 83 NW. U. L. REV. 555 (1988).

20. Ashcroft v. Free Speech Coalition, 535 U.S. 234 (2002).

21. Barber v. Time, Inc., 348 Mo. 1199, 1207 (Mo. 1942).

22. Gilbert v. Medical Economics Co., 665 F.2d 305, 307–308 (10th Cir. 1981).

23. Shulman v. Group W. Productions, Inc. 74 Cal. Rptr. 2d 843, 862 (Cal. 1998).

24. Paul Ohm has argued that it should be illegal for employers to refuse to hire or fire individuals for legal activities performed off duty that are discovered on social networking sites or search-engine results. Jeffrey Rosen, *The Web Means the End of Forgetting*, N.Y. TIMES MAGAZINE (July 21, 2010), http://www.nytimes.com/2010/07/25/magazine/25privacy-t2.html?pagewanted=all.

25. Thomas Jefferson to William Roscoe, Dec. 27, 1820, available at http://www.loc.gov/exhibits/jefferson/75.html.

26. United States v. Alvarez, 132 S. Ct. 2537, 2552 (2012).

27. Jews for Jesus, Inc. v. Rapp, 997 So.2d 1098, 1100 (Fla. 2008); Denver Pub. Co. v. Bueno, 54 P.3d 893 (Col. 2002).

28. Meyerkord v. Zipatoni Co., 276 S.W.3d 319, 325 (Mo. App. E.D. 2008).

29. *See* Comins v. VanVoorhis, 135 So.3d 545 (Fla. Dist. Ct. App. 2014); Thieriot v. The Wrapnews Inc., No. B245022 (Cal. Ct. App. Apr. 15, 2014). Additionally, note that North Dakota, a state that has adopted the Uniform Correction Act, is the only state with a retraction statute that explicitly mentions electronic publications.

30. Public.Resource.org, *Why Is My Court Case on the Internet?*, https://public.resource.org/court_cases.html (accessed June 5, 2015).

31. For future extensions of the robots.txt protocol, *see* BRIAN WASSOM, AUGMENTED REALITY LAW, PRIVACY, AND ETHICS: LAW, SOCIETY, EMERGING AR TECHNOLOGIES 56–57 (2015).

32. *See* http://bulk.resource.org/robots.txt for a list of files "disallowed" for crawlers by Public.Resource.org.

33. Near v. Minnesota, 283 U.S. 697, 706 (1931).

34. Alexander v. U.S., 509 U.S. 544, 550 (1993) (distinguishing the permanent injunction, which prevented future publication of "malicious, scandalous or defamatory" content, overturned in *Near* from the RICO forfeiture at issue in *Alexander*).

35. Graboff v. AAOS and AAOS, No. 2:12-cv-05491-JHS at 1 (E.D.P.A. May 2, 2013).

36. David S. Ardia, *Freedom of Speech, Defamation, and Injunctions*, 55 WM. & MARY L. REV. 1 (2013).

37. *Id*. at 42–51.

38. Cochran v. Tory, No. BC239405, 2002 WL 33966354 (Cal. Super. Ct. Apr. 24, 2002) (order granting permanent injunction), *aff'd*, No. B159437, 2003 WL 22451378, at 1 (Cal. Ct. App. Oct. 29, 2003), *vacated*, 544 U.S. 734 (2005).

39. *Id*.

40. Tory v. Cochran, 544 U.S. 734 (2005).

41. David S. Ardia, *Freedom of Speech, Defamation, and Injunctions*, 55 WM. & MARY L. REV. 1, 50–51 (2013).

42. *Id*. at 2.

43. Justice Blackmun's concurrence, joined by Justice Marshall, in *Wolston v. Reader's Digest Ass'n*, 443 U.S. 157, 171 (1979), maintained that "public figure" status could

fade with the passage of time and that historians may be implicated more than journalists ("Historians, consequently, may well run a greater risk of liability for defamation.").

44. U.S. Dept. of Justice v. Reporters Committee, 489 U.S. 749, 763 (1989).

45. *Id.* at 770 (quoting William H. Rehnquist, *Is an Expanded Right of Privacy Consistent with Fair and Effective Law Enforcement?*, 23 U. Kan. L. Rev. 1 (1974)).

46. Halloran v. Veterans Admin., 874 F.2d 315, 322 (5th Cir. 1989).

47. Swafford v. Memphis Individual Practice Ass'n, 1998 WL 281935 (Tenn. Ct. App. 1999).

48. *Id.* at 10.

49. Frank Pasquale, The Black Box Society (2014).

50. Neil M. Richards, Intellectual Privacy: Rethinking Civil Liberties in the Digital Age 80–89 (2015).

51. Sorrell v. IMS Health Inc., 564 U.S. 2653 (2011).

52. Eugene Volokh, *Freedom of Speech and Information Privacy: The Troubling Implications of a Right to Stop People from Speaking about You*, 52 Stan. L. Rev. 1049 (2000); Ashutosh Bhagwat, *Sorrel v. IMS Health: Details, Detailing, and the Death of Privacy*, 36 Vt. L. Rev. 855 (2012); Jane Bambauer, *Is Data Speech?*, 66 Stan. L. Rev. 57 (2014).

53. Jane Bambauer, *Is Data Speech?*, 66 Stan. L. Rev. 57, 63 (2014).

54. Neil M. Richards, Intellectual Privacy: Rethinking Civil Liberties in the Digital Age 155 (2015).

55. danah boyd and Eszter Hargittai, *Facebook Privacy Settings: Who Cares?*, 15 First Monday (2010), http://firstmonday.org/article/view/3086/2589.

56. Reynol Junco, Engaging Students through Social Media: Evidence-Based Practices for Use in Student Affairs (2014).

57. *Id.* at 117.

58. Kaplan, *Kaplan Test Prep Survey: More College Admissions Officers Checking Applicants' Digital Trails, but Most Students Unconcerned* (Nov. 20, 2014), http://press.kaptest.com/press-releases/kaplan-test-prep-survey-percentage-of-college-admissions-officers-who-visit-applicants-social-networking-pages-continues-to-grow-but-most-students-shrug.

59. *Digital Birth: Welcome to the Online World*, Business Wire (Oct. 6, 2010), http://www.businesswire.com/news/home/20101006006722/en/Digital-Birth-Online-World#.VD17VfldUud.

60. Anupam Chander, *Youthful Indiscretion in an Internet Age, in* The Offensive Internet: Speech, Privacy, and Reputation 124, 125 (Saul Levmore and Martha C. Nussbaum eds., 2010).

61. *Common Sense with Phineas and Ferb* (Disney Channel television broadcast Jan. 27, 2010). Transcript:
Candace: Mom! Phineas and Ferb are making a public service announcement!

PHINEAS: Be careful what you put online! It never goes away! Ever!
[*Video of Heinz Doofenshmirtz falling into a toilet on roller skates plays on computer*]
PHINEAS: Fame is fleeting!
FERB: But the Internet is forever.
PHINEAS: And you never know who's gonna see it!
CANDACE [*holding disk*]: There's no way I'm letting this baby out of my sight!
NORM [*lifting up roof*]: Hello, children! I'll take that!

62. Paulan Korenhof and Bert-Jaap Koops, *Gender Identity and Privacy: Could a Right to Be Forgotten Help ~~Andrew~~ Agnes Online?*, SSRN WORKING PAPER (2013), http://ssrn.com/abstract=2304190 or http://dx.doi.org/10.2139/ssrn.2304190.

63. HAROLD GARFINKEL, STUDIES IN ETHNOMETHODOLOGY 136 (1967).

64. *See* the Transgender Law Center's Equality Map: http://transgenderlawcenter.org/equalitymap.

65. Ilene Seidman and Susan Vickers, *The Second Wave: An Agenda for the Next Thirty Years of Rape Law Reform*, 38 SUFFOLK U. L. REV. 467, 473 (2005) (discussing the importance of privacy for victims of sexual assault).

66. Mary Anne Franks, *Unwilling Avatars: Idealism and Discrimination in Cyberspace*, 20 COLUM. J. GENDER & L. 224 (2011); Danielle Keats Citron and Mary Anne Franks, *Criminalizing Revenge Porn*, 49 WAKE FOREST L. REV. 345 (2014).

67. Ann Wolbert Burgess and Lynda Lytle Holmstrom, *Rape Trauma Syndrome*, 131 AM. J. PSYCHIATRY 981 (1974).

68. Jacqueline R. Rolfs, *The Florida Star v. B.J.F.: The Beginning of the End for the Tort of Public Disclosure*, 1990 WIS. L. REV. 1107 (1990).

69. Florida Star v. B.J.F., 109 S. Ct. 2603, 2613 (1989).

6. CTRL + Z IN THE INTERNATIONAL COMMUNITY

1. Dan Raywood, *Internet to Enter Its Second Stage as Large Domains Control 30 Per Cent of the Total Content*, SC MAGAZINE UK (Oct. 13, 2009), http://www.scmagazineuk.com/internet-to-enter-its-second-stage-as-large-domains-control-30-per-cent-of-the-total-content/article/152156/ ("Out of the 40,000 routed end sites in the Internet, large companies such as Limelight, Facebook, Google, Microsoft and YouTube now generate and consume 30 per cent of all Internet traffic.").

2. While responses to legal requests for information may vary (efforts like Europe v. Facebook, http://europe-v-facebook.org/EN/en.html, and #NOLOGs, https://www.privacyinternational.org/blog/what-does-twitter-know-about-its-users-nologs, may extend user access to those requests deriving from non-EU users, but they are not required to), it is expensive to design country- or region-specific systems.

3. Google, *European Privacy Requests for Search Removals*, TRANSPARENCY REPORT (updated Feb. 15, 2015), http://www.google.com/transparencyreport/removals/europeprivacy/.

4. DP Directive 95/46/EC.

5. Viviane Reding, *Speech at New Frontiers for Social Media Marketing Conference, EU Data Protection Reform and Social Media: Encouraging Citizens' Trust and Creating New Opportunities* (Nov. 29, 2011) (transcript available at http://europa. eu/rapid/press-release_SPEECH-11-827_en.htm).

6. Vivane Reding, *Speech at The Privacy Platform, the Review of the EU Data Protection Framework Event* (Mar. 16, 2011) (transcript available at http://europa. eu/rapid/pressReleasesAction.do?reference=SPEECH/11/183).

7. JOHN PALFREY AND URS GASSER, INTEROP: THE PROMISE AND PERILS OF HIGHLY INTERCONNECTED SYSTEMS 3 (2012).

8. *Id.* at 178.

9. Zippo Mfr. Co. v. Zippo Dot Com, Inc., 952 F. Supp. 1119, 1124 (W.D. Pa. 1997).

10. *Id.*

11. Steven C. Bennett, *The "Right to Be Forgotten": Reconciling EU and US Perspectives*, 30 BERKELEY J. INT'L L. 161, 186–187 (2012).

12. Committee on Civil Liberties, Justice and Home Affairs, Rapporteur Jan Philipp Albrect, *Rapporteur's Report on Draft Report of General Data Protection Regulation*, COM(2012)0011–C7 0025/2012–2012/0011(COD) (Dec. 17, 2012).

13. *Id.* (citing Article 29 Data Protection Working Party, *Working Document on Determining the International Application of EU Data Protection Law to Personal Data Processing on the Internet by Non-EU Based Web Sites*, 5035/01/EN/Final, WP 56 (May 30, 2002)).

14. Yahoo! Inc. v. La Ligue Contre Le Racisme et l'Antisémitisme (LICRA), 433 F.3d 1199, 1217 (9th Cir. 2006).

15. Case No. RG: 00/05308, Association "l'Union des Etudiant Juifs de France," la "Ligue contre le Racisme et l'Antisémitisme" c. Yahoo! et Yahoo France [2000], May 22, 2000, http://www.legalis.net/spip.php?page=jurisprudence-decision&id_article=175. This order was subsequently confirmed by the same court (although the May 22, 2000, order specified a penalty of €100,000, and the later order, on November 20, 2000, specified a penalty of ₣100,000). Case No. RG: 00/05308, Association "l'Union des Etudiant Juifs de France," la "Ligue contre le Racisme et l'Antisémitisme" c. Yahoo! et Yahoo France [2000], November 20, 2000 (Tribunal de Grande Instance de Paris, May 22, 2000) (LICRA and UEJF v. Yahoo! Inc. and Yahoo France), http://www.legalis.net/spip. php?page=jurisprudence-decision&id_article=217.

16. *Id.*

17. *Id.*

18. Yahoo! Inc. v. LICRA, 169 F. Supp. 2d. 1181 (N.D. Cal. 2001).

19. Yahoo! Inc. v. LICRA, 433 F.3d 1199 (9th Cir. 2006).

20. Yahoo! Inc. v. LICRA, 169 F. Supp. 2d. 1181, 1186 (N.D. Cal. 2001).

21. Yahoo! Inc. v. LICRA, 433 F.3d 1199, 1215 (9th Cir. 2006).

22. *Id.*

23. Uta Kohl, Jurisdiction and the Internet: Regulatory Competence over Online Activity 208 (2007).

24. Google, *France—Government Removal Requests*, Transparency Report, http://www.google.com/transparencyreport/removals/government/FR/ (accessed June 5, 2015).

25. Google, *Government Removal Requests*, Transparency Report, https://www.google.com/transparencyreport/removals/government/faq/ (accessed June 5, 2015).

26. Steven C. Bennett, *The "Right to Be Forgotten": Reconciling EU and US Perspectives*, 30 Berkeley J. Int'l L. 161, 186 (2012).

27. DP Regulation, Art. 79(5)(c), LIBE edits.

28. Emma Woollacott, *EU to Vote on Scrapping "Safe Harbor" Data Rules*, Forbes (Dec. 18, 2013), http://www.forbes.com/sites/emmawoollacott/2013/12/18/eu-to-vote-on-scrapping-safe-harbor-data-rules/.

29. European Parliament, *US NSA: Stop Mass Surveillance Now or Face Consequences, MEPs Say*, press release (Mar. 12, 2014), http://www.europarl.europa.eu/news/en/news-room/content/20140307IPR38203/html/US-NSA-stop-mass-surveillance-now-or-face-consequences-MEPs-say.

30. Karin Matussek, *Snowden Leaks Killed U.S.-E.U. Data Deal, Regulator Say*, Bloomberg Business (Jan. 28, 2015), http://www.bloomberg.com/news/articles/2015-01-28/snowden-leaks-killed-u-s-e-u-data-deal-regulator-say.

31. Yuri Kageyama, *Japan Court Orders Google to Remove Search Results*, Associated Press (Oct. 10, 2014), http://hosted.ap.org/dynamic/stories/A/AS_JAPAN_GOOGLE?SITE=AP&SECTION=HOME&TEMPLATE=DEFAULT&CTIME=2014-10-10-12-29-58.

32. European Commission, *Myth-Busting: The Court of Justice of the EU and the "Right to Be Forgotten"* (2014), http://ec.europa.eu/justice/data-protection/files/factsheets/factsheet_rtbf_mythbusting_en.pdf.

33. ECJ, Case C-101/01, Bodil Lindqvist (Nov. 6, 2003).

34. *Id.* at para. 47.

35. Article 29 Data Protection Working Party, *Opinion 5/2009 on Online Social Networking* (WP 163) (Dec. 6, 2009).

36. C / 13/569654 / KG ZA 14–960 PS / BB (Rechtbank Amsterdam (District Court)), Sept. 18, 2014), available at http://uitspraken.rechtspraak.nl/inziendocument?id=ECLI:NL:RBAMS:2014:6118.

37. Caroline Chancé and Carol A. F. Umhoefer, *France: Right to Be Forgotten— Application of the Balancing Test Derived from the Google v. Costeja Case*, Lexology (Feb. 10, 2015).

38. Article 29 Data Protection Working Party, *Guidelines on the Implementation of the Court of Justice of the European Union Judgment on "Google Spain and Inc. v. Agencia Española de Protección de Datos (AEPD) and Mario Costeja González,"* C-131/12, 14/EN WP 225 (Nov. 26, 2014).

39. Google Advisory Council, The Advisory Council to Google on the Right to Be Forgotten Report (Feb. 6, 2015), https://www.google.com/advisorycouncil/.

40. Jack Goldsmith and Tim Wu, Who Controls the Internet? Illusions of a Borderless World 6–9 (2008).

41. Kashmir Hill, *Google Makes Every Person Search in Europe Look Censored*, Forbes (July 2, 2014), http://www.forbes.com/sites/kashmirhill/2014/07/02/google-right-to-be-forgotten-notice/.

42. Council Directive 2000/31, 2000 O.J. (L 178), Art. 14.

43. Council Directive 2000/31, 2000 O.J. (L 178), Art. 15.

44. Payam Tamiz v. Google, Inc. [2013] EWCA Civ. 68, para. 35.

45. *Id.*

46. Delfi AS v. Estonia, no. 64569/09, Eur. Ct. H.R. para. 86 (Oct. 10, 2013).

47. European Commission, *Issued by the Article 29 Data Protection Working Party*, press release (Sept. 18, 2014), http://ec.europa.eu/justice/data-protection/article-29/press-material/press-release/art29_press_material/2014/20140918_wp29_press_release_97th_plenary_cjeu_google_judgment__17sept_adopted.pdf.

48. European Commission, *The Proposed General Data Protection Regulation: The Consistency Mechanism Explained* (2013), http://ec.europa.eu/justice/newsroom/data-protection/news/130206_en.htm.

49. Robert Gellman, *Fair Information Practices: A Basic History, Version 1.91* (2012), http://bobgellman.com/rg-docs/rg-FIPShistory.pdf.

50. *See* Robert Kirk Walker, *Forcing Forgetfulness: Data Privacy, Free Speech, and the "Right to Be Forgotten,"* SSRN Working Paper 42–48 (2012), http://ssrn.com/abstract=2017967 or http://dx.doi.org/10.2139/ssrn.2017967.

51. Paul Alexander Bernal, *A Right to Delete?*, 2 Eur. J. L. & Tech. (2011), http://ejlt.org/article/view/75/144.

52. Jeffrey Rosen, *The Right to Be Forgotten*, 64 Stan. L. Rev. Online 88, 90 (2012), http://www.stanfordlawreview.org/online/privacy-paradox/right-to-be-forgotten.

53. Network Advertising Initiative, *Consumer Opt-Out | NAI: Network Advertising Initiative*, http://www.networkadvertising.org/choices/#completed (accessed June 5, 2015).

54. Harrison, *How Our Opt-Out System Works*, Spokeo People Search Blog (Jan. 12, 2011), https://web.archive.org/web/20110116031332/http://www.spokeo.com/blog/2011/01/how-spokeo-opt-out-system-works/ (for Spokeo's updated process, see http://www.spokeo.com/opt_out/new).

55. Electronic Frontier Foundation, *Do Not Track*, https://www.eff.org/issues/do-not-track (accessed June 5, 2015).

56. *See* Facebook, *Facebook Data Use Policy*, https://www.facebook.com/full_data_use_policy (accessed Aug. 1, 2014; for older version, see https://web.archive.org/web/20140805060652/https://www.facebook.com/full_data_use_policy) (The

policy includes a number of clauses, including the following: "While you are allowing us to use the information we receive about you, you always own all of your information." "We store data for as long as it is necessary to provide products and services to you and others, including those described above. Typically, information associated with your account will be kept until your account is deleted." "It typically takes about one month to delete an account, but some information may remain in backup copies and logs for up to 90 days.").

57. *See, e.g.*, National Telecommunications and Information Administration, U.S. Department of Commerce, *Commercial Data Privacy and Innovation in the Internet Economy: Dynamic Policy Framework* (2010), http://www.ntia.doc.gov/report/2010/commercial-data-privacy-and-innovationInternet-economy-dynamic-policy-framework (proposing the following set of FIPPs: transparency, *individual participation*, purpose specification, *data minimization*, use limitation, data quality and integrity, security, and accountability and auditing).

58. Eugene Volokh and Donald M. Falk, *Google: First Amendment Protection for Search Engine Search Results*, 8 J. L. ECON. & POL'Y 883 (2011).

59. *Id.*

60. *Id.* at 887.

61. Wikipedia, *Talk: Star Wars Kid*, http://en.wikipedia.org/wiki/Talk:Star_Wars_Kid (last modified Jan. 9, 2013).

62. Society of American Archivists, *Code of Ethics for Archivists*, SAA Council Approval/Endorsement (Feb. 2005), http://www2.archivists.org/statements/saa-core-values-statement-and-code-of-ethics.

63. Internet Archive, *Internet Archive's Policies on Archival Integrity and Removal* (2002), http://www2.sims.berkeley.edu/research/conferences/aps/removal-policy.html.

64. Edwin Lane, *Google Removes 12 BBC News Links in "Right to Be Forgotten,"* BBC NEWS (Aug. 19, 2014), http://www.bbc.com/news/technology-28851366.

65. *Briton Guilty of Running Vice Ring*, BBC NEWS (Oct. 23, 2003), http://news.bbc.co.uk/2/hi/uk_news/3206355.stm.

66. Katie Storey, *Evil Killer Ronald Castree Should Never Be Forgotten, Says Father of Lesley Molseed*, MANCHESTER EVENING NEWS (Sept. 25, 2014), http://www.manchestereveningnews.co.uk/news/evil-killer-should-never-forgotten-7834956.

67. Jeff Jonas, *Data Tethering: Managing the Echo*, JEFF JONAS BLOG (Sept. 21, 2006), http://jeffjonas.typepad.com/jeff_jonas/2006/09/data_tethering_.html.

68. *Id.*

69. Frances Robinson, *EU Data Protection Law on Track for Juncker Deadline*, WALL ST. J. (Oct. 10, 2014), http://blogs.wsj.com/brussels/2014/10/10/eu-data-protection-law-on-track-for-juncker-deadline/.

70. Paul M. Schwartz, *The EU-US Privacy Collision: A Turn to Institutions and Procedures* 126 HARV. L. REV. 1966 (2013) (citing Anu Bradford, *The Brussels Effect*, 107 Nw. U. L. REV. 1 (2012)).

71. Anu Bradford, *The Brussels Effect*, 107 Nw. U. L. Rev. 10–17 (2012).
72. Paul M. Schwartz, *The EU-US Privacy Collision: A Turn to Institutions and Procedures* 126 Harv. L. Rev. 1966, 1990–1992 (2013) (citing Anne-Marie Slaughter, A New World Order (2004)).
73. Anne-Marie Slaughter, A New World Order 5 (2004).
74. Ryan J. Barilleaux, *The President, "Intermestic" Issues, and the Risks of Policy Leadership*, 15:4 Perspectives on the Presidency 754 (1985).
75. H. O. Maycotte, *America's "Right to Be Forgotten" Fight Heats Up*, Forbes (Sept. 30, 2014), http://www.forbes.com/sites/homaycotte/2014/09/30/americas-right-to-be-forgotten-fight-heats-up/.
76. *Id.*
77. Jill Lepore, *The Disruption Machine*, New Yorker (June 23, 2014).

Bibliography

Acquisti, Alessandro, and Jens Grossklags, *Privacy Attitudes and Privacy Behavior*, *in* ECONOMICS OF INFORMATION SECURITY 165 (L. Jean Camp and Stephen Lewis eds., 2004).

Adams, Marilyn McCord, *Forgiveness: A Christian Model*, 8 FAITH & PHIL. 277 (1991).

Alexandra Wallace, Student in Anti-Asian Rant, Says She'll Leave UCLA, THE HUFFINGTON POST (Mar. 19, 2011), http://www.huffingtonpost.com/2011/03/19/alexandra-wallace-student_n_837925.html.

ALTMAN, IRWIN, THE ENVIRONMENT AND SOCIAL BEHAVIOR: PRIVACY, PERSONAL SPACE, TERRITORY, AND CROWDING (1975).

Altman, Irwin, *Privacy Regulation: Culturally Universal or Culturally Specific?*, 33 J. SOC. ISSUES 66 (1977).

Ambrose, Meg Leta, *It's about Time: Privacy, Information Life Cycles, and the Right to Be Forgotten*, 16 STAN. TECH. L. REV. 369 (2014).

Ambrose, Meg Leta, *Speaking of Forgetting: Analysis of Possible Non-EU Responses to the Right to Be Forgotten and Speech Exception*, 38:8 TELECOMMUN. POL'Y 800 (2014).

Ambrose, Meg Leta, *You Are What Google Says You Are: The Right to Be Forgotten and Information Stewardship*, 17 INT'L REV. INFO. ETHICS (July 2012).

Ambrose, Meg Leta, and Jef Ausloos, *The Right to Be Forgotten across the Pond*, 3 J. INFO. POL'Y 1 (2013).

Ambrose, Meg Leta, Nicole Friess, and Jill Van Matre, *Seeking Digital Redemption: The Future of Forgiveness in the Internet Age*, 29 SANTA CLARA COMPUTER & HIGH TECH. L.J. 99 (2012).

Andrade, Norberto Nuno Gomes de, *Oblivion: The Right to Be Different . . . from Oneself—Reproposing the Right to Be Forgotten*, 13 IDP 122 (2012).

Angwin, Julia, *The Web's New Gold Mine: Your Secrets*, WALL ST. J. (July 30, 2010), http://online.wsj.com/article/SB10001424052748703940904575395073512989404.html.

Ardia, David S., *Freedom of Speech, Defamation, and Injunctions*, 55 WM. & MARY L. REV. 1 (2013).

Article 29 Data Protection Working Party, *Guidelines on the Implementation of the Court of Justice of the European Union Judgment on "Google Spain and Inc. v. Agencia Española de Protección de Datos (AEPD) and Mario Costeja González,"* C-131/12, 14/EN WP 225 (Nov. 26, 2014).

Article 29 Data Protection Working Party, *Opinion 5/2009 on Online Social Networking* (WP 163) (Dec. 6, 2009).

Article 29 Data Protection Working Party, *Working Document on Determining the International Application of EU Data Protection Law to Personal Data Processing on the Internet by Non-EU Based Web Sites*, 5035/01/EN/Final, WP 56 (May 30, 2002).

Ausloos, Jef, *The "Right to Be Forgotten"—Worth Remembering?*, 28 COMPUTER L. & SEC. REV. 143 (2012).

Bambauer, Jane, *Is Data Speech?*, 66 STAN. L. REV. 57 (2014).

Bannon, Liam J., *Forgetting as a Feature, Not a Bug: The Duality of Memory and Implications for Ubiquitous Computing*, 2 CODESIGN 3 (2006).

Barbas, Samantha, *The Death of the Public Disclosure Tort: A Historical Perspective*, 22 YALE J. L. & HUMAN. 171 (2010).

Barilleaux, Ryan J., *The President, "Intermestic" Issues, and the Risks of Policy Leadership*, 15:4 PERSPECTIVES ON THE PRESIDENCY 754 (1985).

Barnes, Bill, *Nothing but Net*, SLATE (Feb. 28, 1997), http://www.slate.com/articles/technology/webhead/1997/02/nothing_but_net.html.

BARNES, JULIAN, FLAUBERT'S PARROT (1984).

BATTELLE, JOHN, THE SEARCH: HOW GOOGLE AND ITS RIVALS REWROTE THE RULES OF BUSINESS AND TRANSFORMED OUR CULTURE (2006).

Battle, Cynthia L., and Ivan W. Miller, *Families and Forgiveness*, in HANDBOOK OF FORGIVENESS 233 (Everett L. Worthington Jr. ed., 2005).

Baumeister, Roy F., Ellen Bratslavsky, Catrin Finkenauer, and Kathleen D. Vohs, *Bad Is Stronger than Good*, 5 REV. GEN. PSYCHOL. 323 (2001).

Baumeister, Roy F., Julie Juola Exline, and Kristin L. Sommer, *The Victim Role, Grudge Theory, and Two Dimensions of Forgiveness*, in DIMENSIONS OF FORGIVENESS: PSYCHOLOGICAL RESEARCH & THEOLOGICAL PERSPECTIVES 79 (Everett L. Worthington Jr. ed., 1998).

BELL, GORDON, AND JIM GEMMELL, TOTAL RECALL: HOW THE E-MEMORY REVOLUTION WILL CHANGE EVERYTHING (2009).

Benhow, S. Mary P., *File Not Found: The Problem of Changing URLs for the World Wide Web*, 8 INTERNET RESEARCH: NETWORK APPLICATIONS & POL'Y 247 (1998).

BENKLER, YOCHAI, THE WEALTH OF NETWORKS: HOW SOCIAL PRODUCTION TRANSFORMS MARKETS AND FREEDOM (2007).

Benn, Stanley I., *Privacy, Freedom, and Respect for Persons, in* PRIVACY, NOMOS XIII: YEARBOOK OF THE AMERICAN SOCIETY FOR POLITICAL AND LEGAL PHILOSOPHY 1 (J. Ronald Pennock and John W. Chapman eds., 1971).

BENNETT, COLIN J., AND CHARLES RAAB, THE GOVERNANCE OF PRIVACY: POLICY INSTRUMENTS IN GLOBAL PERSPECTIVE (2006).

Bennett, Steven C., *The "Right to Be Forgotten": Reconciling EU and US Perspectives*, 30 BERKELEY J. INT'L L. 161 (2012).

Bernal, Paul Alexander, *A Right to Delete?*, 2:2 EUR. J. L. & TECH. (2011), http://ejlt. org/article/view/75/144.

BEUC (European Consumers' Organisation), *A Comprehensive Approach on Personal Data Protection in the European Union: European Commission's Communication* (Jan. 24, 2011), http://ec.europa.eu/justice/news/consulting_public/0006/ contributions/organisations/beuc_en.pdf.

Bezanson, Randall P., *The Libel Tort Today*, 45 WASH. & LEE L. REV. 535 (1988).

Bhagwat, Ashutosh, *Sorrel v. IMS Health: Details, Detailing, and the Death of Privacy*, 36 VT. L. REV. 855 (2012).

Bibas, Stephanos, *Forgiveness in Criminal Procedure*, 4 OHIO ST. J. CRIM. L. 329 (2007).

Bielski, Zosia, *If a Teacher's Decades-Old Erotic Films Can Resurface Online, What Rights Should We Have to Digital Privacy?*, GLOBE AND MAIL (Oct. 22, 2014), http://www.theglobeandmail.com/life/relationships/if-a-teachers-decades-old-erotic-films-can-resurface-online-what-rights-should-we-have-to-digital-privacy/ article21218588/.

Bijker, Wiebe E., Thomas P. Hughes, Trevor Pinch, and Deborah G. Douglas, eds., THE SOCIAL CONSTRUCTION OF TECHNOLOGICAL SYSTEMS: NEW DIRECTIONS IN THE SOCIOLOGY AND HISTORY OF TECHNOLOGY (2012).

Borris, Eileen R., *Forgiveness and the Healing of Nations, in* PARALLEL EVENT OF THE 55TH COMMISSION ON THE STATUS OF WOMEN, UNIVERSAL PEACE FEDERATION (2011), http://www.upf.org/education/ speeches/3464-eileen-r-borris-forgiveness-and-the-healing-of-nations.

boyd, danah, *Why Youth (Heart) Social Network Sites: The Role of Networked Publics in Teenage Social Life, in* MACARTHUR FOUNDATION SERIES ON DIGITAL LEARNING—YOUTH, IDENTITY, AND DIGITAL MEDIA 119 (David Buckingham ed., 2008).

boyd, danah, and Eszter Hargittai, *Facebook Privacy Settings: Who Cares?*, 15 FIRST MONDAY (2010), http://firstmonday.org/article/view/3086/2589.

boyd, danah, Eszter Hargittai, Jason Schultz, and John Palfrey, *Why Parents Help Their Children Lie to Facebook about Age: Unintended Consequences of the "Children's Online Privacy Protection Act,"* 16 FIRST MONDAY (2011), http://firstmonday.org/ojs/index.php/fm/article/view/3850.

Bradford, Anu, *The Brussels Effect*, 107 NW. U. L. REV. 1 (2012).

Brandimarte, Laura, *Discounting the Past: Bad Weighs Heavier than Good* (2010), unpublished manuscript, available at http://heinz.cmu.edu/research/384full.pdf.

Brewington, Brian E., and George Cybenko, *How Dynamic Is the Web?*, 33 COMPUTER NETWORKS 257 (2000).

BRILLOUIN, LEON, SCIENCE AND INFORMATION THEORY (2d ed., 1962).

BRIN, DAVID, THE TRANSPARENT SOCIETY: WILL TECHNOLOGY FORCE US TO CHOOSE BETWEEN PRIVACY AND FREEDOM? (1999).

Briton Guilty of Running Vice Ring, BBC NEWS (Oct. 23, 2003), http://news.bbc.co.uk/2/hi/uk_news/3206355.stm.

Bullying Statistics, *Bullying and Suicide*, http://www.bullyingstatistics.org/content/bullying-and-suicide.html (accessed June 23, 2015).

Burgess, Ann Wolbert, and Lynda Lytle Holmstrom, *Rape Trauma Syndrome*, 131 AM. J. PSYCHIATRY 981 (1974).

Cahn, Edmond, *The Firstness of the First Amendment*, 65 YALE L.J. 464 (1956).

Capurro, Rafael, and Birger Hjorland, *The Concept of Information*, 37 ANN. REV. INFO. SCI. & TECH. 343 (2003).

Castellano, Pere Simón, *The Right to Be Forgotten under European Law: A Constitutional Debate*, 16 LEX ELECTRONICA (2012).

Cavoukian, Ann, and Jeff Jonas, *Privacy by Design in the Age of Big Data*, PRIVACY BY DESIGN (2012), http://privacybydesign.ca/content/uploads/2012/06/pbd-big_data.pdf.

Chancé, Caroline, and Carol A. F. Umhoefer, *France: Right to Be Forgotten— Application of the Balancing Test Derived from the Google v. Costeja Case*, LEXOLOGY (Feb. 10, 2015).

Chander, Anupam, *Youthful Indiscretion in an Internet Age, in* THE OFFENSIVE INTERNET: SPEECH, PRIVACY, AND REPUTATION 124 (Saul Levmore and Martha C. Nussbaum eds., 2010).

Cho, Daegon, Soodong Kim, and Alessandro Acquisti, *Empirical Analysis and User Behaviors: The Impact of Real Name Policy, in* PROC. OF 45TH HAWAII INTERNATIONAL CONFERENCE ON SYSTEM SCIENCE (HICSS 2012).

Cho, Junghoo, and Hector Garcia-Molina, *The Evolution of the Web and Implications for an Incremental Crawler, in* PROC. OF THE 26TH INT'L CONF. ON VERY LARGE DATA BASES 200 (2000).

Citron, Danielle Keats, *Cyber Civil Rights*, 89 B.U. L. REV. 61 (2009).

Citron, Danielle Keats, and Mary Anne Franks, *Criminalizing Revenge Porn*, 49 WAKE FOREST L. REV. 345 (2014).

Cockburn, Bruce, *The Trouble with Normal, on* THE TROUBLE WITH NORMAL (True North 1983).

Cohen, Jonathan R., *Apology and Organizations: Exploring an Example from Medical Practice*, 27 FORDHAM URB. L.J. 1447 (2000).

COHEN, JULIE E., CONFIGURING THE NETWORKED SELF: LAW, CODE, AND THE PLAY OF EVERYDAY PRACTICE (2012).

Cohen, Julie E., *What Privacy Is For*, 126 HARV. L. REV. 1904 (2013).

Cohen, Patricia, *Questioning Privacy Protections in Research*, N.Y. TIMES (Oct. 23, 2011), http://www.nytimes.com/2011/10/24/arts/rules-meant-to-protect-human-research-subjects-cause-concern.html?pagewanted=all.

College Gossip Website Shuts Down, Citing Economy. USA TODAY (Feb. 5, 2009). http://www.usatoday.com/tech/webguide/Internetlife/2009-02-05-juicycampus_N.htm.

Committee on Civil Liberties, Justice and Home Affairs, Rapporteur Jan Philipp Albrect, *Rapporteur's Report on Draft Report of General Data Protection Regulation*, COM(2012)0011–C7 0025/2012–2012/0011(COD) (Dec. 17, 2012).

Common Sense with Phineas and Ferb. Disney Channel television broadcast Jan. 27, 2010.

Cosgrove, Charles H., *The Declaration of Independence in Constitutional Interpretation: A Selective History and Analysis*, 32 U. RICH. L. REV. 107 (1998).

Council of Europe, *Convention for the Protection of Individuals with Regard to Automatic Processing of Personal Data* (1981), http://www.conventions.coe.int/Treaty/en/Treaties/Html/108.htm.

Cross Tab, *Online Reputation in a Connected World* (Jan. 2010), http://www.job-hunt.org/guides/DPD_Online-Reputation-Research_overview.pdf (accessed Aug. 1, 2015).

Cyberbullying-Linked Suicides Rising, Study Says, CBC NEWS (Oct. 20, 2012), http://www.cbc.ca/news/technology/story/2012/10/19/cyberbullying-suicide-study.html.

Daley, Suzanne, *On Its Own, Europe Backs Web Privacy Fights*, N.Y. TIMES (Aug. 9, 2011), http://www.nytimes.com/2011/08/10/world/europe/10spain.html?pagewanted=all&_r=0.

Das, Sauvik, and Adam Kramer, *Self-Censorship on Facebook*, PROC. OF SEVENTH INTERNATIONAL AAAI CONFERENCE ON WEBLOGS AND SOCIAL MEDIA (2013).

Davenport, Claire, *Spain Refers Google Privacy Complaints to EU's Top Court*, REUTERS (Mar. 2, 2012), http://www.reuters.com/article/2012/03/02/us-eu-google-idUSTRE8211DP20120302.

DE AZEVEDO CUNHA, MARIO VIOLA, MARKET INTEGRATION THROUGH DATA PROTECTION: AN ANALYSIS OF THE INSURANCE AND FINANCIAL INDUSTRIES IN THE EU (2013).

DᴇCᴇᴡ, Jᴜᴅɪᴛʜ Wᴀɢɴᴇʀ, Iɴ Pᴜʀsᴜɪᴛ ᴏꜰ Pʀɪᴠᴀᴄʏ (1997).

Digital Birth: Welcome to the Online World, Bᴜsɪɴᴇss Wɪʀᴇ (Oct. 6, 2010), http://www.businesswire.com/news/home/20101006006722/en/Digital-Birth-Online-World#.VD17VfldUud.

Doe, George, *With Genetic Testing, I Gave My Parents the Gift of Divorce*, Vᴏx (Sept. 9, 2014), http://www.vox.com/2014/9/9/5975653/with-genetic-testing-i-gave-my-parents-the-gift-of-divorce-23andme.

Driver, Michael J., and Theodore J. Mock, *Human Information Processing Decision Style Theory, and Accounting Information Systems*, 50 Aᴄᴄᴏᴜɴᴛɪɴɢ Rᴇᴠ. 490 (1975).

Duhigg, Charles, *How Companies Learn Your Secrets*, N.Y. Tɪᴍᴇs (Feb. 16, 2012).

Easterbrook, Frank, *Approaches to Judicial Review*, *in* Pᴏʟɪᴛɪᴄs ᴀɴᴅ ᴛʜᴇ Cᴏɴsᴛɪ-ᴛᴜᴛɪᴏɴ: Tʜᴇ Nᴀᴛᴜʀᴇ ᴏꜰ ᴀɴᴅ Exᴛᴇɴᴛ ᴏꜰ Iɴᴛᴇʀᴘʀᴇᴛᴀᴛɪᴏɴ 29 (Judith A. Baer ed., 1990).

Eᴀᴇʀʟᴇ, Eᴅᴡᴀʀᴅ J., Dɪɢɴɪᴛʏ ᴀɴᴅ Lɪᴀᴇʀᴛʏ: Cᴏɴsᴛɪᴛᴜᴛɪᴏɴᴀʟ Vɪsɪᴏɴs ɪɴ Gᴇʀᴍᴀɴʏ ᴀɴᴅ ᴛʜᴇ Uɴɪᴛᴇᴅ Sᴛᴀᴛᴇs 85 (2002).

Editorial Board, *Wrong Responses to Charlie Hebdo*, N.Y. Tɪᴍᴇs (Jan. 15, 2015).

Electronic Frontier Foundation, *Do Not Track*, https://www.eff.org/issues/do-not-track (accessed June 5, 2015).

Enright, Robert D., *Forgiveness Education with Children in Areas of Violence and Poverty*, *in* Fᴏʀɢɪᴠᴇɴᴇss: A Sᴀᴍᴘʟɪɴɢ ᴏꜰ Rᴇsᴇᴀʀᴄʜ Rᴇsᴜʟᴛs 11 (American Psychological Association, 2006), http://www.apa.org/international/resources/forgiveness.pdf.

Enright, Robert D., Suzanne Freedman, and Julio Rique, *The Psychology of Interpersonal Forgiveness*, *in* Exᴘʟᴏʀɪɴɢ Fᴏʀɢɪᴠᴇɴᴇss 46 (Robert D. Enright and Joanna North eds., 1998).

Enright, Robert D., Jeanette Knutson, Anthony Holter, Casey Knutson, and Padraig Twomey, *Forgiveness Education with Children in Areas of Violence and Poverty*, *in* Fᴏʀɢɪᴠᴇɴᴇss: A Sᴀᴍᴘʟɪɴɢ ᴏꜰ Rᴇsᴇᴀʀᴄʜ Rᴇsᴜʟᴛs 11 (American Psychological Association, 2006), http://www.apa.org/international/resources/forgiveness.pdf.

European Commission, *Commission Proposes a Comprehensive Reform of the Data Protection Rules* (Jan. 25, 2012), http://ec.europa.eu/justice/newsroom/data-protection/news/120125_en.htm.

European Commission, *Data Protection Reform—Frequently Asked Questions*, press release, MEMO/10/542 (Nov. 4, 2010), http://europa.eu/rapid/press-release_MEMO-10-542_en.htm?locale=fr.

European Commission, *European Commission Sets Out Strategy to Strengthen EU Data Protection Rules*, press release, IP/10/1462 (Nov. 4, 2010).

European Commission, *Issued by the Article 29 Data Protection Working Party*, press release (Sept. 18, 2014), http://ec.europa.eu/justice/data-protection/article-29/press-material/press-release/art29_press_material/2014/20140918_wp29_press_release_97th_plenary_cjeu_google_judgment__17sept_adopted.pdf.

European Commission, *Myth-Busing: The Court of Justice of the EU and the "Right to Be Forgotten"* (2014), http://ec.europa.eu/justice/data-protection/files/factsheets/factsheet_rtbf_mythbusting_en.pdf.

European Commission, *Proposal for a Regulation of the European Parliament and of the Council*, COM(2012) 11 final (Jan. 25, 2012) (DP Regulation), http://ec.europa.eu/justice/data-protection/document/review2012/com_2012_11_en.pdf.

European Commission, *The Proposed General Data Protection Regulation: The Consistency Mechanism Explained* (2013), http://ec.europa.eu/justice/newsroom/data-protection/news/130206_en.htm.

European Commission, *Safer Internet Day 2009: Commission Starts Campaign against Cyber-bullying*, press release, MEMO/09/58 (Feb. 10, 2009).

European Parliament, *US NSA: Stop Mass Surveillance Now or Face Consequences, MEPs Say*, press release (Mar. 12, 2014), http://www.europarl.europa.eu/news/en/news-room/content/20140307IPR38203/html/US-NSA-stop-mass-surveillance-now-or-face-consequences-MEPs-say.

European Parliament, Committee on Civil Liberties, Justice and Home Affairs, *Report on Draft European Parliament Legislative Resolution*, A7–0402/001–207 (Mar. 6, 2014) (DP Regulation, LIBE edits), http://www.europarl.europa.eu/sides/getDoc.do?pubRef=-//EP//NONSGML+AMD+A7–2013–0402+001–207+DOC+PDF+V0//EN.

Exline, Julie Juola, Everett L. Worthington Jr., Peter Hill, and Michael E. McCullough, *Forgiveness and Justice: A Research Agenda for Social and Personality Psychology*, 7 PERSONALITY & SOC. PSYCHOL. REV. 337 (2003).

Facebook, *Facebook Data Use Policy*, https://www.facebook.com/full_data_use_policy (accessed Aug. 1, 2014; for older version, see https://web.archive.org/web/20140805060652/https://www.facebook.com/full_data_use_policy).

Fastenberg, Dan, *Facebook Firings: Top 10 Cases and the NLRB's New Guidelines*, AOL JOBS (Sep. 2, 2011), http://jobs.aol.com/articles/2011/09/02/facebook-firings-top-ten-cases-and-the-nlrbs-new-guidelines/.

Fee, Gayle, and Laura Raposa, *Caitlin Davis' Life Is Not So Cheery Now*, BOSTON HERALD (Nov. 5, 2008), http://bostonherald.com/track/inside_track/view/2008_11_05_Caitlin_Davis_booted_from_Patriots__cheering_squad.

Feldman, Stuart I., *A Conversation with Brewster Kahle*, 2 QUEUE 24 (June 2004), http://queue.acm.org/detail.cfm?id=1016993.

Fetterly, Dennis, Mark Manasse, Marc Najork, and Janet L. Wiener, *A Large-Scale Study of the Evolution of Web Pages*, 34 SOFTWARE PRAC. & EXPERIENCE 213 (2004).

Fincham, Frank D., Steven R. H. Beach, and Joanne Davila, *Forgiveness and Conflict Resolution in Marriage*, 18 J. FAM. PSYCHOL. 72 (2004).

Fincham, Frank D., Julie H. Hall, and Steven R. H. Beach, *Til Lack of Forgiveness Doth Us Part: Forgiveness in Marriage*, in HANDBOOK OF FORGIVENESS 207 (Everett L. Worthington Jr. ed., 2005).

Firozi, Paulina, *Law School Admissions Use Facebook, Google to Screen Applicants, Study Finds*, DAILY NW. (Oct. 30, 2011), http://dailynorthwestern.com/2011/10/30/blogs/oncampus/law-school-admissions-use-facebook-google-to-screen-applicants-study-finds.

Flock, Elizabeth, *Should We Have a Right to Be Forgotten Online?*, WASH. POST (Apr. 20, 2011), http://www.washingtonpost.com/blogs/blogpost/post/should-we-have-a-right-to-be-forgotten-online/2011/04/20/AF2iOPCE_blog.html.

Frankel, David, *The Excavator: Creator or Destroyer?*, 67 ANTIQUITY 875 (Dec. 1993).

Franks, Mary Anne, *Unwilling Avatars: Idealism and Discrimination in Cyberspace*, 20 COLUM. J. GENDER & L. 224 (2011).

FRAUENFELDER, MARK, RULE THE WEB: HOW TO DO ANYTHING AND EVERYTHING ON THE INTERNET—BETTER, FASTER, EASIER (2007).

FRENCH, PETER A., THE VIRTUES OF VENGEANCE (2001).

Freund, Paul, *Address to the American Law Institute, in* PROCEEDINGS OF THE 52ND ANNUAL MEETING OF THE AMERICAN LAW INSTITUTE (1975).

Fried, Charles, *Privacy*, 77 YALE L.J. 475 (1968).

FRIEDMAN, LAWRENCE M., GUARDING LIFE'S DARK SECRETS (2007).

FRIEDMAN, LAWRENCE M., PRIVATE LIVES: FAMILIES, INDIVIDUALS, AND LAW (2005).

FUSTER, GLORIA GONZÁLEZ, THE EMERGENCE OF PERSONAL DATA PROTECTION AS A FUNDAMENTAL RIGHT OF THE EU (2014).

GARFINKEL, HAROLD, STUDIES IN ETHNOMETHODOLOGY (1967).

Gavison, Ruth, *Privacy and the Limits of Law*, 89 YALE L.J. 421 (1980).

Gellman, Robert, *Fair Information Practices: A Basic History, Version 1.91* (2012), http://bobgellman.com/rg-docs/rg-FIPShistory.pdf.

Germain, Carol Anne, *URLs: Uniform Resource Locators or Unreliable Resource Locators*, 60 C. AND RESEARCH LIBR. 359 (2000).

Gillespie, Tarleton, Pablo J. Boczkowski, and Kirsten A. Foot, eds., MEDIA TECHNOLOGIES: ESSAYS ON COMMUNICATION, MATERIALITY, AND SOCIETY (2014).

Glazer, Rashi H., *Measuring the Value of Information: The Information-Intensive Organization*, 32 IBM SYSTEMS J. 99 (1993).

Glensy, Rex D., *The Right to Dignity*, 43 COLUM. HUM. RTS. L. REV. 65 (2011).

GOLDSMITH, JACK, AND TIM WU, WHO CONTROLS THE INTERNET? ILLUSIONS OF A BORDERLESS WORLD (2008).

Gomes, Daniel, and Mario J. Silva, *Modelling Information Persistence on the Web, in* PROC. OF THE 6TH INT'L CONF. ON WEB ENGINEERING 193 (2006).

Google, *Company Overview* (Mar. 1, 2012), http://www.google.com/about/company/.

Google, *European Privacy Requests for Search Removals*, TRANSPARENCY REPORT (updated Feb. 15, 2015), http://www.google.com/transparencyreport/removals/europeprivacy/.

Google, *France—Government Removal Requests*, TRANSPARENCY REPORT, http://www.google.com/transparencyreport/removals/government/FR/ (accessed June 5, 2015).

Google, *Government Removal Requests*, Transparency Report, http://www. google.com/transparencyreport/removals/government/faq/ (accessed June 5, 2015).

Google, *Privacy Policy* (Mar. 1, 2012), http://www.google.com/intl/en/policies/ privacy/.

Google Advisory Council, The Advisory Council to Google on the Right to Be Forgotten Report (Feb. 6, 2015), https://www.google. com/advisorycouncil/.

Google Launches Challenges to Max Mosley's Privacy Bid, BBC News (Jan. 14, 2015), http://www.bbc.com/news/uk-30816523.

Google Sets Up "Right to Be Forgotten" Form after EU Ruling, BBC News (May 30, 2014), http://www.bbc.com/news/technology-27631001.

Granick, Jennifer, *Convicted Murderer to Wikipedia: Shhh!*, Electronic Frontier Foundation (Nov. 10, 2009), https://www.eff.org/deeplinks/2009/11/ murderer-wikipedia-shhh.

Gray, Jim, and Catharine van Ingen, *Empirical Measurements of Disk Failure Rates and Error Rates*, Microsoft Research Technical Report MSR-TR-2005–166 (Dec. 2005).

Griffin, James, *First Steps in an Account of Human Rights*, 9 Eur. J. Phil. 306 (2001).

Halliday, Josh, *Max Mosley Sues Google in France and Germany over "Orgy" Search Results*, Guardian (Feb. 25, 2011), http://www.theguardian.com/media/2011/nov/25/ max-mosley-google-france-germany.

Hampton, Keith, Lee Rainie, Weixu Lu, Maria Dwyer, Inyoung Shin, and Kristen Purcell, *Social Media and the "Spiral of Silence,"* Pew Research Center (Aug. 26, 2014), http://www.pewinternet.org/files/2014/08/PI_Social-networks-and-debate_082614.pdf.

Harrison, *How Our Opt-Out System Works*, Spokeo People Search Blog (Jan. 12, 2011), https://web.archive.org/web/20110116031332/http://www.spokeo.com/ blog/2011/01/how-spokeo-opt-out-system-works/.

Hartzog, Woodrow, and Frederic Stutzman, *The Case for Online Obscurity*, 101 Cal. L. Rev. 1 (2013).

Hauch, Jeanne M., *Protecting Private Facts in France: The Warren & Brandeis Tort Is Alive and Well and Flourishing in Paris*, 68 Tul. L. Rev. 1219 (1994).

Hendel, John, *In Europe, a Right to Be Forgotten Trumps the Memory of the Internet*, Atlantic (Feb. 3, 2011).

Hill, David G., Data Protection: Governance, Risk Management, and Compliance (2009).

Hill, Kashmir, *Google Makes Every Person Search in Europe Look Censored*, Forbes (July 2, 2014), http://www.forbes.com/sites/kashmirhill/2014/07/02/ google-right-to-be-forgotten-notice/.

Hill, Kashmir, *How the Past Haunts Us in the Digital Age*, Forbes (Oct. 4, 2011), http://www.forbes.com/sites/kashmirhill/2011/10/04/ how-the-past-haunts-us-in-the-digital-age/.

Hogan, Bernie, *Pseudonyms and the Rise of the Real-Name Web, in* A COMPANION TO NEW MEDIA DYNAMICS 290 (John Hartley, Jean Burgess, and Alex Bruns eds. 2013).

Holmgren, Margaret R., *Forgiveness and the Intrinsic Value of Persons*, 30 AM. PHIL. Q. 341 (1993).

Holson, Laura M., *The New Court of Shame Is Online*, N.Y. TIMES (Dec. 23, 2010), http://www.nytimes.com/2010/12/26/fashion/26shaming.html?ref=todayspaper&_r=0.

HOUSE OF LORDS, EU DATA PROTECTION LAW: "RIGHT TO BE FORGOTTEN"?, EUROPEAN UNION COMMITTEE, 2ND REPORT OF SESSION 2014–15 (July 30, 2014), http://www.publications.parliament.uk/pa/ld201415/ldselect/ldeucom/40/40.pdf.

Human Rights Committee, *General Comment 16* (23rd sess., 1988), COMPILATION OF GENERAL COMMENTS AND GENERAL RECOMMENDATIONS ADOPTED BY HUMAN RIGHTS TREATY BODIES, U.N. Doc. HRI/GEN/1/Rev.1 at 21 (1994).

Internet Archive, *Internet Archive's Policies on Archival Integrity and Removal* (2002), http://www2.sims.berkeley.edu/research/conferences/aps/removal-policy.html.

Internet Archive, *Wayback Machine: Frequently Asked Questions*, https://www.archive.org/about/faqs.php (accessed June 6, 2015).

Italian Data Protection Authority, *Oblivion Rights*, doc. Web n. 1336892 (Nov. 9, 2005).

Jakoby, Jacob, Donald E. Speller, and Carol A. Kohn, *Brand Choice as a Function of Information Overload: Replication and Extension*, 1:1 J. CONSUM. RESEARCH 33 (1974).

JASANOFF, SHEILA, DESIGNS OF NATURE (2005).

Jasanoff, Sheila, *Ordering Knowledge, Ordering Society, in* STATES OF KNOWLEDGE 13 (Sheila Jasanoff ed., 2004).

Jasanoff, Sheila, ed., STATES OF KNOWLEDGE (2004).

JEFFRESS, ROBERT, WHEN FORGIVENESS DOESN'T MAKE SENSE (2001).

Jenkins, Holman W., Jr., *Google and the Search for the Future*, WALL ST. J. (Aug. 14, 2010), http://online.wsj.com/article/SB10001424052748704901104575423294099527212.html.

Johnson, David R., and David Post, *Law and Borders: The Rise of Law in Cyberspace*, 48 STAN. L. REV. 1367 (1996).

Jonas, Jeff, *Data Tethering: Managing the Echo*, JEFF JONAS BLOG (Sep. 21, 2006), http://jeffjonas.typepad.com/jeff_jonas/2006/09/data_tethering_.html.

JUNCO, REYNOL, ENGAGING STUDENTS THROUGH SOCIAL MEDIA: EVIDENCE-BASED PRACTICES FOR USE IN STUDENT AFFAIRS (2014).

Kageyama, Yuri, *Japan Court Orders Google to Remove Search Results*, ASSOCIATED PRESS (Oct. 10, 2014), http://hosted.ap.org/dynamic/stories/A/AS_JAPAN_GOOGLE?SITE=AP&SECTION=HOME&TEMPLATE=DEFAULT&CTIME=2014-10-10-12-29-58.

Kahle, Brewster, *Preserving the Internet*, SCIENTIFIC AMERICAN (July 27, 1998), http://web.archive.org/web/19980627072808/http://www.sciam.com/0397issue/0397kahle.html.

Kaplan, *Kaplan Test Prep Survey: More College Admissions Officers Checking Applicants' Digital Trails, but Most Students Unconcerned* (Nov. 20, 2014), http://press.kaptest.com/press-releases/kaplan-test-prep-survey-percentage-of-college-admissions-officers-who-visit-applicants-social-networking-pages-continues-to-grow-but-most-students-shrug.

Karremans, Johan C., Paul A. M. Van Lange, and Rob W. Holland, *Forgiveness and Its Associations with Prosocial Thinking, Feeling, and Doing beyond the Relationship with the Offender*, 31 PERSONALITY & SOC. PSYCHOL. BULL. 1315 (2005).

Karvonen, Kristiina, Sanna Shibasaki, Sofia Nunes, Puneet Kaur, and Olli Immonen, *Visual Nudges for Enhancing the Use and Produce of Reputation Information, in* PROC. CEUR WORKSHOP (2010), http://ceur-ws.org/Vol-612/paper1.pdf.

Kelln, Brad R. C., and John H. Ellard, *An Equity Theory Analysis of the Impact of Forgiveness and Retribution on Transgressor Compliance*, 25 PERSONALITY & SOC. PSYCHOL. BULL. 864 (1999).

Kilian, Wolfgang, *Germany, in* GLOBAL PRIVACY PROTECTION: THE FIRST GENERATION 80 (James B. Rule and Graham Greenleaf eds., 2008).

Kim, Jinyoung, and Viktor R. Carvalho, *An Analysis of Time Stability in Web Search Results, in* PROC. OF THE 33RD EUROPEAN CONF. ON ADVANCES IN INFO. RETRIEVAL 466 (2011).

Kobayashi, Mei, and Koichi Takeda, *Information Retrieval on the Web*, 32 ACM COMPUTING SURVEYS 144 (2000).

Koehler, Wallace, *A Longitudinal Study of Web Pages Continued: A Consideration of Document Persistence*, 9:2 INFO. RESEARCH paper 174 (2004), http://informationr.net/ir/9-2/paper174.html.

KOHL, UTA, JURISDICTION AND THE INTERNET: REGULATORY COMPETENCE OVER ONLINE ACTIVITY (2007).

Koops, Bert-Jaap, *Forgetting Footprints, Shunning Shadows: A Critical Analysis of the "Right to Be Forgotten" in Big Data Practice*, 8:3 SCRIPTed 1 (2011).

Korenhof, Paulan, and Bert-Jaap Koops, *Gender Identity and Privacy: Could a Right to Be Forgotten Help ~~Andrew~~ Agnes Online?*, SSRN WORKING PAPER (2013), http://ssrn.com/abstract=2304190 or http://dx.doi.org/10.2139/ssrn.2304190.

Lane, Edwin, *Google Removes 12 BBC News Links in "Right to Be Forgotten,"* BBC NEWS (Aug. 19, 2014), http://www.bbc.com/news/technology-28851366.

Law Reform Commission, Ireland, *Issues Paper on Cyber-Crime Affecting Personal Safety, Privacy and Reputation Including Cyber-Bullying*, LRC IP 6–2014 (2014).

Lee, Dave, *Google Removing BBC Link Was "Not a Good Judgement,"* BBC NEWS (July 3, 2014), http://www.bbc.com/news/technology-28144406.

Leonhard, Woody, *"Zombie Cookies" Won't Die: Microsoft Admits Use, HTML 5 Looms as New Vector*, INFOWORLD (Aug. 22, 2011), http://www.infoworld.com/t/Internet-privacy/zombie-cookies-wont-die-microsoft-admits-use-and-html5-looms-new-vector-170511.

Lepore, Jill, *The Disruption Machine*, NEW YORKER (June 23, 2014).

LESSIG, LAWRENCE, CODE: VERSION 2.0 (2006).

LUENBERGER, DAVID G., INFORMATION SCIENCE (2006).

Luskin, Frederick, *The Stanford Forgiveness Projects, in* FORGIVENESS: A SAMPLING OF RESEARCH RESULTS 14 (American Psychological Association, 2006), http://www.apa.org/international/resources/publications/forgiveness.pdf.

Lyman, Peter, and Howard Besser, *Defining the Problem of Our Vanishing Memory: Background, Current Status, Models for Resolution, in* TIME & BITS: MANAGING DIGITAL CONTINUITY 11 (Margaret MacLean and Ben H. Davis eds., 1998).

MacLean, Margaret, and Ben H. Davis, eds., TIME & BITS: MANAGING DIGITAL CONTINUITY (1998).

Manders-Huits, Noëmi, and Jeroen van den Hoven, *Moral Identification in Identity Management Systems, in* THE FUTURE OF IDENTITY IN THE INFORMATION SOCIETY 77 (Simone Fischer-Hübner, Penny Duquenoy, Albin Zuccato, and Leonardo Martuc eds., 2008).

Marano, Hara Estroff, *Our Brain's Negative Bias,* PSYCHOLOGY TODAY (June 20, 2003), http://www.psychologytoday.com/articles/200306/our-brains-negative-bias.

MARGALIT, AVISHAI, THE ETHICS OF MEMORY (2002).

Marsh, Stephen, and Pamela Briggs, *Examining Trust, Forgiveness and Regret as Computational Concepts, in* COMPUTING WITH SOCIAL TRUST 9 (Jennifer Golbeck ed., 2009).

Match.com Presents Singles in America 2012, UP TO DATE (blog), Match.com, http://blog.match.com/SIA/ (accessed June 23, 2015).

Matussek, Karin, *Snowden Leaks Killed U.S.-E.U. Data Deal, Regulator Say,* BLOOMBERG BUSINESS (Jan. 28, 2015). http://www.bloomberg.com/news/articles/2015-01-28/snowden-leaks-killed-u-s-e-u-data-deal-regulator-say.

Mauger, Paul A., J. F. Perry, T. Freeman, D. C. Grove, A. G. McBride, and K. E. McKinney, *The Measurement of Forgiveness: Preliminary Research,* 11 J. PSYCHOL. CHRIST. 170 (1992).

Maycotte, H. O., *America's "Right to Be Forgotten" Fight Heats Up,* FORBES (Sept. 30, 2014), http://www.forbes.com/sites/homaycotte/2014/09/30/americas-right-to-be-forgotten-fight-heats-up/.

MAYER-SCHÖNBERGER, VIKTOR, DELETE: THE VIRTUE OF FORGETTING IN THE DIGITAL AGE (2009).

Mayo Clinic, *Forgiveness: Letting Go of Grudges and Bitterness* (Nov. 11, 2014), http://www.mayoclinic.org/healthy-living/adult-health/in-depth/forgiveness/art-20047692.

McArdle, Megan, *Sink and Swim,* ATLANTIC (June 1, 2009).

McDonald, Aleecia M., and Lorrie Faith Cranor, *The Cost of Reading Privacy Policies,* 4 ISJLP 543 (2008).

Michaels, Ralf, *The Functional Method of Comparative Law, in* THE OXFORD HANDBOOK OF COMPARATIVE LAW 339 (Mathias Reimann and Reinhard Zimmermann eds., 2006).

Ministry of Justice and the Rt. Hon. Chris Grayling MP, *New Law to Tackle Revenge Porn*, press release (Oct. 12, 2014).

Moore, Michael, *The Moral Worth of Retribution*, in RESPONSIBILITY, CHARACTER, AND THE EMOTIONS 179 (Ferdinand Schoeman ed., 1987).

Mooris, Alex, *Hunter Moore: The Most Hated Man on the Internet*, ROLLING STONE (Oct. 11, 2012), http://www.rollingstone.com/culture/news/the-most-hated-man-on-the-Internet-20121113.

Morain, Dan, *Anthony Kennedy Speaks about History, Civics, Flag Burning, and Emerging Issues*, SACRAMENTO BEE (June 29, 2014), http://www.sacbee.com/2014/06/29/6512694/anthony-kennedy-speaks-about-history.html#storylink=cpy.

Moran, Lee, and Beth Stebner, *Now FBI Launch Investigation into Founder of "Revenge Porn" Site Is Anyone Up?*, DAILY MAIL (May 23, 2012), http://www.dailymail.co.uk/news/article-2148522/Hunter-Moore-founder-revenge-porn-site-Is-Anyone-Up-investigated-FBI.html.

Morris, Herbert, *Murphy on Forgiveness*, 7 CRIM. JUST. ETHICS 15 (1988), http://dx.doi.org/10.1080/0731129X.1988.9991836.

Morrissey, Tracie Egan, *Racist Teens Forced to Answer for Tweets about the "N*****" President*, JEZEBEL (Nov. 9, 2012), http://jezebel.com/5958993/racist-teens-forced-to-answer-for-tweets-about-the-nigger-president.

Movius, Lauren B., and Nathalie Krup, *U.S. and EU Privacy Policy: Comparison of Regulatory Approaches*, 3 INT'L J. COMM. 169 (2009).

Mungin, Lateef, *Bullied Canadian Teen Leaves Behind Chilling YouTube Video*, CNN (Oct. 12, 2012), http://www.cnn.com/2012/10/12/world/americas/canada-teen-bullying/.

Murphy, Jeffrie G., *Forgiveness in Counseling: A Philosophical Perspective*, in BEFORE FORGIVING: CAUTIONARY VIEWS OF FORGIVENESS IN PSYCHOTHERAPY 41 (Sharon Lamb and Jeffrie G. Murphy eds., 2002).

Murphy, Jeffrie G., *Forgiveness, Mercy, and the Retributive Emotions*, 7:2 CRIM. JUST. ETHICS 3 (1988).

Murphy, Jeffrie G., *Forgiveness, Self-Respect, and the Value of Resentment*, in HANDBOOK OF FORGIVENESS 33 (Everett L. Worthington Jr. ed., 2005).

Murphy, Jeffrie G., *Two Cheers for Vindictiveness*, 2 PUNISHM. & SOC'Y 131 (2000).

Nakashima, Ellen, *Feeling Betrayed, Facebook Users Force Site to Honor Their Privacy*, WASH. POST (Nov. 30, 2007), http://www.washingtonpost.com/wp-dyn/content/article/2007/11/29/AR2007112902503.html.

National Telecommunications and Information Administration, U.S. Department of Commerce, *Commercial Data Privacy and Innovation in the Internet Economy: Dynamic Policy Framework* (2010), http://www.ntia.doc.gov/report/2010/commercial-data-privacy-and-innovationInternet-economy-dynamic-policy-framework.

NELSON, HAROLD L., AND DWIGHT L. TEETER JR., LAW OF MASS COMMUNICATIONS (2d ed. 1973).

Network Advertising Initiative, *Consumer Opt-Out | NAI: Network Advertising Initiative*, http://www.networkadvertising.org/choices/#completed (accessed June 5, 2015).

Neumann, Elisabeth Noelle, *The Spiral of Silence: A Theory of Public Opinion*, 24 J. COMMUN. 43 (1974).

NEWMAN, ABRAHAM L., PROTECTORS OF PRIVACY (2008).

Nimmer, Melville B., *The Right to Speak from Time to Time: First Amendment Theory Applied to Libel and Misapplied to Privacy*, 56 CAL. L. REV. 935 (1967).

Nissenbaum, Helen, *A Contextual Approach to Privacy Online*, 140 DAEDALUS 32 (2011), http://www.amacad.org/publications/daedalus/11_fall_nissenbaum.pdf.

Nissenbaum, Helen, *Privacy as Contextual Integrity*, 79 WASH. L. REV. 119 (2004).

Norberg, Patricia A., *The Privacy Paradox: Personal Information Disclosure Intentions versus Behaviors*, 41 J. CONSUMER AFF. 100 (2007).

North, Joanna, *The "Ideal" of Forgiveness: A Philosopher's Exploration*, *in* EXPLORING FORGIVENESS 15 (Robert D. Enright and Joanna North eds., 1998).

North, Joanna, *Wrongdoing and Forgiveness*, 62 PHILOSOPHY 499 (1987).

Ohm, Paul, *Broken Promises of Privacy: Responding to the Surprising Failure of Anonymization*, 57 UCLA L. REV. 1701 (2010).

Ohm, Paul, *Good Enough Privacy*, 2008 U. CHI. LEGAL F. 1 (2008).

O'Kane, Ciaran, *BlueKai Explain Their Data Exchange Platform and Hint at European Move*, EXCHANGEWIRE (blog) (Aug. 10, 2009), http://www.exchangewire.com/blog/2009/08/10/bluekai-explain-their-data-exchange-platform-and-hint-at-european-move/.

Olson, Walter, *Facebook Opens Takedown Hotline for Public School Officials*, CATO INSTITUTE (Oct. 3, 2013), http://www.cato.org/blog/facebook-opens-takedown-hotline-public-school-officials.

Oltermann, Philip, *"Revenge Porn" Victims Receive Boost from German Court*, GUARDIAN (May 22, 2014).

O'Reilly, Charles A., *Individuals and Information Overload in Organisations: Is More Necessarily Better?*, 23 ACADEMY OF MANAGEMENT J. 684 (1980).

PALFREY, JOHN, AND URS GASSER, INTEROP: THE PROMISE AND PERILS OF HIGHLY INTERCONNECTED SYSTEMS (2012).

PARISER, ELI, THE FILTER BUBBLE (2011).

PASQUALE, FRANK, THE BLACK BOX SOCIETY (2014).

Paul-Choudhury, Sumit, *Digital Legacy: The Fate of Your Online Soul*, NEW SCIENTIST (May 15, 2012), http://www.newscientist.com/article/mg21028091.400-digital-legacy-the-fate-of-your-online-soul.html.

Perma, *About*, https://perma.cc/about (accessed June 12, 2015).

Pino, Giorgio, *The Right to Personal Identity in Italian Private Law: Constitutional Interpretation and Judge-Made Rights*, *in* THE HARMONIZATION OF PRIVATE LAW IN EUROPE 225 (Mark Van Hoecke and François Ost eds., 2000).

Post, Robert C., *The Social Foundations of Privacy: Community and Self in the Common Law Tort*, 77 CAL. L. REV. 957 (1989).

Prosser, William, *Privacy*, 48 CAL. L. REV. 383 (1960).

Public.Resource.org, *Why Is My Court Case on the Internet?*, https://public.resource.org/court_cases.html (accessed June 5, 2015).

Public Session: Panel Discussion, in TIME & BITS: MANAGING DIGITAL CONTINUITY 36 (Margaret MacLean and Ben H. Davis eds., 1998).

Raywood, Dan, *Internet to Enter Its Second Stage as Large Domains Control 30 Per Cent of the Total Content*, SC MAGAZINE UK (Oct. 13, 2009), http://www.scmagazineuk.com/internet-to-enter-its-second-stage-as-large-domains-control-30-per-cent-of-the-total-content/article/152156/.

Reding, Viviane, *Speech at New Frontiers for Social Media Marketing Conference, EU Data Protection Reform and Social Media: Encouraging Citizens' Trust and Creating New Opportunities* (Nov. 29, 2011) (transcript available at http://europa.eu/rapid/press-release_SPEECH-11-827_en.htm).

Reding, Viviane, *Speech at The Privacy Platform, the Review of the EU Data Protection Framework Event* (Mar. 16, 2011) (transcript available at http://europa.eu/rapid/pressReleasesAction.do?reference=SPEECH/11/183).

REGAN, PRISCILLA M., LEGISLATING PRIVACY: TECHNOLOGY, SOCIAL VALUES, AND PUBLIC POLICY (1995).

Regan, Priscilla M., *The United States, in* GLOBAL PRIVACY PROTECTION: THE FIRST GENERATION 50 (James B. Rule and Graham Greenleaf eds., 2008).

Rehnquist, William H., *Is an Expanded Right of Privacy Consistent with Fair and Effective Law Enforcement?*, 23 U. KAN. L. REV. 1 (1974).

Reiman, Jeffrey H., *Driving to the Panopticon: A Philosophical Exploration of the Risks to Privacy Posed by the Highway Technology of the Future*, 11 SANTA CLARA COMPUTER & HIGH TECH. L.J. 27 (1995).

Rein, Lisa, *Brewster Kahle on the Internet Archive and People's Technology*, O'REILLY P2P.COM (Jan. 22, 2004), http://openp2p.com/pub/a/p2p/2004/01/22/kahle.html.

Reputation.com, *A Bad Online Reputation Could Cost You the Election*, http://www.reputation.com/reputationwatch/articles/a-bad-online-reputation-could-cost-you-the-election (accessed June 28, 2015).

Reputation.com, *The Real-World Effect of Online Reputation Management*, http://www.reputation.com/reputationwatch/articles/real-world-effects-of-online-reputation-management (accessed June 28, 2015).

Reputation.com, *Suppress Negative Content Online: ReputationDefender*, https://www.reputation.com/reputationdefender (accessed June 28, 2005).

Restatement (Second) of Torts (2012).

Richards, Neil M., *Intellectual Privacy*, 87 TEX. L. REV. 387 (2008).

RICHARDS, NEIL M., INTELLECTUAL PRIVACY: RETHINKING CIVIL LIBERTIES IN THE DIGITAL AGE (2015).

Richards, Neil M., and Daniel J. Solove, *Privacy's Other Path: Recovering the Law of Confidentiality*, 96 GEO. L.J. 123 (2007).

Robinson, Frances, *EU Data Protection Law on Track for Juncker Deadline*, WALL ST. J. (Oct. 10, 2014), http://blogs.wsj.com/brussels/2014/10/10/eu-data-protection-law-on-track-for-juncker-deadline/.

Roesner, Franziska, Brian T. Gill, and Tadayoshi Kohno, *Sex, Lies, or Kittens? Investigating the Use of Snapchat's Self-Destructing Messages*, 8437 FINANCIAL CRYPTOGRAPHY AND DATA SECURITY 64 (2014).

Rolfs, Jacqueline R., *The Florida Star v. B.J.F.: The Beginning of the End for the Tort of Public Disclosure*, 1990 WIS. L. REV. 1107 (1990).

Rosen, Jeffrey, *The Delete Squad*, NEW REPUBLIC (Apr. 29, 2013).

Rosen, Jeffrey, *Free Speech, Privacy, and the Web That Never Forgets*, 9 J. ON TELECOMM. & HIGH TECH. L. 345 (2011).

Rosen, Jeffrey, *The Right to Be Forgotten*, 64 STAN. L. REV. ONLINE 88 (2012), http://www.stanfordlawreview.org/online/privacy-paradox/right-to-be-forgotten.

ROSEN, JEFFREY, THE UNWANTED GAZE: THE DESTRUCTION OF PRIVACY IN AMERICA (2000).

Rosen, Jeffrey, *The Web Means the End of Forgetting*, N.Y. TIMES MAGAZINE (July 21, 2010), http://www.nytimes.com/2010/07/25/magazine/25privacy-t2.html?pagewanted=all.

ROSENZWEIG, ROY, CLIO WIRED: THE FUTURE OF THE PAST IN THE DIGITAL AGE (2011).

ROTHENBERG, JEFF, AVOIDING TECHNOLOGICAL QUICKSAND (1998).

Rouvroy, Antoinette, and Yves Poullet, *The Right to Informational Self-Determination and the Value of Self-Development: Reassessing the Importance of Privacy for Democracy*, in REINVENTING DATA PROTECTION? 45 (Serge Gutwirth, Yves Poullet, Paul de Hert, Cécile de Terwangne, Sjaak Nouwt eds., 2009).

Ruderman, Zoe, *The First Ever Live-Tweeted Breakup*, COSMOPOLITAN (Nov. 9, 2011).

Rumsey, Mary, *Runaway Train: Problems of Permanence, Accessibility, and Stability in the Use of Web Resources in Law Review Citations*, 94 LAW LIBR. J. 27 (2002).

Rusbult, Caryl E., Peggy A. Hannon, Sevaun L. Stocker, and Eli J. Finkel, *Forgiveness and Relational Repair*, in HANDBOOK OF FORGIVENESS 185 (Everett L. Worthington Jr. ed., 2005).

Salkin, Allen, *What's in a Name? Ask Google*, N.Y. TIMES (Nov. 25, 2011), http://www.nytimes.com/2011/11/27/fashion/google-searches-help-parents-narrow-down-baby-names.html?_r=2&ref=technology.

Schwartz, John, *Two German Killers Demanding Anonymity Sue Wikipedia's Parent*, N.Y. TIMES (Nov. 12, 2009).

Schwartz, Paul M., *Data Protection Law and the Ethical Use of Analytics*, CENTRE FOR INFORMATION POLICY LEADERSHIP (2010), http://www.huntonfiles.com/files/webupload/CIPL_Ethical_Undperinnings_of_Analytics_Paper.pdf.

Schwartz, Paul M., *The EU-US Privacy Collision: A Turn to Institutions and Procedures*, 126 HARV. L. REV. 1966 (2013).

Schwartz, Paul M., and Karl-Nikolaus Peifer, *Prosser's Privacy and the German Right of Personality: Are Four Privacy Torts Better than One Unitary Concept?*, 98 CAL. L. REV. 1925 (2010).

Segal, David, *Mugged by a Mug Shot Online*, N.Y. TIMES (Oct. 5, 2013).

Seidman, Ilene, and Susan Vickers, *The Second Wave: An Agenda for the Next Thirty Years of Rape Law Reform*, 38 SUFFOLK U. L. REV. 467, 473 (2005).

Seltzer, Wendy, *Free Speech Unmoored in Copyright's Safe Harbor: Chilling Effects of the DMCA on the First Amendment*, 24 HARV. J. L. & TECH. 171 (2010).

Singer, Natasha, *They Loved Your G.P.A. Then They Saw Your Tweets*, N.Y. TIMES (Nov. 9, 2013), http://www.nytimes.com/2013/11/10/business/they-loved-your-gpa-then-they-saw-your-tweets.html?_r=0.

Siry, Lawrence, and Sandra Schmitz, *A Right to Be Forgotten? How Recent Developments in Germany May Affect the Internet Publishers in the US*, 3:1 EUR. J. L. & TECH. (2012), http://ejlt.org/article/viewFile/141/222%3E.

SLAUGHTER, ANNE-MARIE, A NEW WORLD ORDER (2004).

Snead, O. Carter, *Memory and Punishment*, 64 VAND. L. REV. 1195 (2011).

Social Network, The (Columbia Pictures 2010).

Society of American Archivists, *Code of Ethics for Archivists*, SAA Council Approval/ Endorsement (Feb. 2005), http://www2.archivists.org/statements/saa-core-values -statement-and-code-of-ethics.

SOLOVE, DANIEL J., THE FUTURE OF REPUTATION: GOSSIP, RUMOR, AND PRIVACY ON THE INTERNET (2007).

Solove, Daniel J., *Privacy Self-Management and the Consent Dilemma*, 126 HARV. L. REV. 1880 (2013).

SOLOVE, DANIEL J., UNDERSTANDING PRIVACY (2008).

Spencer, Neil, *How Much Data Is Created Every Minute?*, VISUAL NEWS (June 9, 2012), http://www.visualnews.com/2012/06/19/ how-much-data-created-every-minute/?view=infographic.

SPINELLO, RICHARD A., CASE STUDIES IN INFORMATION AND COMPUTER ETHICS (1997).

Sprenger, Polly, *Sun on Privacy: "Get Over It,"* WIRED (Jan. 26, 1999).

Stanley, James E., *Max Mosley and the English Right to Privacy*, 10 WASH. U. GLOBAL STUD. L. REV. 641 (2011).

Star-Ledger Staff, *Dharun Ravi Sentenced to Jail in Tyler Clementi Webcam Spying Case*, NJ.COM (May 21, 2012), http://www.nj.com/news/index.ssf/2012/05/dharun_ravi_ sentenced_to_jail.html.

Staub, Ervin, and Laurie Anne Pearlman, *Promoting Reconciliation and Forgiveness after Mass Violence: Rwanda and Other Settings*, in FORGIVENESS: A SAMPLING OF RESEARCH RESULTS 31 (American Psychological Association, 2006), http:// www.apa.org/international/resources/forgiveness.pdf.

Storey, Katie, *Evil Killer Ronald Castree Should Never Be Forgotten, Says Father of Lesley Molseed*, MANCHESTER EVENING NEWS

(Sept. 25, 2014), http://www.manchestereveningnews.co.uk/news/
evil-killer-should-never-forgotten-7834956.

Student in Asian Tirade Video Quits University after "Death Threats and Harassment,"
DAILY MAIL (Mar. 19, 2011), http://www.dailymail.co.uk/news/article-1367923/
Alexandra-Wallace-YouTube-video-Student-Asian-race-row-quits-Californian-
university.html.

Sunstein, Cass R., *Low Value Speech Revisited,* 83 NW. U. L. REV. 555 (1988).

Tabuchi, Hiroko, *Facebook Wins Relatively Few Friends in Japan,* N.Y. TIMES B1 (Jan.
10, 2011).

Tan, Gillian, Douglas MacMillan, and Jack Marshall, *News and Ads to Debut on
Snapchat,* WALL ST. J. (Aug. 19, 2014), http://online.wsj.com/articles/snapchat-
discussing-new-content-service-with-advertisers-and-media-firms-1408486739.

Taylor, Mary K., and Diane Hudson, *"Linkrot" and the Usefulness of Web Site Bibliographies,* 39 REF. & USER SERV. Q. 273 (2000).

Todd, Amanda, *My Story: Struggling, Bullying, Suicide, Self Harm,* YOUTUBE (2012),
http://www.youtube.com/watch?v=ojo5LJryiKE.

Toussaint, Loren, and Jon R. Webb, *Theoretical and Empirical Connections between
Forgiveness, Mental Health, and Well-Being, in* HANDBOOK OF FORGIVENESS
349 (Everett L. Worthington Jr. ed., 2005).

Tugendhat, Michael, *The Data Protection Act of 1998 and the Media, in* THE YEARBOOK
OF COPYRIGHT AND MEDIA LAW: VOLUME V: 2000 115 (Eric M. Barendt,
Alison Firth, Stephen Bate, Julia Palca, John Enser, and Thomas Gibbons eds., 2001).

Umansky, Natalie, *10 Outrageous Tweets That Got People Fired,* ODDEE (Feb. 21,
2014), http://www.oddee.com/item_98873.aspx.

UMBREIT, MARK S., THE HANDBOOK OF VICTIM OFFENDER MEDIATION:
AN ESSENTIAL GUIDE TO PRACTICE AND RESEARCH (2002).

Urban, Jennifer, and Laura Quilter, *Efficient Process or "Chilling Effects"? Takedown Notices under Section 512 of the Digital Millennium Copyright Act,* 22 SANTA CLARA
COMPUTER & HIGH TECH. L.J. 621 (2006).

Vasalou, Asimina, and Jeremy Pitt, *Reinventing Forgiveness: A Formal Investigation of
Moral Facilitation, in* TRUST MANAGEMENT, THIRD INTERNATIONAL CON-
FERENCE, iTRUST 2005 146 (Peter Herrmann, Valérie Issarny, and Simon Shiu
eds., 2005).

Velleman, J. David, *The Genesis of Shame,* 30 PHIL. & PUB. AFF. 27 (2001).

Volokh, Eugene, *Freedom of Speech and Information Privacy: The Troubling Implications of a Right to Stop People from Speaking about You,* 52 STAN. L. REV. 1049
(2000).

Volokh, Eugene, and Donald M. Falk, *Google: First Amendment Protection for Search
Engine Search Results,* 8 J. L. ECON. & POL'Y 883 (2011).

Wacks, Raymond, *Why There Will Never Be an English Common Law Privacy Tort, in*
NEW DIMENSIONS IN PRIVACY LAW: INTERNATIONAL AND COMPARA-
TIVE PERSPECTIVES 154 (Andrew T. Kenyon and Megan Richardson eds., 2010).

Walker, Robert Kirk, *Forcing Forgetfulness: Data Privacy, Free Speech, and the "Right to Be Forgotten,"* SSRN WORKING PAPER (2012), http://ssrn.com/abstract=2017967 or http://dx.doi.org/10.2139/ssrn.2017967.

Warren, Christina, *10 People Who Lost Jobs over Social Media Mistakes*, MASHABLE (June 16, 2011), http://mashable.com/2011/06/16/weinergate-social-media-job -loss/.

Warren, Samuel D., and Louis D. Brandeis, *The Right to Privacy*, 4 HARV. L. REV. 193 (1890).

WASSOM, BRIAN, AUGMENTED REALITY LAW, PRIVACY, AND ETHICS: LAW, SOCIETY, EMERGING AR TECHNOLOGIES (2015).

Weber, Rolf H., *The Right to Be Forgotten: More than a Pandora's Box?*, 2 JIPITEC 120 (2011), http://www.jipitec.eu/issues/jipitec-2-2-2011/3084/jipitec%202%20-%20a%20 -%20weber.pdf.

Weiss, Rick, *On the Web, Research Work Proves Ephemeral*, WASH. POST (Nov. 24, 2003), http://faculty.missouri.edu/glaserr/205fo3/Article_WebPub.html.

Werro, Franz, *The Right to Inform v. the Right to Be Forgotten: A Transatlantic Clash, in* LIABILITY IN THE THIRD MILLENNIUM 285 (Aurelia Colombi Ciacchi, Christine Godt, Peter Rott, and Leslie Jane Smith eds., 2009).

Wersig, Gernot, *Information Theory, in* INTERNATIONAL ENCYCLOPEDIA OF INFORMATION AND LIBRARY SCIENCE 312 (John Feather and Paul Sturges eds., 2003).

WESTIN, ALAN F., PRIVACY AND FREEDOM (1967).

Westin, Alan F., *Science, Privacy, and Freedom: Issues and Proposals for the 1970's*, 66 COLUMBIA L. REV. 1205 (1966).

WHITE HOUSE, NATIONAL STRATEGY FOR TRUSTED IDENTITIES IN CYBERSPACE, ENHANCING ONLINE CHOICE, EFFICIENCY, SECURITY, AND PRIVACY (2011), http://www.whitehouse.gov/sites/default/files/rss_viewer/NSTIC-strategy_041511.pdf.

WHITMAN, JAMES Q., HARSH JUSTICE: CRIMINAL PUNISHMENT AND THE WIDENING DIVIDE BETWEEN AMERICA AND EUROPE (2003).

Whitman, James Q., *The Two Western Cultures of Privacy: Dignity versus Liberty*, 113 YALE L.J. 1151 (2004).

Wikipedia, "Biographies of Living Persons," http://en.wikipedia.org/wiki/ Wikipedia:Biographies_of_living_persons#Presumption_in_favor_of_privacy (last modified Feb. 3, 2013).

Wikipedia, *Talk: Star Wars Kid*, http://en.wikipedia.org/wiki/Talk:Star_Wars_Kid (last modified Jan. 9, 2013).

Wikipedia, *Wikipedia: Notability*, http://en.wikipedia.org/wiki/Wikipedia:Notability (last modified July 5, 2015).

Wikipedia, *Wikipedia Talk: Talk Pages Not Indexed by Google*, http://en.wikipedia.org/ wiki/Wikipedia_talk:Talk_pages_not_indexed_by_Google (last modified Aug. 22, 2014).

Winter, Jessica, *The Advantages of Amnesia*, BOSTON.COM (Sept. 23, 2007), http://www.boston.com/news/education/higher/articles/2007/09/23/the_advantages_of_amnesia/?page=full.

Witvliet, Charlotte van Oyen, *Traumatic Intrusive Imagery as an Emotional Memory Phenomenon: A Review of Research and Explanatory Information Processing Theories*, 17 CLIN. PSYCHOL. REV. 509 (1997).

Witvliet, Charlotte van Oyen, Thomas E. Ludwig, and Kelly L. Vander Laan, *Granting Forgiveness or Harboring Grudges: Implications for Emotion, Physiology, and Health*, 12 PSYCHOL. SCI. 117 (2001).

Wohl, Michael J. A., and Nyla R. Branscombe, *Forgiving the Ingroup or the Outgroup for Harm Doing, in* FORGIVENESS: A SAMPLING OF RESEARCH RESULTS 23 (American Psychological Association, 2006), http://www.apa.org/international/resources/forgiveness.pdf.

Wood, Shawn Paul, *Top 10 Social Media Fails of 2013*, MEDIABISTRO (Dec. 16, 2013) http://www.mediabistro.com/prnewser/pr-newsers-top-10-social-media-fails-of-2013_b80443.

Woollacott, Emma, *EU to Vote on Scrapping "Safe Harbor" Data Rules*, FORBES (Dec. 18, 2013), http://www.forbes.com/sites/emmawoollacott/2013/12/18/eu-to-vote-on-scrapping-safe-harbor-data-rules/.

World Internet Users Statistics Usage and World Population Stats, INTERNET WORLD STATS, http://www.internetworldstats.com/stats.htm (accessed June 23, 2015).

Worthington, Everett L., Jr., *Empirical Research in Forgiveness: Looking Backward, Looking Forward, in* DIMENSIONS OF FORGIVENESS: PSYCHOLOGICAL RESEARCH AND THEOLOGICAL PERSPECTIVES 321 (Everett L. Worthington Jr. ed., 1998).

Xanthoulis, Napoleon, *Conceptualising a Right to Oblivion in the Digital World: A Human Rights–Based Approach*, SSRN WORKING PAPER SERIES (2012), http://ssrn.com/abstract=2064503 or http://dx.doi.org/10.2139/ssrn.2064503.

Zechmeister, Jeanne S., and Catherine Romero, *Victim and Offender Accounts of Interpersonal Conflict: Autobiographical Narratives of Forgiveness and Unforgiveness*, 82 J. PERSONALITY & SOC. PSYCHOL. 675 (2002).

Zimmer, Michael, *The Externalities of Search 2.0: The Emerging Privacy Threats When the Drive for the Perfect Search Engine Meets Web 2.0*, 13:3 FIRST MONDAY (Mar. 2008), http://www.uic.edu/htbin/cgiwrap/bin/ojs/index.php/fm/article/view/2136/1944.

ZITTRAIN, JONATHAN, THE FUTURE OF THE INTERNET . . . AND HOW TO STOP IT (2009).

Zittrain, Jonathan, Kendra Albert, and Lawrence Lessig, *Perma: Scoping and Addressing the Problem of Link and Reference Rot in Legal Citations*, 14:2 LEGAL INFO. MANAGEMENT 88 (2014).

Index

About the Author

Meg Leta Jones is Assistant Professor at Georgetown University, teaching and writing about technology law and policy in the Communication, Culture, and Technology Department.